ART AND ANGER

ART

and

ANGER

Essays on Politics and the Imagination

ILAN STAVANS

University of New Mexico Press
Albuquerque

Books by Ilan Stavans in English

FICTION

The One-Handed Pianist and Other Stories

NONFICTION

Bandido: Oscar 'Zeta' Acosta and the Chicano Experience
The Hispanic Condition: Reflections on Culture and Identity in America
Imagining Columbus: The Literary Voyage

EDITOR

Tropical Synagogues: Short Stories by Jewish Latin American Writers
Growing Up Latino: Memoirs and Stories (co-edited with Harold Augenbraum)

TRANSLATION

Sentimental Songs by Felipe Alfau

The essays in this collection first appeared, in somehwat different form, in the following publications: "Letter to a German Friend" in *Midstream*; "Two Peruvians" and "Of Arms and the Essayist" in *Utne Reader* and *Transition*; "The First Book," in *The Washington Post Book World*; "The Verbal Quest" in *Metamorphoses* and *Translation Review*; "The Master of Aracataca" and "Translation and Identity" in *Michigan Quarterly Review*; "Las Mariposas," "Pessoa's Echoes," "Discoveries," "The Adventures of Maqroll," and "Tongue Snatcher" in *The Nation*; "*Vuelta*: A Succinct Appraisal" in *Salmagundi*; "Art and Anger" and "Mexico: Four Dispatches" in *In These Times*; "Felipe Alfau" in *Commonweal* and as Preface to *Sentimental Songs* by Felipe Alfau (Dalkey Archive Press, 1992); "The Latin Phallus: A Survey" in *Transition* and in *Muy Macho*, Ray Gonzalez, ed. (Doubleday, 1996); "The Brick Novel" in *The Bloomsbury Review*; and "Hello Columbus" in *Hungry Mind* and *Imagining Columbus: The Literary Voyage* (Twayne, 1993).

Library of Congress Cataloging-in-Publication Data
Stavans, Ilan.
Art and anger: essays on politics and the imagination / Ilan Stavans. — 1st ed.
   p.   cm.
Includes index.
ISBN 0-8263-1744-8.
1. Latin American literature—20th century—History and criticism.
I. Title.
PQ7081.S74 1995
864—dc20
95-50199

for Liora Stavchansky

CONTENTS

PREFACE

Saul Bellow is right: it is not always pleasant to read what you wrote almost a decade ago. I began writing these miscellaneous essays about a year after I moved to New York City—or better, after I moved into the English language. To say that the transition was an arduous one is to undermine its true significance: I was aware since day one that my writing skills in Shakespeare's tongue were quite precarious; still, I was ready to do anything not to become an intellectual parasite, a pariah. I grew up with Yiddish and Hebrew around, aside from Spanish of course; translingualism, then, could be seen as a challenge, not an impediment. I immediately took to earnest the old dictum attributed to Anzia Yezier- ska, which described Jewish writers as "communicating vessels across cultural and linguistic lines." As I began writing in borrowed words, I devoted myself to the enterprise of explaining Hispanic culture to Anglo- Saxon readers. But I did so while remaining loyal to my native tongue, hence living two parallel lives: in Spanish I wrote about H. P. Lovecraft and B. Traven; in English, about Fernando Pessoa and Mario Vargas Llosa. Every so often I would have *tête-à-tête* with my *doppelgänger,* which re- sulted in a moment of intense confusion and despair, making me feel as the personification of a no-man's-land. Did I belong north or south of the border? Or was it perhaps in (and on) the border? Eventually I came to realize that a writer's career is about mutation and that, as an immi- grant, I was undergoing a profound process of reeducation, of cultural reexamination. As a result, in more than one way this volume is only half of an ongoing autobiography, a record of my metamorphosis and acknowledgment of the many masks I wear in English. (The other half is to be found in Spanish.) These nineteen collected essays are a sideboard of my reflections on politics and the imagination as perceived through the veil of translation. No wonder a sense of dislocation and foreignness permeates them all. They seem to me the product of a writer happily at home in the homelessness of the diaspora, which, by the way, is the exact same feeling I get as I reread my collected Spanish essays.

Rereading, once again I hasten to say, has been difficult, even dissatisfying. I recalled a Cyril Connolly statement that "literature is the art of writing something that will be read twice; journalism what will be read once." A part of what made it to print had been written with both eyes in the present. On occasion I would be thrilled by having produced something good, and like Bellow singing the tune of little Jack Horner, I would say "Oh, what a good boy am I!" The names of Borges and Octavio Paz, for instance, kept on reappearing time and again, as if I was looking to cast the support of them as my precedents. Paz is clearly a man of letters I have much admired but have also felt deeply annoyed by; his politics often repel me, and his convoluted liaison with Mexico's government, while not unique, aggravates me. Like him, I understand the essay as an indispensable literary form to investigate urgent and long-standing social, psychological, and artistic concerns. As for Borges, a thinker of the highest caliber, he seemed to have inhabited a time capsule, a baroque, self-sufficient universe beyond earthly morality. To paraphrase Fran Leibowitz, for him life was something to do when you couldn't dream. While writing, I often found myself recalling what they said on matters of importance. And yet, both hold no real clue to my true literary dilemmas.

Which brings me to my title selection. I have come to realize that much of what I wrote in the last decade is about creativity and fury, the pen and the sword—what Lionel Trilling accurately called "the bloody crossroads where literature and politics meet." I can see how my views on writing are linked to messianic religion: the written word as a passport to the future, as a bridge toward one's deeper realms and the divide, literature as an attempt to decipher our human inadequacies. There is no art without anger, but anger alone doesn't make good art.

ART AND ANGER

1 / LETTER TO A GERMAN FRIEND

D ear Thomas K.: Sorry I didn't answer your unexpected letter of May 8th, 1989, before, but I was quite surprised by it and needed some time to process its content. How would you have reacted if a perfect stranger astonished you the same way? I'll tell you how I did: I loved finding a Luftpost envelope in my mailbox, stamped in the Deutsche Demokratischer Republik. Surprises nowadays come in the form of a telephone call. The epistolary genre is agonizing; nobody wants to communicate through writing anymore, so romance and friendship, trapped in the technological wire, are losing a poetic side.

Twice you apologize for your rotten and precarious English. You say you learned it by yourself and it's ungrammatical. Don't worry! Words serve you well in the task of describing your curiosity, puzzlement, and existential dilemma. Besides, there's nothing to fear, English is not my mother tongue either. We're communicating in an alien yet neutral ground, neither yours nor mine. This, I believe, is a good beginning.

You explain you're a twenty-one-year-old Christian resident of Konitz, a small village in the hills of Thuringia, East Germany, who last July traveled with a few college friends just across the border to West Czechoslovakia. During a visit to Prague you entered the Old Jewish Cemetery and found while wandering around the tombstones a spare piece of paper: on one side it contained my home address, on the opposite, a wish to God.

It struck you as intriguing that a Jew would correspond with Heaven. So you copied the address on a memo pad and allegedly left the wish unread. Some nine months later, you write to me.

Prague, which the Third Reich intended to be a museum gathering the folklore and paraphernalia of the extinct Jewish people, left a lasting impression on you. Possessed by what the eyes saw, you returned home to discover that your soul was now inhabited by a force questioning the surrounding reality and putting in doubt past beliefs. So you looked for documentary films and books capable of explaining the horrors of a holocaust perpetrated by your forefathers. And a dark, unpleasant shadow emerged, evidence of a sinful, malevolent ancestry.

But the research also brought you to an honest admiration for the stubborn survival instinct of the Jews. The melancholic air of Prague can certainly ignite a profound reaction like the one you had. I know it because I was there.

"We are children of one Father," you claim, "all brothers. All we want is to live in peace. So why the ethnic discrimination and racial excesses of today? Why so much aversion not only against the Jewish, but against foreigners and ethnic minorities in West Germany, the European community, and the rest of the world? Why wars in Ireland, Lebanon, and Israel?" You're asking difficult questions, Thomas.

Unfortunately, you happen to have reached a skeptic hedonist who thinks the world is neither developing nor regressing into a primitive and inhuman state, but stabilized at a dead end. If you had read my secret message (in English), you would have understood how irreverent it was. While I often request from God health and success in an enterprise for me and those around, I also question his rule.

You ask me for a self-portrait. Here it is:

I'm from Mexico, a country that opened its friendly hands to immigrants and refugees before and during the Second World War and where several thousand Jews made their home. To move to the United States I had to learn to respect, honor, and understand a pantheon of heroes, values, and loyalties alien to me before. Contrary to what's expected, it wasn't difficult. An immense number of illegal Mexican workers, fooling the border patrol, cross the Rio Grande every month. They look for better opportunities. But if living conditions are miserable in the native land, exploitation here is a form of welcome. Happily, since I'm a member of the People of the Book, changing homes and globetrotting, especially in peaceful times like ours—sorry, Thomas, if I contradict you but, when compared to fifty years ago, these are pleasant and fruitful decades—, didn't bring uncontrollable obstacles. I was able to master the idiom quickly and was academically active from the beginning. Unlike some of my fellow Mexicans, I wasn't looking for better-quality housing or a sufficient salary. What I needed was intellectual freedom and a challenging environment in order to create. You see, Mexico is still intolerant in many respects, hesitant to debate ideas democratically, and lacking in a tradition that celebrates the spirit as producer and consumer of aesthetic beauty.

I got married in June of 1988 to an American Jew. The bridge that unites me to my wife, beyond love, is a collective memory, one evident in the culture we share. Her ancestors were Czech, mine Polish. Before and during the Holocaust the two families lived in terrible penury. Few survived, and the dead, many of them incinerated, saw their last days in camps like Auschwitz.

On our honeymoon we decided to return to family towns in Poland and Czechoslovakia that had been turned into mythology in our childhood. Parents and relatives believed the project was wrong; after all, marriage is a pact with the future, not the past. Yet voices in us refused to remain silent and demanded a settlement with death. In my ears one of these voices repeatedly whispered: "The annihilation of family members was the result of pure chance: Your granduncles perished, you're alive. Why? Because God rules the universe in a game of roulette. You got the lucky number!"

We kept a travel diary and when I received your letter, I returned to it. The entries describe our impressions of the Warsaw Ghetto, the bunker of Anielewicz and his heroic squad where everybody struggled against the Nazis until the very end, and the fancy Czech resort Karlovy Vary, where the educated of the nineteenth century took therapeutic baths. Reading its touching paragraphs, I refreshed the memory of our wonderful pilgrimage.

In Prague we met Mr. Alexander Dawidowicz. My wife had found his name and number in a tourist guide whose editor was convinced this tiny, old employee of Chedoc, the state-owned travel agency, knew everything about the city's Hebraic past: details, forgotten gossip, and legends of rivalry and treason between rabbis and noblemen. We stayed at the Park Hotel, a decrepit, architecturally outmoded building which the Czechs perceive as luxurious, and called Mr. Dawidowicz immediately after we settled in. Next day he came to us. What a delightful octogenarian: His old-fashioned suits, heavy-graded spectacles, inexhaustible knowledge, and *joie de vivre* make him a character Mendele and Agnon would have adored. For us he ended up becoming Prague's most invaluable treasure.

Of course he wanted a few dollars for his friendship. So what? Alexander not only took us around, he practically adopted us as grandchildren. Exhilaration is the word that best describes his amazement when hearing his name was published in a tourist book. He was also very happy when we told him we wanted to see Kafka's different homes and *gymnasium.* "The Party detests Kafka and refuses to print his books," he told us, "but he's no doubt the best Czech *littérateur* of all times."

I'm telling you all about Alexander because, indeed, he was a decisive figure in our trip. While he disliked talking about himself, we persuaded him to explain facts and mementos about the Holocaust. What we discovered was an optimistic yet tragic biography. During the war, because of his enlistment in the army, Alexander couldn't possibly save his wife and children from the Nazis. He was stationed in the Ukraine, near the Black Sea, and on his return he found ghosts, death, and silence in Prague. His entire family had vanished, all swallowed in the mouth of an unmerciful destiny. Remorse took over. Alexander felt guilty for having abandoned his loved ones, and suicide became an alternative. Fortunately, he rejected it and chose perpetuation. It was not easy! It took close to a decade to find a wife; his youngest son today is around fifteen, and his wife, whom he introduced to us, is in her late thirties.

So there you have it, Thomas: Alexander Dawidowicz is the magnificent evidence of that Jewish stubbornness you so much admire. Had my relatives survived, a plausible life pattern would have been Alexander's. In our various encounters we had endless conversations about Israel, God, and the present. I asked him if Jews would ever stop existing in Czechoslovakia. "They are not allowed to!" he answered. We idealized his courage—a courage, I must say, expressed every day in the histrionic art of guiding visitors across Prague's labyrinthine map. For as you well know, in recent decades Czechoslovakia has become an attractive sight for German tourists (among them yourself). Its overwhelming beauty and strategic location bring people from all over but especially from Dresden, Munich, and Berlin, making both Germanies an important financial pillar of the fragile Czech economy. Alexander, victimized in the past by Germans, now "humbly smiles" (his words) while showing the Smetana Museum, the bridges over the Moldau River, the Vaclavske Namesti Square, and the Jewish quarter. He comments on their baroque architecture and symbolism while never insinuating revenge. "No matter what I think or feel, it is not for me to judge," he announced while confessing to have had troubling nightmares for years.

It was he who took us to the Old Synagogue, where I was the tenth man in a Friday-night service, and guided us through the Old Jewish Cemetery. We went from tomb to tomb deciphering the hazy Hebrew letters. One impressed me in particular: that of the great Maharal of Prague, who is believed to have created a Golem with his wisdom of Kabbalah. This one is revered by both Orthodox and even many secular Jews in every corner of the world, and wax spreads over it from melted candles placed as marks of devotion. It's here that I wrote a wish to God.

Since I didn't have a spare sheet of paper, I wrote it on the back of a business card. I felt bad after doing it. "God ought not to be addressed on that sort of stationery!," I said to myself. I also remember commenting to my wife: "What if somebody finds my card? What if that person decides to trace me? You'll think it's hokey that I foresaw receiving your letter. Well, I didn't! I'm not a prophet. It crossed my mind, for a second or two, that leaving my address behind in such an open space could be understood (if not by anybody, at least by God) as an invitation to an unexpected encounter. Little did I know that by doing it, I was promoting a future correspondence with a German.

I'll explain: By choosing Poland and Czechoslovakia as sights for our honeymoon, we were unconsciously rejecting Germany. Of course we never had it in mind to travel to Leipzig or Frankfurt, but selecting Eastern Europe was an indirect repudiation. Capable of reviving old wounds, we knew images of cruel Nazi and Russian soldiers would emerge. We wanted that! We wanted to unmask our past and accept its fatalistic status. And to be honest, nothing would have offended us more than being involved with Germans. When Alexander wanted us to accompany his tours with German groups, we refused. (During our rendezvous in the Old Jewish Cemetery, we did talk to a Turkish German girl, but she was Jewish, or at least thought she was.)

What am I trying to express? That Judaism is less a religion than a past collectively shared. When my wife and I left Warsaw, our final stop, we believed ourselves to be ready for a common future. The whispering voices inside our ears were now acknowledging that if only accidents rule Nature, each individual must take full responsibility for his own life and live it to its limits. After all, the apparent state of things can suddenly change from one minute to the next and bring the end (in the form of war, a terrorist act, or an unexpected assassination).

Why did a Christian German like you pick up my personal message? For weeks I saw in your behavior a cycle in history—the dialogue between a Jew and his God is once more intercepted by the enemy. But that's a mistaken interpretation. Your humane letter, Thomas, is a gesture of reconciliation I confess not to have wanted while I was in Eastern Europe. Yet by writing on a business card, perhaps unwillingly, I left the door open for it. A few weeks after your letter arrived I still wasn't ready for a reevaluation of feelings. Back in New York, why should I? Today, I am ready, I know.

Our civilized life is a precarious and insecure state of mind. It's a pendulum that alternates progress with barbarism, light with darkness. And I'm afraid it'll always do so! There's no end to war, Thomas, because war is a pivotal modulator of human energy. Victims eventually become victimizer, and vice versa. While one must never forget, it is essential to recognize that everybody destructs and is guilty of something.

You're still young, my friend. Maybe you'll disagree that human evil is inevitable. I truly hope so! Optimists are needed to combat our world's defects. Sorry again for the delay in responding and for not hiding the pessimism of my skeptical spirit.

Yours truly,

Post Script: By the way, in the message to God I impugn Him for having forgotten my relatives during the Holocaust. And I also requested three short-run wishes, two of which have been granted already. I've accomplished, as well, two errands He wanted me to perform.

We are not through with our epistolary encounter. Telephone calls to Heaven haven't been invented as yet, and the correspondence between us, permeated with poetry, continues.

[1989]

2 / TWO PERUVIANS

To abandon one's life for a dream is to know
its true worth.

—*Montaigne*

At what precise moment did Peru fuck itself up? Mario Vargas Llosa posed the query in his 1969 novel *Conversation in the Cathedral,* a multilayered narrative about Peru's haves and have-nots; and the query runs through public discourse on Peru at home and abroad. There is no easy answer, of course. Was it during the disastrous war with Chile in 1879, which threw a roadblock before the country's economic progress? Was it after the tyrannical two-part regime of President Augusto B. Leguía (1908–12, 1919–30), a national patriarch who promoted economic development in the interest of the small wealthy minority? Or during the dictatorship of General Manuel Odría (1948–56)? Did it happen when Fernando Balaúnde Terry, a moderate reformer and a populist, became president in a 1963 democratic election, only to be deposed five years later by a military junta headed by General Juan Alvarado Velasco? When the same Balaúnde Terry returned in the early eighties to govern as a Conservative? Or was it when Alan García, a highly popular Social Democrat, came to office in 1985 and refused to pay Peru's foreign debt to the International Monetary Fund?

Whatever date one might settle on, the devastation now seems incurable, as if apocalypse has already taken place. Massive emigration, a useless, overgrown bureaucracy, a decade-long guerrilla insurrection with tentacles that seem to be everywhere and headquarters nowhere—all this has turned the banana republic, comprising a narrow strip of 500,000 square miles, into the dead zone of the Pacific coast.

For many, life has come to seem unbearable, the future elusive. During the eighties, Peru's skyrocketing inflation was as unpredictable as the lottery. While the GNP maintained a downward spiral, dynamite explosions and the assassinations of civilians and diplomats became part of the texture of everyday life—and they still are. With a population of some 24 million (50 percent Indian, 37 percent mestizo, and 13 percent white) concentrated in Lima, a megalopolis holding a third of the citizenship, Peru today is South America's time bomb. As its inefficient, bankrupt government flounders, ideological fundamentalists are at the brink of seizing power. If, in the Hispanic hemisphere, Fidel Castro's Cuba represents order under repression, contemporary Peru presents the mirror image of regression through chaos. Confusion, anomie, lawlessness—the present is in shambles.

Politically fractured and socially disfigured, today the nation is divided into two essentially opposed ideological projects, facing off belligerently: one identified with the principles and traditions of our fin-de-siècle Western way of life, the other attached to Marxism-Leninism and to the glories of the Inca empire—especially its last hero, Atahualpa, who was captured and killed by the conquistador Francisco Pizarro. Progress versus dogmatism, civilization versus barbarism—a bloody, all-too-common contest south of the Rio Grande.

Inasmuch as Peruvian society is led more by passion than reason, its multitudes clamor to be guided by a single mind. What they seek is not the direction of enlightened logic, but the personified will of a common dream, a common fear, a common desire to avenge collective injury. Their enthusiasm has been divided between two prominent figures, who together represent the spiritual cleavage of contemporary Peru.

On stage left stands Carlos Abimael Guzmán Reynoso, alias Presidente Gonzalo, the obese, bearded, psoriasis-suffering mastermind of the guerrilla movement Sendero Luminoso, or Shining Path. Guzmán: a man who claims his five to seven thousand kamikaze followers have been preparing the one true path to a political paradise on earth. Guzmán: a man who, since his capture on September 12, 1992, and his uneffected death sentence a month later, has been ill, depressed, and rapidly losing weight as prisoner no. 1509, living out his days in solitary confinement—first in San Lorenzo, also known as El Frontón, an island prison of the Pacific coast, then in a specially constructed underground cell in Callao, where he is to spend the rest of his existence.

On stage right stands Mario Vargas Llosa, a tall, handsome, and elegantly dressed novelist and presidential candidate, who first achieved international esteem in 1963 with his debut novel *The Time of the Hero*. Vargas Llosa: a man who has come to personify Peru's Europeanized oligarchy and whom many see as the nation's link to reason and enlightenment.

So there you have it: a man of action and a man of letters—a sword and a pen. One a merciless ideological agitator, the other a refined prose stylist and a dilettante; one a dialectical materialist captivated by Mao Zedong and the Chinese Cultural Revolution, the other an idealist and epicure whose literary imagination inclines toward Faulkner and Flaubert (among his favorite books are *Light in August* and *Madame Bovary*). Guzmán and Vargas Llosa, perfect strangers, have become twin emblems of Peru's search for a solution to its sorrowful reality.

Fate had them born two years apart in the very same southern state, Arequipa: Guzmán on December 4, 1934, Vargas Llosa on March 28, 1936. It is a state that shares its name with its capital, Peru's second largest city, founded by the Spaniards in 1540 not far from Lake Titicaca, and home to scores of romantic poets and revolutionaries. Guzmán and Vargas Llosa came from different social classes, lower-middle and upper-middle respectively, with no record of a tête-à-tête; and yet, as Vargas Llosa has acknowledged, it's not impossible that as children they saw each other at a bus stop or as passersby in Arequipa's downtown commercial district.

Both are members of a distinguished Peruvian generation commonly referred to in intellectual circles as *la generación del '50,* which also includes the writers Julio Ramón Ribeyro, Sebastián Salazar Bondy, José Miguel Oviedo, and José María Arguedas; the painter Fernando de Szyszlo; and the politician Hector Cornejo Chávez. Torn between a heartfelt patriotism and an adversarial relation to the status quo, between sympathy toward the aboriginal minority and an allegiance to global modernization, this generation, with Guzmán and Vargas Llosa representing its polar extremes, has had an enormous impact on Peru's recent history.

In spite of the families' different financial condition, the two men went to branches of La Salle, a prestigious Catholic school, Guzmán in Arequipa and Vargas Llosa in Cochabamba, Bolivia, where the boy and his mother—separated from her husband and seeking help after a troubled marriage—had moved in 1937, when Mario's grandfather was named consul. Each was an only child (the novelist had two stepbrothers) and has the personality of one. Each grew up in the absence of a paternal figure (Vargas Llosa met his father at age ten); each was marked by a traumatic encounter with urban life in his early adolescence.

Born out of wedlock to a mother who is said to have twice attempted an abortion, Guzmán as a boy is remembered by teachers and classmates as a hardworking, unusually dedicated student. Rejected by his biological father, a small-time businessman in the provinces, he was educated by his mother until she died when he was twelve. Only then did his father take him back, pledging to continue his education. In the La Salle secondary school, Guzmán discovered a passion for political philosophy; he and a group of friends founded a club to analyze capitalism's discontents and to study the connections between metaphysics and militancy, between Marxism and Hegel's dialectics.

Arequipa—from *Ari quepay,* meaning "Yes, stay around" in Quechua (alongside Spanish, Peru's other official tongue)—was a remarkable setting for an incubating activist. A shadow box of Peru's economic contradictions, the city was in turmoil during the fifties, stricken by successive labor strikes and organized unrest that would be imprinted forever in Guzmán's memory. Indeed, his conviction that violence was the only road toward secular redemption dates back to his early twenties. As a pariah—an illegitimate child welcomed by neither parent—he grew convinced that the ills afflicting the society he knew reflected a larger inequality that was rooted in the Spanish conquest during the sixteenth century and perpetuated by foreign powers who had continued to subjugate his countrymen.

Vargas Llosa returned to Peru at the age of nine, at first living with his mother in the northern coastal town of Piura near the border with Ecuador (the setting of his second novel, *The Green House*), then, after his parents reconciled, moving to Lima in 1946. The transition from small town to big city was difficult and his personal encounter with the troubled capital quite shocking. "Piura was a wonderful town," he would later on write, "full of happenings that sparked the imagination. There was La Magachería, a district of huts made of reeds and mud, where the best taverns were found, as well as La Gallinacera, the district between the river and the canal." Lima, on the other hand, was unappealing: "I hated the metropolis from the beginning because of the unhappiness I felt there."

When he was fourteen, his father sent him to the Leoncio Prado Military School, a rigid educational institution portrayed in his first novel. "My father, who had found out I was writing poems, feared for my future . . . and for my 'manhood.'" The army environment, his father believed, would be an antidote to these perilous tendencies. Vargas Llosa spent two years, 1950–52, as a boarding student at the school, which he later described as "a microcosm of Peruvian society." He then returned once more to Piura, where his work began appearing in newspapers and where, at the age of seventeen, he finished his first of many plays, a naturalistic drama titled *The Flight of the Inca.*

Half persuaded by his father's view of poetry as an unmanly and unremunerative vocation, he entered the San Marcos University to study law, an established and safe career. Even so, his passion for literature remained unvanquished. In 1958 he won a prize for a short story from the *Revue Française,* and his award was a fully paid trip to Paris, where he was able to retread the footsteps of his beloved idols, Victor Hugo and Flaubert, and to try to befriend Jean-Paul Sartre and Albert Camus (he only met the latter, briefly). On his return to Peru, he visited the Amazon jungle, a theater of colors and animality he would put at center stage in his literary universe. But the allure of the indigenous would not suffice for him. Unable to satisfy his cosmopolitanism at home, he again returned to Europe—Spain this time—and enrolled in graduate studies at Madrid's Universidad Central.

During the fifties, General Odría's corrupt, brutal, and oppressive dictatorship suffused everything Peruvian. Barbarism—often state-sponsored barbarism—reigned. Guzmán, who, like Vargas Llosa, would become a law student, lived in Arequipa at the time. He entered the University of San Agustín immediately after his high school graduation. By then he had no trouble identifying with victims.

The nation's independence had been achieved in 1821, thanks to generals José de San Martín and Simón Bolívar, and to the defeat of Spain in the battles of Ayacucho and Junín. But once European control was gone, Peru remained sharply divided between the wealthy aristocracy, mostly Creoles, and the poverty-ridden Indian majority. Where was the justice in that? But Guzmán's commitment to the oppressed was not without hope. He imagined a utopian future in which natives would rule in an equal fashion, a universe where whites would have no role to play unless they gave up their undeserved privileges.

Ambitious and spirited, he simultaneously registered in two academic fields, law and philosophy, and would write two theses, one about the democratic bourgeois state and the other on Kant's theory of space. Judging from these texts and from the manifestos and communiqués he would publish later on in *El Diario,* the Shining Path's official party publication, Guzmán's writing skills were always mediocre. His long paragraphs are tortured by what seems to be a convoluted train of thinking. His prose is unpolished, tending toward a sermonic drone. And yet his large number of acolytes bear witness to his powers of absolute persuasion. Besides, his lack of verbal panache would in the end matter little: the loaded gun, not the embellished word, would become Guzmán's most effective weapon. Even from his student days, politics monopolized his attention. Deepening cynicism about the possibilities of peaceful parliamentary socialism turned a Social Democrat into a fervent Marxist-Leninist, one who views Peru's government as a Satan on earth.

Guzmán left Arequipa in 1962. He had been teaching at San Agustín for a while but was soon hired away by the University of San Cristóbal of Huamanga in the south-central city of Ayacucho. Famous for its nickel, gold, and silver mines, and as a historic site of victory by General Antonio José de Sucre against the Spanish army, this Peruvian city, with a population of 27,000 in the mid-sixties, was driven by a radical economic divide between upper and lower classes. Guzmán's experience in Ayacucho heightened his awareness of the inequality under which a large segment of the Peruvian population labored.

"My greatest and deepest impression was to meet and discover the Ayacucho peasants," Guzmán would state during the fifteen-day interrogation that ensued upon his September 1992 arrest. "Their reality shook my eyes and mind. . . . They endure an oppressive semifeudal burden. I saw people working as slaves on ranches." Outraged by what he had witnessed, he decided to organize a national student assembly and began studying Mao Zedong in depth. He then traveled to China, in

1965 and 1967, to fully submerge himself in Communist affairs and to witness first-hand the agitations of the Cultural Revolution—a campaign set forth by Chairman Mao to revitalize the popular fervor toward Marxism and to renew his nation's basic public institutions. First in China and then in Albania, Guzmán met top-level Marxist leaders and was able to solidify overseas contacts and reaffirm his ideological allegiances.

There was no turning back. Having seen the Red Guards, allied with the army, attack so-called bourgeois elements in intellectual and artistic circles and the bureaucracy, Guzmán was convinced that a similar state of affairs needed to be organized at home. "Honor and glory to the Peruvian people!"—the throaty cry would resound for almost three decades. He would recruit and indoctrinate the young and the poor, preparing them to fight the aggressor within, imperialism's fifth columnists who were ready to do anything to dismantle the country's dignity. Peru's salvation, it was clear to him, lay in the establishment of a Communist regime similar to that of Mao's China. Presumably in an effort to "naturalize" Maoist thought, Guzmán, on his return to Ayacucho, gave his full attention to the work of José Carlos Mariátegui—Peru's original socialist commentator, nicknamed Amauta after a handful of Inca teachers and philosophers—drawing clear parallels between his beliefs and Mao's. And so it was that Mariátegui came to play a crucial role in the shaping of Shining Path.

One can only speculate whether he would have been pleased by this. Born in 1894 in Moquegua, Mariátequi was a self-educated man who was unable to finish primary school for lack of money but who, at the age of nineteen, was already a respected journalist for the Lima newspaper *La Prensa*. He had been strongly influenced by Georges Sorel's thinking and came to believe the only solution to Peru's problems was a process of revolution. During his twenties he met and became friends with Victor Raúl Haya de la Torre (1895–1979), a young activist who would found a political organization known by the name of Alianza Popular Revolucionaria Americana, or APRA (later on Alan García's party), and would have become Peru's elected president in 1962 had a military coup not prevented him from taking office.

Like his effusive follower, Abimael Guzmán, Mariátegui traveled abroad—to Spain, to Italy (where he met Antonio Gramsci and

Benedetto Croce), to Germany. On his return he finished a number of books, many of them composed of essays and reviews published in newspapers and weekly magazines, including his famous 1928 title *Seven Interpretative Essays on Peruvian Reality*. Paying special attention to the forgotten Inca population, the book offers a Marxist analysis of the country's most urgent social, economic, and political problems, showing how the nation's infrastructure is conditioned by colonial and semifeudal elements. Breaking with Haya de la Torre and the APRA, Mariátegui went on to create the Partido Socialista del Perú, or PSP, which enthusiastically joined the Communist International Movement and was later redefined as Partido Comunista del Perú, or PCP.

Although Mariátegui died at the age of thirty-six, the party grew steadily until the early sixties, when a few global controversies—including debates over the 'true value' of Castro's revolution in Cuba, the Sino-Soviet split, and Khrushchev's denunciation of Stalin—caused the party to fragment. By 1975, it had been divided into some twenty different organizations, with two factions retaining most of the power: a pro-Soviet group favoring a peaceful transition to communism through reform and a pro-Maoist one that promoted change through violence. For a while those members leaning toward Mao called themselves Partido Comunista del Perú-Bandera Roja, or Red Flag.

After a few more internal quarrels, yet another faction was born in 1970: the Partido Comunista Peruano por el Sendero Luminoso de Mariátegui, PCP-SL, or Shining Path. Its leader was Abimael Guzmán, a man who, having invested a considerable part of the sixties in internal political struggles, was now emerging as a key figure in leftist politics. Not for him the temporizing of some of his comrades. He was convinced that conditions for radical revolution were already present in Peru—the only things needed were a date and a cathartic explosion.

Meanwhile, all through the next decade, Vargas Llosa was in the process of becoming, in the eyes of Europe and the United States, the nation's most prominent citizen—Peru's favorite son, but stationed, like a diplomat, in Europe—intelligent, outspoken, sexy, and cosmopolitan. A litterateur, a sophisticated op-ed commentator, and a very articulate keynote speaker, he had championed democracy in international forums (after an ill-fated flirtation with Castro's 1959 revolution), and was known for his stylish novels and plays, which were frequently set in Piura, Lima, and Arequipa. For his works, he was recipient of a number of prestigious awards, including the Biblioteca Breve Prize, the Rómulo Gallegos, the Premio de la Crítica, and the PEN-Faulkner Award; he was also a regular contender for the Nobel Prize. When Carmen Balcells, a very capable Barcelona literary agent, took him as client (she also represented Gabriel García Márquez, Isabel Allende, and other writers from the so-called Latin American literary boom), his name was immediately established in the international literary arena.

While Shining Path was being created, Vargas Llosa was finishing a doctorate from the Universidad Central, for which he submitted a voluminous dissertation (over a thousand manuscript pages) called "García Márquez: History of a Deicide." Published in book form in 1971 but never reprinted or translated into any other language, this study of the life, times, and artistic contribution of the Colombian author of *One Hundred Years of Solitude* provided the Peruvian an opportunity to elaborate his own theory of the "total novel," one seeking to encompass through narrative art a comprehensive social reality: it would parse the various segments of society, every nuance of their hopes, dream, and sorrows. Inspired by Balzac's epigram, "Il faut avoir fouillé toute la vie sociale pour être un vrai romancier, vu que le roman est l'histoire privée des nations," Vargas Llosa had put this idea to work in his first three novels and took it even further in his encyclopedic *The War of the End of the World*, a title generally used as a divider between the writer's creative periods. Some 560 pages long in its 1981 Spanish original, the novel is a rewriting of a Brazilian classic, Euclides Da Cunha's *Os Sertões*, known in English as *Rebellion in the Backlands*. A combination of biography, journalism, documentary history, and narrative fiction considered by many "the Bible of Brazilian nationalism," Da Cunha's magnum opus is about an 1886 uprising in Canudos, an old cattle ranch on the banks of the Vasa-Barris River, laid low by the type of poverty that inhabits Latin American shantytowns. Critics are sharply divided regarding the actual value of Vargas Llosa's work, originally commissioned as a screenplay by a Brazilian filmmaker: while some consider it too ambitious to hold the reader's attention, others, including me, regard the book as an outstanding piece of fiction—the tribute of a twentieth-century Hispanic writer to his precursor. But whatever the final assessment might be, a consensus holds this to be the author's last novel of real distinction, at least for now; his aesthetic standards having been impoverished by the high demands of stardom. At the apex of his career, Vargas Llosa has had trouble focusing his attention on the type of meganarratives he had trained his audience to expect. His literary work since *The War of the End of the World* has been reduced to slim transitional novels, what Graham Greene used to call "entertainments"—works with more looks than substance. It was in the late seventies that he had matured and recognized his true voice—in just the years that Guzmán's lasting impact was about to begin.

Guzmán began suffering health problems in 1972. In June of that year, he asked for a leave of absence from the University of San Cristóbal to get a complete medical checkup at a hospital in Lima, followed by another series of doctor's appointments in subsequent months. His psoriasis, which specialists diagnosed as chronic and believed would deteriorate rapidly in Ayacucho because of its high altitude, had become a real impediment. What Guzmán needed was a place at sea level, like Lima or La Cantuba. Around that time he got a scholarship to finish "Mariátegui's Philosophy," a seminal study in which he displayed his commitment to his idol and one of the last intellectual projects he accomplished in Ayacucho—with the exception, of course, of masterminding Shining Path's secret birth.

He resigned from his academic job in 1976. Until then he had used colleagues and students to spread his gospel. But now an inner calling assured him a different strategy was needed in order to destabilize Peru's status quo. He had been living the divided life of Mr. Verloc in Conrad's *The Secret Agent*: in a world of fatuous civil servants and corrupt policemen, he dreamed of becoming a chilling terrorist and began organizing an underground guerrilla army. Vargas Llosa's egotism, his globetrotting ways, held absolutely no appeal for Guzmán. Peru had to be transformed from within, and Guzmán cared little if foreigners saw his Maoist utopia as an anarchic killing field of utter madness, despair, and desolation. Paradise on earth could wait no longer.

And so he disappeared from the public eye. He became a ghost, a mythical figure—an abstract entity. No one knew his whereabouts: his presence could be felt everywhere, but physically he was a shadow, a wraith. While Guzmán was never an invalid, his skin disease had a direct impact on his politics. And accompanied by a susceptibility to migraines, quick changes of mood, and a sense of vulnerability expressed in impatience and easy anger, it made him a more tyrannical figure. Because of his psoriasis, he had to restructure Shining Path to control its actions from a habitat benign to his health; otherwise he would have had to interrupt his strategy to "descend" to a place where he could recover in peace. (Interestingly, the legendary Argentine guerrilla Ernesto "Che" Guevara, whom Guzmán often ridiculed to show how tenderness can destroy a life, suffered frequent asthma attacks that impeded his will to fight.) Thus Shining Paths' *incahuas*—literally "the Inca's House," a term used by Haya de la Torre to describe a clandestine party's secret headquarters—had to be adapted to its leader's physical disabilities.

In any event, Guzmán spent his days and nights plotting the first terrorist attack. It took place in 1980, when a group of student sympathizers set fire to the ballot boxes in the remote Andean village of Chuschi. Although it looked like a peripheral incident of violence, the horror had begun. Guzmán's ultimate goal was to establish a People's Republic of the New Democracy in Peru: a greater good in the name of which any sort of mayhem and brutality would ultimately be justified. In conventions and meetings, he sermonized about the "troublesome" contradictions of Peruvian reality and would read out loud passages by Mao as well as segments of Washington Irving's now forgotten *Life of Mahomet* (to demonstrate "how when men are unified by a common cause, they act together hand-in-hand") and Shakespeare's *Macbeth* ("to show how treason can poison the human mind").

Vargas Llosa was overseas at the time. With residences in London and Barcelona he would spend most of his time across the Atlantic and would make only an occasional trip home to reinvigorate his professional and family ties, to keep his "Peruvian persona" alive. He had unsuccessfully tried to return to live there several years before but quickly gave up the idea; "I left Europe and didn't live in my country again for any length of time until 1974," he later recounted. "I was twenty-two when I left and thirty-eight when I returned. In many ways, I was a totally different person when I came back. . . . Peru is for me a kind of incurable disease, and my feeling for her is intense, bitter, and full of the violence that characterizes passion." But a year later he again crossed the ocean to Europe. (He has spent comparatively little time in the United States, first in 1968 at Washington State University and later at academic institutions like Syracuse and Princeton.) Named president of PEN Club International, he enjoyed the glittering lifestyle of a successful *homme de lettres* that only Europe can offer. He was constantly interviewed by journalists and asked to comment on world affairs, appearing in academic congresses, and dined by diplomats. He also tried his luck as a film director and wrote a number of dramatic plays. His emerging profile had less to do with sober intellect than with a sparkling, perhaps irresponsible wit; in middle age, he seemed more the *enfant terrible* than elder statesman.

As Guzmán's *El diario* and other Peruvian periodicals have insisted, frivolity in Vargas Llosa was always a synonym for indiscretion. A case in point is his 1977 novel *Aunt Julia and the Script Writer,* which became a long-running television miniseries and was turned into a Hollywood-style movie (retitled *Tune in Tomorrow* and set in New Orleans, starring Peter Falk, Barbara Hershey, and Keanu Reeves). The novel tells two parallel stories, that of Varguitas, a young promising writer in Lima who works for a radio station in the fifties, and Pedro Camacho, the scriptwriter who is responsible for popular radio soap operas adored by a large Peruvian audience. As Varguitas gets more fascinated with Camacho's fantasy, his personal life unravels in a humorous fashion: he falls in love with his aunt Julia and, in spite of the family's opposition, he marries her in a secret ceremony. Based on the writer's real-life liaison with Julia Urquidi Illanes, a Bolivian and the force behind Vargas Llosa's early success, whom he married in 1955 at age nineteen (she was twenty-nine), the novel created a scandal. When Urquidi read it she is said to have exploded in fury: truth had been distorted, her privacy destroyed, her reputation ruined (the press called her "a seducer of minors").

Indiscretion generates more indiscretion, says Blaise Pascal in his *Pensées.* In revenge Urquidi wrote *Varguitas' Silence,* a confession published in La Paz, Bolivia, in 1983; in it she sets the record straight, basing her arguments on actual letters and portraying Vargas Llosa as "a paranoiac daydreamer." The polemic, not unlike another one launched by an article in the *New York Times Magazine* where the novelist ridiculed one of his sons for his Rastafarian tastes, is relevant only insofar as it illustrates a facet of the writer's flamboyant personality: his rashness.

Frivolity and guerrilla warfare—the pen and the sword. While Vargas Llosa continued to receive international applause, Guzmán's nightmarish methods of indoctrination and terror shook the Peruvian population. After killing adults and children alike, Shining Path would cut out their eyes and tongues, hang their bodies from trees, and set entire villages on fire. The targets, although varied, were rarely indiscriminate: the attack would single out peasants who refused to join the guerrillas' ranks, eyewitnesses, and innocents whose death could send a message to the Lima government. The army responded with equal harshness. Among contemporary guerrilla movements, the Shining Path is comparable only to Pol Pot's Khmer Rouge. And yet, as Tina Rosenberg has pointed out, the 27,000 deaths in Peru since 1980 have not been perpetrated solely by Guzmán's squads: the brutal and incredibly inept Peruvian military has contributed more than its share.

Shining Path's paraphernalia is borrowed from Communist parties in Spain, Italy, and what used to be the Soviet Union. But if the music of its anthems and marches is inauthentic, the wording is original:

> *Communist Party, conduct us to a new life,*
> *Make doubt and fear vanish like smoke;*
> *We have the strength, the Future is ours.*
> *Communism is a goal and will be a reality.*

And this:

> *And people listen carefully*
> *When returning from a day's work;*
> *It's Gonzalo! sings the fire,*
> *Gonzalo means armed struggle.*
>
> *Gonzalo! the masses roar*
> *and the Andes tremble*
> *expressing ardent passion,*
> *Sure and well-aimed faith.*

Sonia Goldenberg, author of *Report on the Unknown Peru,* reports that Guzmán's movement has tentacles beyond regional borders that portray him and the Shining Path as the only hope for an egalitarian future for Peru. Its major organization, the Committee to Support the Revolution in Peru, paints graffiti and hangs posters in urban centers worldwide and places ads in mainstream periodicals (in the United States, it gets the support of the Revolutionary Communist Party, which distributes Maoist literature from Atlanta to Honolulu) to condemn massacres of political prisoners and oppose foreign military intervention.

Latin America has a long-standing tradition of writers who involve themselves in political affairs. Perhaps the first, and certainly among the best known, is Domingo Faustino Sarmiento, a nineteenth century Argentine intellectual heavily influenced by the novels of James Fenimore Cooper and Benjamin Franklin's *Autobiography,* who wrote the groundbreaking *Facundo: Civilization and Barbarism* in 1845 (it was translated into English twenty-three years later by Mrs. Horace Mann). The book was part biography, part novel, part nonfictional account of Juan Facundo Quiroga, a gaucho leader, and its political impact was tremendous. Sarmiento became his country's most important citizen, and when he ran for president after a life in exile, the vote easily placed him in office (1868–74). Many have followed his path, including Ernesto Cardenal, Alejo Carpentier, Octavio Paz, and Carlos Fuentes-—authors who, at one point or another in their literary careers, became ministers of culture, ambassadors, and cultural attachés in Europe and the Far East.

Since his beginnings as a writer, Vargas Llosa had been vocal about political issues: he had written about the Arab Israeli conflict, the Irish Republican Army, and Castro's ideology, among other topics. But until 1987, he never succumbed to the temptation to enter politics, although such a temptation was present. In fact, he refused the invitations by Fernando Balaúnde Terry, during his return to presidential power in the early eighties, to become ambassador in London and Washington, minister of education, minister of foreign relations, and, finally, to fill the office of prime minister. Vargas Llosa constantly rejected the offers— with one exception: he did accept the unpaid, month-long appointment to head the commission investigating a 1982 massacre of eight journalists in Uchuraccay, a remote region of the Andes, after which he published a report, translated into English as "Inquest in the Andes." "A big mistake," he would later on say. "I was mercilessly attacked and slandered for months by the press" for accepting the appointment. A temporary job, it had seemed, apparently nothing of great importance. He was dead wrong, of course. Whatever his misgivings, though, politics was not a side interest for him; it constantly occupied his thoughts. So when he officially entered politics a few years later, what surprised people was only how long it had taken.

In July 1987, by his own account (published in *Granta* and expanded into a 538-page memoir published in book form by Seix Barral in Barcelona in 1993) he was in Punta Sal, a resort in the far north of Peru, when he heard Alan García's annual speech to Congress on the radio. García had been in office for two years and was having a difficult time controlling the insatiable beast of the nation's foreign debt. In the past, García had had a confrontation with the International Monetary Fund and the World Bank because he refused to continue paying huge amounts of the foreign debt. His policies, although immensely popular, didn't fit in Vargas Llosa's own vision of how Peru could be rebuilt. In the speech, the President announced what others like Salvador Allende in Chile, José López Portillo in Mexico, and Siles Suazo in Bolivia had done: the nationalization of the country's banks. An uproar followed. The strategy was clear—to target the monetary institutions as responsible for Peru's inflation and deeply rooted poverty. This was not an unexpected move, one might add. During the seventies, still enchanted with Castro's communism, Latin American politicians saw capitalism and the United States as evil forces that had only compounded the region's difficulties. By contrast, they understood the role of the state to be omniscient and benign, what Octavio Paz called "the philanthropic ogre." Since only a small segment of the population was affluent and controlled the nation's wealth, the solution was to mobilize the government to counterbalance social and economic inequalities. And before that, in 1938, Lázaro Cárdenas, then Mexico's president and, like Alan García, hugely popular, struck at rich American oil companies by declaring the mineral resources the sole property of the Mexican people. Suddenly, a vast foreign industry lost its ground and was declared illegal. Cárdenas—who was father of today's opposition leader Cuauhtémoc Cárdenas, the founder and head of the National Democratic Front—appealed to the masses for immediate support. He invited peasants and blue-collar workers to donate money, jewelry, goods, and other valuable possessions—anything to help compensate the owners who had been stripped of their companies. Alan García's plan wasn't very different.

Vargas Llosa had found him power hungry and immature. They had met for an interview that lasted an hour and a half at the government's palace in Lima. According to the writer's account, they talked about a number of topics, including Shining Path's attack on the palace with handmade bazookas. It was clear the politician was hoping to get the backing of the writer. But after their dialogue, the novelist appeared on television to state that instead of voting for García in the coming elections, he had chosen to support the candidate of the Christian Popular Party, Luis Bedoya Reyes. And in a move that infuriated the president even more, the novelist published an open letter in June 1986 in which he blamed García for the massacre of Shining Path rioters in three prisons.

The story behind the massacre was a widespread topic of conversation among Peruvians. By the mideighties, Shining Path had branches everywhere in the highlands—most prominently in Ayacucho, Junín, Cerro de Pasco, Apurímac, and Huancavelica. And though the vigor of the insurgency seemed undiminished by it, many Guzmán followers had been captured. They populated Peru's prisons under miserable conditions yet remained loyal to the cause. So much so that on June 18, 1986, an uprising in three Lima jails took place: Lurigancho, Santa Bárbara, and El Frontón. After taking seven policemen hostage, the prisoners demanded better health facilities and the unification of Shining Path followers in a single building. Frustrated by the ineptness of his own forces, President Alan García ended the mutiny by sending the military to quell the insurrection. After soldiers assaulted the three prisons with heavy artillery, close to 250 inmates were killed—at Lurigancho, for instance, nobody survived, and El Frontón lay in ruins after the incident. The action shocked the public and the international uproar was tremendous. García's own political credibility was just one of the casualties.

After listening to Alan García's address on the radio, Vargas Llosa wrote an article on August 2, 1987 for the newspaper *El Comercio* in which he talked of the perils of a totalitarian Peru and declared his opposition to the president's policy. A day later, together with intellectuals, artists, and highly regarded professionals like painter Fernando de Szyszlo and architect Freddy Cooper, he joined a group that drafted a manifesto calling for more democratic freedom for citizens and less dictatorial power for the state. Those two days transformed him forever. Suddenly, Vargas Llosa found himself in the spotlight: he was the most famous, and vocal, antagonist to Alan García's plan. And on August 21 he gave a speech in the Plaza San Martín, the first in which he faced his new persona: Vargas Llosa, politician.

It was also the start of a new freedom movement, Libertad, which grew very quickly and is now registered as an official Peruvian party. The movement actually had its origins in Fernando de Szyszlo's studio in September 1987. (Vargas Llosa used one of his paintings as inspiration in his erotic novel *In Praise of the Stepmother*.) As the writer himself put it, in its birth this new party had as its greatest goal "to attract young people and show them that the real revolution for a country like ours would be one that replaced arbitrariness with the rule of law, and convince them that liberal reform could make Peru a prosperous modern country."

Before the presidential campaign, Vargas Llosa was said to be nurturing five projects: a theatrical piece set in the Lima of the fifties about an old Quixote who tries to save the colonial-era balconies that are threatened by demolition; a novel set in the Andes; an essay on Victor Hugo's *Les Misérables*; a play about a change-of-gender surgical operation and its humorous consequences in the friendship of two men, former schoolmates, who meet at the Savoy Hotel in London; and a novel about Flora Tristán, a Franco-Peruvian revolutionary. Since politics dominated his days, none of these projects would be accomplished.

As candidate, the novelist made an early alliance, called Frente Democrático, with the Popular Action Party of Fernando Balaúnde, as well as with the Christian Popular Party. The campaign did not go as smoothly as he had hoped, however, and in the middle of it, feeling suffocated and regretful, he quit and fled to Spain. It seemed he had had second thoughts about the wisdom of running for office—mainly because he and his wife Patricia had received constant death threats, some by Alan García's supporters, but also because his dream to change Peru's economic and social course seemed an impossible one. And while he eventually doubled back and returned to campaigning, the harm was done. (Alvaro, one of his three children, was his press officer. He later wrote a campaign memoir, *The Devil on Campaign,* where his father's inner life is well described.) The country suffered from an incurable disease, Vargas Llosa believed: corruption and incompetence. His life had changed, he wrote in his memoir: "I had ceased to be private. Until I left Peru . . . after the second round of voting for the presidency, I lost the privacy that I had always guarded jealously."

In spite of Vargas Llosa's goodwill and heavy publicity apparatus organized by the reputable U.S. agency of Sawyer Miller (which also advised Corazón Aquino on her campaign for the presidency of the Philippines), the decisive winner of the presidential election was Alberto K. Fujimori, a fifty-one year old Peruvian of Japanese descent, who had been an unknown agronomy professor and headed La Molina's Agronomist University. The outcome came as a surprise to almost everybody, including world leaders such as U.S. President George Bush and Britain's Prime Minister Margaret Thatcher. Interestingly enough, Abimael Guzmán did not regard the two with the same degree of antipathy. El Chinito—the little Chinaman, a nickname given to Fujimori in spite of his Japanese ancestry—was a rival he wanted dead; the novelist, on the other hand, while symbolizing European intervention and the hierarchy of those Western values Presidente Gonzalo thoroughly dislikes, was treated less aggressively in 1990 and thereafter by *El Diario.* Its editorials, as the Peruvian journalist Gustavo Gorriti Ellenbogen has found, portrayed Vargas Llosa in a more benign fashion—even as "a man of wisdom." He certainly isn't seen as a friend, but neither is he seen as "a pig, a brute and tyrannical type" personified by Fujimori. The curious distinction the Shining Path drew between the two might have to do with ethnicity. Since Guzmán is known to express contempt for anything foreign, he perceived Fujimori, raised in popular Lima neighborhoods in an "un-Peruvian" Japanese household, as an image of external intervention. By contrast, Vargas Llosa is the embodiment of patriotism turned bourgeois. A lesser sin, apparently.

In retrospect, Vargas Llosa says that only three speeches he wrote made him proud: the one prepared in the garden of a friend's house—without the intrusive presence of bodyguards, reporters, and telephones—that launched his candidacy in the Plaza de Armas of Arequipa on June 4, 1989; the one that closed it in the Paseo de la República in Lima the next year; and the address he gave at the Libertad headquarters as soon as it became known he had lost the election. "Democracy," he said in that final occasion, "is driven by the electoral process, and in elections that are victories and defeats. But the work that had been done by the members of Libertad cannot be judged in this way. I know, I am certain, that Peru too will come to know and acknowledge this. That the seeds that we have sown together during these two and a half years will continue to germinate and finally produce those fruits that we desire for Peru: the fruits of modernity, justice, prosperity, peace and *libertad*."

Once again he was wrong. At one point in the campaign, in a public debate, Fujimori said to Vargas Llosa "It seems that you would like to make Peru a Switzerland, Doctor." In truth, the novelist *had* hoped to turn his into a country of cultured, prosperous, and free people, without poverty or unemployment or illiteracy, and certainly without an army. Quite the opposite happened. During his first few months as president, Fujimori borrowed from Vargas Llosa the shock-treatment therapy that was now renamed "Fujishock"—a package of neoliberal reform measures the novelist-candidate had proposed to help remedy Peru's financial insolvency. The national situation swiftly worsened. If before the election 7 million Peruvians were under the poverty level, in 1993 the numer increased to 12 million; a cholera epidemic left thousands dead throughout the country and spread to South and Central America; the incidence of tuberculosis grew to the highest in the region.

Once Fujimori came to office, moreover, Shining Path made a commitment to intensify its attacks in the provinces and in Lima. With Vargas Llosa in Europe and thus out of the picture, the struggle between Guzmán and the government was fearfully relentless. Peruvians began to talk of their country as ruled by two presidents: El Chinito and Presidente Gonzalo. Which one could outrule his opponent? On April 5, 1992, Fujimori struck what is now called *autogolpe*, a self-coup in which he closed down Congress, announced the complete reconstruction of the legal system, purged elderly judges, and suspended individual liberties. For decades Peru had been plagued with corruption, he claimed, and a drastic restructuring was urgently needed. Vargas Llosa was in Berlin's

Wissenchafts Kolleg at the time, finishing that narrative inspired by his presidential campaign *El pez en el agua*. In fact, since his defeat to Fujimori he has returned to Peru just twice—to attend the marriage of his daughter Morgana and to make Libertad an official Peruvian party. Although he wrote op-ed articles deploring the *autogolpe* for *El País* in Spain and the *New York Times*, by and large he has become a dilettante, his best and most comfortable role.

Vargas Llosa's book-length memoir is a compelling exercise in self-deception. Constructed in such a way that two separate narratives find a common message only in the last page, the volume's odd-numbered chapters recall the novelist's childhood and adolescence, the dogmatic paternal figure he reencountered in 1946–47, his education and early readings, his marriage to Tía Julia, up until his departure for Europe in 1958. Even-numbered chapters, on the other hand, detail every aspect of the presidential campaign and end in 1990, when Vargas Llosa leaves Peru once more, to fully devote himself to writing.

A few elements in the book are puzzling—above all first the author's messianism. Throughout the narrative, Vargas Llosa is convinced he and he alone is the savior, the redeemer of Peru's national sickness, his ideas a prescription from heaven. He uses a disproportionate amount of space to rage at and vilify his enemies, who, by definition, are corrupt, inefficient, nearsighted, or simply stupid. He attacks attachés, confidants, and even onetime partners like Hernando de Soto, an economist and the author of *The Other Path*, a 1989 international bestseller about the "informals," black marketeers who work outside the law in Lima, which had a foreword by Vargas Llosa that he now regrets having written. But Vargas Llosa's analysis is also marked by welcome insights. In one section, he studies the behavior of Peruvian artists and writers, what Gramsci called "organic intellectuals," to conclude convincingly that one of the most dramatic features of underdeveloped countries is the way in which the Left persuades the educated to adopt socialist gestures to hide their mediocrity and their personal frustration.

What's unforgivable in *El pez en el agua* is that, in such a compulsive account of the Peruvian cosmos, Vargas Llosa only mentions Guzmán in passing—and that only in the nine-page-long epilogue. His presence as an emblematic national figure is never acknowledged, his dangerous power never studied. There's only one explanation for this omission: in spite of his political involvements, Vargas Llosa remains essentially disconnected from Peru's inner soul, a stranger in a strange land. In fact, he lost the election precisely because he was seen as a member of the oligarchy, a member of the ruling class. Presidente Gonzalo, on the other hand, has deeply transformed the way things are conceived and perceived in Peru. For all his many atrocious crimes, he is considered to speak for a segment of the population which, even if small, directly affects the nation's present. Such irony makes one think of an analysis offered by Alfredo Bryce Echenique, author of the masterpiece *A World for Julius,* Peru's second-most important novelist, and once a student of Vargas Llosa, who has been living in Europe since 1972. In an article called "Peru: Our Daily Violence," published in the Spanish magazine *Claves,* he argues that the two selves, the Westernized and the *cholo,* divided across racial lines, have always existed by ignoring each other— the less they interact the better, and if they are doomed, it is simply because they refuse to face each other.

Fujimori's lucky day was September 12, 1992, when the members of the Dirección Nacional Contra el Terrorismo, or DINCOTE, finally captured Abimael Guzmán, with minimum fuss, in a house that functioned as a modern dance studio located in a quiet Lima neighborhood. (His closest allies are women, and one of them, Maritza Garrido Lecca, was once a ballerina.) Although Peru's embattled constitution prohibits the death penalty, Fujimori, after shutting down Congress, has openly declared his will to make Guzmán an exception by placing him on death row. This wasn't the first time Presidente Gonzalo had been arrested. Gorriti Ellenbogen's *Sendero: History of Peru's Millenary War* details how the police captured him in January 1979, linking him to a number of well-publicized strikes. He was taken to the State Security offices and interrogated by high authorities. Ironically, though, he was released after confessing to having a Marxist-Leninist ideology but "not to [being] Shining Path's commander-in-chief." Considered by his followers the Fourth Sword of Marxism (Marx, Lenin and Mao are the other three), Abimael Guzmán is now Latin America's most famous prisoner.

Is he still a threat? Peru is inhabited by other guerrilla groups, including Victor Polay's Tupac Amaru Revolutionary Movement (MRTA), which began action in 1984 and is considerably smaller than Shining Path. Unlike Guzmán, the MRTA followers revere Che Guevara and have links to Cuba. But Presidente Gonzalo dismisses the group and its idol as a supporting cast, a bourgeois extremity of the nation's government. The Shining Path is another story. As Tina Rosenberg argues, Shining Path, which controls a "liberated territory" in Peru's jungle, has broken most of the rules of guerrilla warfare, of urban and rural subversion, and has left international intelligence services thoroughly perplexed. Since Guzmán's imprisonment, bombs and assassinations have not ceased. On the contrary, a seemingly headless Shining Path seemed to be launching a counterattack, a wave of revenge for its leaders's arrest.

Fujimori's decline is imminent: his tyranny, the fourth such regime in Peru's twentieth-century history, will sooner or later bring more un-certainty. This semifeudal, quasi-modern Banana Republic is torn apart: Vargas Llosa's westernized supporters are in a face-off against Guzmán's reactionary militarism. And so the question returns, as it does time and again: At what precise moment did Peru fuck itself up?

Or should one say that the nation was always divided—that it was defective from birth? Wandering around the globe in a self-imposed exile, the novelist continues to write, his sharp pen explicating, or per-haps distorting, Peru's impossible dilemma. Carlos Abimael Guzmán Reynoso, alias Presidente Gonzalo, caged in an underground cell and metamorphosed into a media artifact, has in turn become a living mar-tyr, a monument, his Shining Path certain to have a role in the country's future. If Peru eventually becomes South America's Iran, complete with a fanatical ayatollah ready to cut international ties, Marxist-Leninist ide-ology will sweep the nation like a tide crashing upon a sand castle. By then the white European minority will long be gone, of course, replaced by mythical Inca heroes. Mao Zedong in Macondo: market economy and democracy alike stand to be a casualties of ideological absolutism. Guzmán and Vargas Llosa: two aspects of the country's identity, their lives mapping out the forking paths to Peru's future.

[1993]

3 / THE FIRST BOOK

I disliked books when I was a child. They symbolized isolation, concealment, silence, and boredom. I also thoroughly disliked bookish kids and instantly befriended those preferring outdoor adventures: I
wanted action, to go places—to be a mountain climber, to ascend pyramids, to build fortresses in the jungle against fictitious invaders. I
dreamed of exploring the Chiapas rain forest, navigating the Usumazinta
River, penetrating mysterious caves in Tabasco, and conquering dormant volcanoes like Popocatépetl. What least appealed to me was staying alone within the four walls of my room, suffocated and forgotten.

But I did read. My parents made sure that books were common, familiar objects at home. In fact, as I recollect, it seems that I carefully
selected the titles to read: If I was going to spend endless amounts of
time staring at pages, I wanted marvelous odysseys in return. In my eyes
a book was successful when I found a hero to emulate. I would pretend
to be Gulliver in Lilliput or Brobdingnag, the protagonist of H. G. Wells's
The Time Machine disoriented in the middle of a battle between the
Morlocks and the Eloi. I cared very little about the shape and order of
the words themselves. What mattered was the fantasy invoked.

Some early literary recollections are of an illustrated volume on
monks, which, I discovered many years later, had been written by Mar-
guerite Yourcenar. I also recall a poorly developed German tale, *An Au-
tomobile Named Julia*, about a couple of siblings who turn a dilapidated
vehicle into a race car. The vehicle's magical transformation attracted
me: from junk to marvel, from being undesired to becoming an object
of pride. In some mysterious way the book was about oblivion and resurrection, about death and reincarnation. Happily, not long ago I found

it hidden in a drawer and my three-year-old son is now under its spell.

I thoroughly enjoyed riffling through the pages of encyclopedias and studying their maps and graphics. In fact, most of the few books I read were mediocre and forgettable translations of heroic adventures set in distant places. Jules Verne's *Journey to the Center of the Earth* and *20,000 Leagues Under the Sea* were compelling as ideas, but felt endless as stories. I read an abridged version of Ernest Hemingway's *The Old Man and the Sea,* which I thought unusual for its description of human courage and endurance. I also had a copy of Rudyard Kipling's *The Jungle Book*; I fantasized being Mowgli, brought up as a wolf cub, capable of communicating with elephants, giraffes, monkeys, and snakes. I was compelled by Kipling's *Kim* and his *Just So Stories* as well, but ended up less mesmerized by these.

Bizarre descriptions of enigmatic societies enchanted me. My all-time favorite was Emilio Salgari, a prolific Italian writer who, inexplicably, never made in onto the Anglo-American bookshelf. I acquired almost his entire oeuvre, some twenty-five volumes, published by Editorial Porrúa in Mexico in its legendary series "Sepan Cuantos . . . ."

Even though I was hardly ever in the mood to read, when I did find myself with a book in hand, it was usually Salgari, perhaps *Sandokan, The Pirates of Malaysia,* or *Captain Thunder,* all piquant voyages to never-never lands full of suspense, audacity, and false identities.

Ironically, my native country, Mexico, played almost no role in my incipient, if precarious literary life. The explanation has less to do with parental guidance than with the state of affairs at the time. In the early seventies Mexico still had no juvenile book industry to speak of. None of the writers through which I would later on dicover my cultural landscape—Juan Rulfo, Agustín Yáñez, Alfonso Reyes, Octavio Paz, Carlos Fuentes—had ever bothered to write for children. This also explains why the only Spanish titles I remember reading were *Platero and I,* a dull prose poem about the Andalusian wanderings of a poet with his donkey, by Juan Ramón Jiménez, winner of the 1956 Nobel Prize for Literature, and an abridged version of *Don Quixote* with drawings by Gustave Doré, which I found foolish.

My irreverence and disrespect for books ended abruptly the day of my first encounter with what I think of as the Book—the model, the book of books, a Platonic archetype whose virtue is not lessened by the passing of time. It was a decisive event in my life, an epiphany that made me understand, once and for all, the importance of the printed word in society and its future role in my own life. Since then I cannot but experience the universe as an open-ended narrative and think of God as a magisterial novelist, wise, savvy, romantic, even corny at times.

The synagogue where this all took place was a modern structure—plain, tasteless, cold, made of huge chambers. I must have been in my early teens, a young adolescent, still a bit of a rascal, naive, who approached life as an indecipherable labyrinth. I recall running frenetically up and down the aisles.

At one point I remember covering my face with a prayer shawl, pretending to be a ghost. Then I saw the ark. Of course, I had seen it many times before but somehow its sacredness became apparent to me that very moment. I had a feeling of foreboding: Something strange, something ineluctable was approaching. The ark's curtain opened and before my eyes were the scrolls: luminous, impeccable, royal, ornamented with baroque jewelry, just like a lost treasure from a Salgari novel.

A man from the congregation took out a scroll and kissed it. The scroll was embraced by other members of the congregation and carried around the assembly, at which point other kisses, innumerable, pious, from mouths young and old, descended on it. People were paying respect to the written word. I realized for the first time that books really mattered. Or better, that one of them reigned over all the rest: the Book.

After that day my books at home seemed different: I felt empathy toward them, immense love. I dreamed of memorizing every single word they contained. I wanted to be next to them at all times, keep them well protected, reopen them for the sheer pleasure of enjoying the texture and shape of a written page.

I immediately began collecting books, investigating their process of production, holding them in my hands with care and affection. I began contrasting translations with originals. During the next few years, I slowly began to reflect on the role of the Book in my life. I realized it was a covenant, a pact between my past and future. It had been written by people like me, concerned with daily affairs but, also, with memory and remembrance. It's always the same book; what changes are its readers. And so the act of reading acquired new meaning for me. Words began to matter as much as content. Rather than being lifeless, mere conduits for escapist adventures, they became the embodiment of a pact: a pact to make life meaningful, to link dream and awareness, to establish a dialogue between my ancestors and my descendants. Written words had life.

Today I pride myself on my personal library: ambitious, fortifying, multilingual, irrevocably limited, and imperfect. It was born in Mexico and enriched in the Middle East, Spain, the United States, the Caribbean, Africa, and South America. I have numerous editions of *Don Quixote*, which I now think was part of God's original design of the universe. I have relocated my entire Salgari collection and have almost every title by Swift and H. G. Wells. I also pride myself on possessing a voluminous section devoted to Mexican and other Hispanic books, all dancing around a unifying heart: Borges's complete works.

I spend many hours in my library, writing and rewriting, reading and rereading adventures, mystical tales, and essays about people and books. A considerable portion of my day is made of voyages to the center of a novel and in adventurous excursions to encyclopedias and dictionaries. I often feel I have no existence outside these volumes: I live with and by the Book.

[1995]

4 / LAS MARIPOSAS

Not long ago, I heard Julia Alvarez call attention to an intriguing linguistic tic in her native Dominican culture: When you ask somebody what's up and no easy reply can be found, people are likely to say, *Entre Lucas y Juan Mejía.* "Between the devil and the deep blue sea" isn't the right equivalent in English, Alvarez added, "because you aren't describing the sensation of being caught between a pair of bad alternatives."

> "So-so" isn't the meaning either, because the Dominican expression isn't at all meant to suggest bland stasis, mediocrity. It's much more intriguing than that. "How are you doing?" "I'm between Lucas and Juan Mejía." And who are these guys? . . . The very story that inspired the saying is gone. So . . . you have to go on and tell the tale of why you feel the way you do. What are the forces you're caught between? How did you get there? And how does it feel to be there?

Alvarez's *oeuvre* is precisely about this type of crisis—the identity of the in-betweens—and about why she feels the way she does in somebody else's country and language (she immigrated to the United States with her family when she was ten). Although this subject is ubiquitous in ethnic literature in general, her pen lends it an authenticity and sense of urgency seldom found elsewhere. In fact, in the current wave of Latina novelists she strikes me as among the least theatrical and vociferous, the one listening most closely to the subtleties of her own artistic call. She stands apart stylistically, a psychological novelist who uses language skill-fully to depict complex inner lives for her fictional creations.

Alvarez's journey from Spanish into English, from Santo Domingo to New York City, from Lucas to Juan Mejía, was the topic of *How the García Girls Lost Their Accents*, a set of loosely connected autobiographical stories published in book form in 1991, about well-off Dominican sisters exiled in *el norte*. The critical reception was mixed, though readers whole-heartedly embraced the book as charming and compassionate—a sort of minor echo of Laura Esquivel's *Like Water for Chocolate*—and it was welcomed with the type of jubilation often granted to works by suddenly emergent minorities. After all, Dominican literature, in Spanish or English, is hardly represented in bookstores and college courses in the United States. Indeed, not since the early twentieth-century larger-than-life scholar and essayist Pedro Henríquez Ureña delivered the Charles Eliot Norton lectures at Harvard University in 1940–41, on the topic of literary currents in Hispanic America, had a writer from the Dominican Republic been the target of such admiration here.

In spite of Alvarez's fairly conservative, yet semi-experimental approach to literature, what makes her a peculiar, nontraditional Dominican writer is her divided identity. "I am a Dominican, hyphen, American," she once said. "As a fiction writer, I find that the most exciting things happen in the realm of that hyphen—the place where two worlds collide or blend together."

Alvarez's novelistic debut evidenced a writer whose control of her craft was sharp but less than complete. Some of the autonomous segments of *García Girls* were not knit together well, for example, leaving the reader holding several frustratingly loose ends. Now, three years later, such shortcomings have been largely erased, as her haunting second novel easily surpasses her earlier achievement. And while this vista of the political turmoil left behind by émigrés like the García girls still may not be proportional to her talents, it is extraordinary in that it exhibits quick, solid maturing as an artist. In spite of its title, *In the Time of the Butterflies* is not crowded with magic realist scenes à la Gabriel García Márquez and Isabel Allende. Instead, it's a fictional study of a tragic event in Dominican history, when, on November 25, 1960, three outspoken Mirabal sisters, active opponents of the dictatorship of Rafael Leónidas Trujillo, were found dead near their wrecked Jeep, at the bottom of a fifteen-foot cliff in the northern part of the country. Today the Mirabals are known throughout the Caribbean as The Butterflies—Las Mariposas. Alvarez uses her novel to explore their tragic odyssey and, metaphorically, to bring them back to life.

The novel's 300-plus pages are full of pathos and passion, with beautifully crafted anecdotes interstitched to create a patchwork quilt of memory and ideology. We see the sisters as teens, fighting with Papá, marrying, leading double lives, commenting on the Cuban revolution, becoming rebels themselves, going on to bury husbands and sons. The organization is symmetrical: The book's major parts are laid out in four sections, one devoted to each of the three murdered sisters and one to the fourth sister, who escaped their fate. We have thus a quatrain of novellas, only one of which doesn't end in tragedy. Here's how Alvarez has Dedé, the surviving Mirabal sister, remark on the assassination:

> It seems that at first the Jeep was following the truck up the mountain. Then as the truck slowed for the grade, the Jeep passed and sped away, around some curves, out of sight. Then it seems that the truck came upon the ambush. A blue-and-white Austin had blocked part of the road; the Jeep had been forced to a stop; the women were being led away peaceably, so the truck driver said, *peaceably* to the car.

While the Mirabal incident might seem a bit obscure to American readers (most of Dominican history, perhaps even the U.S. invasion, does), it offers an amazing array of creative opportunities to reflect on the labyrinthine paths of the Hispanic psyche. Others in the Dominican Republic have used this historical episode as a springboard to reflect on freedom and ideology, among them Pedro Mir in his poem "Amén de Mariposas" and Ramón Alberto Ferreras in his book *Las Mirabal*. Alvarez takes a decidedly unique approach: She examines the martyrdom of these three Dominican women as a gender battlefield—three brave, subversive wives crushed by a phallocentric regime. In an openly misogynistic society, the Mirabals are initially dealt with by the government in a delicate, somewhat condescending fashion, which of course doesn't exclude the oppressive power from annihilating them in the end.

The official newspaper of the Trujillo regime, *El Caribe*, treated the deaths of Minerva, Patria, and María Teresa Mirabal and their driver, Rufino de la Cruz, all between twenty-five and thirty-seven years of age, as an accident. Not only did it report the incident without much explanation, it failed to mention the sisters' anti-Trujillo activities. Nor did it acknowledge that a fourth sister wasn't among the victims and had thus survived. Assuming her role as historian and marionetteer, Alvarez fills in the gaps. She didn't know the sisters personally, and she laments at the end of her volume that the reluctance of people in the Dominican Republic to speak out or open up to strangers, as well as the chaotic state of affairs in the nation's libraries and research centers, made it difficult for her to gather historical data. But her task was hardly biographical. "I wanted to immerse my readers in an epoch in the life of the Dominican Republic that I believe can only finally be understood by fiction, only finally be redeemed by the imagination," she writes. "A novel is not, after all, a historical document, but a way to travel through the human heart."

Alvarez writes, for instance, that Trujillo himself had a crush on Minerva, who responded publicly by slapping him in the face. She also analyzes the religious education María Teresa received and later metamorphosed into anti-authoritarian animosity. Much in the *Butterflies* novel resembles *How the García Girls Lost Their Accents*: Hispanic domesticity is at center stage, analyzed in light of the intricate partnerships and rivalries of the four sisters. The male chauvinism that dominates the Hispanic family is meant to mirror and complement Trujillo's own machismo, with home and country approached as micro- and macrocosms. The style is deliberately fragmentary and openly Faulknerian. Alvarez's pages made me think, time and again, of the Israeli writer A. B. Yehoshua: By intertwining disparate literary forms (journals, first-person accounts, correspondence, drawings, etc.) Alvarez allows each Mirabal to acquire her own voice. Pasted together, their voices provide a sense that Truth is a collective invention.

Unlike many Latino writers of her generation, Alvarez abandons the United States in theme and scenario to analyze the role of women under dictatorships in the Southern Hemisphere. Trujillo's presence is felt from afar, as an overwhelming shadow controlling and destroying human happiness—so overarching is the dictator, in fact, that it seems to me he becomes the central character. The Mirabal sisters fight *el líder* as both a real and a ghostlike figure. Their opposition is also an attack against phallocentrism as an accepted way of life in Hispanic societies. In this respect, *In the Time of Butterflies* ought to be equated with a number of Latin American works about dictators (known in Spanish as *novelas del dictador*), including Miguel Angel Asturias's *El Señor Presidente* and Augusto Roa Bastos's *I, the Supreme*. And it is a first-rate addition to the shelf of works by Latina literary artists who write about chauvinism, from Delmira Agustini to Rosario Ferré. In her Postscript, Alvarez writes:

> During [Trujillo's] terrifying thirty-one-year
> regime, any hint of disagreement ultimately resulted
> in death for the dissenter and often for members of
> his or her family. Yet the Mirabals had risked their
> lives. I kept asking myself, What gave them that
> special courage? It was to understand that question
> that I began this story.

Fiction as an instrument to decodify a tyranny's hidden and manifest tentacles. Fiction as a tool of journalism and vice versa. Fiction as a device to reclaim a stolen aspect of history. Ironically, it is precisely at this level that Alvarez's volume is simultaneously invigorating and curiously disappointing. The author herself appears at the beginning of the plot: It is 1994 and, as an American woman with broken Spanish, she is eager to interview Dedé. Dedé offers much data about her sisters' journey, from their convent education to their first love affairs and subsequent marriages to high-profile activists in the fifties. Indeed, Dedé serves as the backbone to the entire story. But Alvarez leaves reaction to the Mirabals' assassination to a twenty-page epilogue, in which we find out about public outrage and the spectacular, media-oriented trial of their murderers, which took place a year after Trujillo was killed in 1961. Interleaving news clips, court testimony, interviews, and other paraphernalia throughout her narrative might have helped—anything, to insert the Mirabals more firmly in the flux of Dominican memory.

Notwithstanding this structural handicap, *In the Time of the Butterflies* is enchanting, a novel only a female, English-speaking Hispanic could have written. By inserting herself in the cast as *la gringa norteamericana*, Alvarez links the old and the new. At a time when many Latino writers seem so easily satisfied exploring the ghetto, in fictional terms of drugs, crime, and videotape, Alvarez, a writer on a different kind of edge, calls attention to the Latin American foundations of Hispanic fiction in English and dares once again to turn the novel into a political artifact. The inside covers of her book are illustrated with typography listing women and men assassinated by Trujillo. Recalling the Vietnam Memorial in Washington, D.C., the names seem endless, an homage to patriotic anonymity. Alvarez pays tribute to only three of these names, but the rest are also evoked in her lucid pages. Her novel is a wonderful examination of how it feels to be a survivor, how it feels to come from a society where justice and freedom are unwelcome and where the answer to the question "How are you?" often has to be, *Entre Lucas y Juan Mejía.*

[1994]

5 / THE MASTER OF ARACATACA

The invention of a nation in a phase . . .
—*Wallace Stevens*

For God's sake!—quick!—quick! put me to sleep—or,
quick!—waken me!—quick!—I say to you that I am dead!
—*Edgar Allan Poe*

Honor to whom honor is due: Gabriel García Márquez, whose labyrinthine imagination has enchanted millions worldwide since 1967, when his masterpiece *One Hundred Years of Solitude* was first published in Buenos Aires, has reinvented Latin America. Macondo, his fictional coastal town in the Caribbean, has become such a landmark—its geography and inhabitants constantly invoked by teachers, politicians, and tourist agents—that it is hard to believe it is a sheer fabrication.

What makes this south-of-the-border Yoknapatowpha irresistible is the idiosyncrasy of its inhabitants, who often defy the rules and principles of Western civilization. As V. S. Pritchett once argued, the Colombian novelist "is a master of a spoken prose that passes unmoved from scenes of animal disgust and horror to the lyrical evocation, opening up vistas of imagined or real sights which may be gentle or barbarous." A parade of both gentleness and barbarity, Macondo makes beauty of chaos. García Márquez's fictional topos makes Latin America's ancient battle between the forces of progress and those of regression, between civilization and anarchy, look like a mere theatrical prop—an adjuvant to art.

John Updike put it simply: García Márquez dreams perfect dreams for us. But not always, we must qualify—in fact, quite rarely. For the radiant glare of his finest work has obscured the dismal truth: García Márquez's literary career is curiously disappointing. Aside from his masterpiece, his writing often seems uneven, repetitive, obsessively overwritten, forced: cynical in ways even this master of the cycle never intended.

Perhaps it couldn't have been otherwise. So arrestingly powerful is his magnum opus that all beside it looks pallid. I shall never forget the suggestion of a celebrated Uruguayan colleague, who argued at a writer's conference that, after 1967, García Márquez's annus mirabilis, it would have been best had he mysteriously vanished, become prematurely posthumous. This was an unfair, strange, even villainous thought, no doubt, but one that spoke to the curiously monotonous nature of the Colombian's art.

Whatever the lapses of his pen, however, there can be no doubt as to his stature. Alongside Miguel de Cervantes, he is considered today the premier Hispanic writer, *Don Quixote of La Mancha* and *One Hundred Years of Solitude* being the most durable and widely read bestsellers in the Spanish-speaking world, with billions of copies in print and translations into every imaginable language. Who would have thought that this obscure journalist of *El Espectador in Bogotá* (a city he considers "the ugliest in the world"), an admirer of Graham Greene, Virginia Woolf, and William Faulkner, could end up traveling to Stockholm in 1982 to receive the Nobel Prize for literature—and this on the basis of a single genealogical narrative?

Indeed, critics such as Irving Howe, Tzvetan Todorov, and Ermir Rodríguez Monegal claim García Márquez has helped renew the novel as a literary genre. And so he has. After the earlier legacy of the high modernists had almost reduced the form to a philosophical battlefield where, it sometimes seemed, only pessimistic insights were worth writing about, he has imbued prose fiction with a sense of wonder and joy that is both critically and popularly acclaimed around the world. John Leonard believes you emerge from the Colombian's marvelous universe "as if from a dream, the mind on fire. A dark, ageless figure at the hearth, part historian, part haruspex, in a voice by turns angelic and maniacal, first lulls to sleep your grip on a manageable reality, then locks you into legend and myth." Alfred Kazin compared his masterpiece to *Moby Dick* and Mario Vargas Llosa calls his ex-friend "a total novelist"—able to encapsulate, through words, the complexities of our vast universe. It's hard to imagine a modern voice with more echoes.

But aside from the memorable Buendía saga—its intricate structure destined to remain a much-envied model of creative intelligence—will readers ever witness another achievement of this order? Can García Márquez ever stop imitating, even plagiarizing, himself as he has frequently done since the mid-seventies? Is the sense of déjà-vu conveyed by his post-1967 titles a normal reaction to the decades-long accumulation of his literary talent, the audience always sensing an inevitable return to the same set of metaphors, once fresh and now trite? Or is it that any writer at any given time, Shakespeare aside, is capable of handling only a limited number of ideas and images and that the Colombian has used and abused them all? Can *One Hundred Years of Solitude* leave room for another *coup de maître*?

It could be argued, of course, that García Márquez, more than many, has earned the right to repeat himself. Since *Leafstorm,* a novella he began at age nineteen (later collected with a handful of stories and printed in English in 1972), a dozen volumes by the Colombian have become available in the United States. (Spanish editions of his books include some twenty different titles, including volumes of journalistic pieces and screenplays.) Prolific as he is, his settings, from Macondo to a fictionalized Magdalena River, inhabit a region only about fifty square miles long; very rarely does he place a story line elsewhere—say in Mexico, Chile, or Europe. His characters share provincial values in a universe where memory and modernity are antagonists; García Márquez specializes in making the so-called Third World look exotic and anachronistic, in touch with nature and its own roots. His exuberant, grandiloquent style, however, reveals a writer who spends his life creating one sublime book—a book of books whose pages reflect all things at all times, the sort of conceit to which Walt Whitman was devoted.

What's most puzzling, to my mind at least, is that, in spite of his dazzling international esteem, García Márquez remains a literary subject in search of a biographer. While discussions of his work exist in profusion, his intellectual odyssey remains in shadow, as does his carefully guarded private life. We don't even know for sure in what year he was born. In 1971 Vargas Llosa published an ambitious and voluminous literary study of him, *History of a Deicide,* the first seventy pages of which gave the most accurate profile of García Márquez up to that time; but political differences between the Peruvian and the Colombian kept the volume out of print and unavailable, and today the document seems hopelessly dated. In 1983, a volume of conversations with his long-time friend Plinio Apuleyo Mendoza, shedding light on his intellectual anxieties, came out in England. Otherwise, what little is known about this man remains scattered in interviews (with William Kennedy, with Ernesto González

Bermejo, with Harley D. Oberhelman, and with some thirty others) and reviews in literary journals and yellowing newspaper pages.

To complicate matters further, García Márquez, a sly humorist, often enjoys deceiving interviewers by revamping his own life story, giving out confusing information and spinning anecdotes and gossip to evade answers. Unfortunately, nothing remotely resembling a true literary biography, á la Leon Edel's *Henry James* or Carlos Baker's *Ernest Hemingway*, is available, while only a few scholarly volumes on the writer's life and work have been published by scholarly imprints, including essay collections put out by the University of Texas Press and G. K. Hall. Thanks to the Colombian's loquacious tendency to embellish the past, even the circumstances surrounding the composition of *One Hundred Years of Solitude* remain shrouded by myth. Ever since 1967, it would seem, García Márquez has been busy fabricating his own eternity. A biographer is needed to bring perspective to his story, at once to render his aspired heroism in human scale and to render his routine existence in the form of narrative art. For the biographer's craft, at its best, is one that at once reduces and magnifies its subject, discovering the ordinariness within the art, but also making art of that very ordinariness.

A serious consideration of García Márquez's ups and downs would probably divide his years into five parts. The first part, 1928 to 1954, includes his birth and childhood years in Aracataca, his adolescence in Bogotá, his early stories, his years in Cartagena as a law student and journalist, and his writing for Bogotá's newspaper *El Espectador*. The second part, 1955 to 1966, takes us from his first published novel, *Leafstorm* (La hojarasca)—encompassing the influences of Joseph Conrad, Faulkner, Hemingway, Graham Greene, and John Dos Passos on his work, Colombia's political upheaval in the mid-fifties, and his travels to Paris and marriage to Mercedes Barcha—to the publication of his celebrated novella *No One Writes to the Colonel* (El coronel no tienen quién le escriba). The third part, 1967 to 1972, includes the origin, impact, and contribution of García Márquez's magnum opus, *One Hundred Years of Solitude* (Cien años de soledad); the writer's friendship with famous Latin American intellectuals like Julio Cortázar, Alvaro Mutis, Mario Vargas Llosa, and Carlos Fuentes; his permanent residence in Mexico City and Cuba; and his increasing international stardom. The fourth part, 1973 to 1982, spans the years between his stunning success and his reception of the Nobel Prize for literature, just after the publication of *Chronicle of a Death Foretold* (Crónica de una muerte anunciada). And the fifth part, from 1983 onward, begins with García Márquez's second major work *Love in the Time of Cholera* (El amor en los tiempos del cólera), and includes his mature political views and friendship with Fidel Castro, his semibiographical account of Simón Bolívar's last days in *The General in His Labyrinth* (El general en su laberinto), his fight against cancer, the shaping of his "European" short stories in the collection *Strange Pilgrims* (Doce cuentos peregrinos), his physical and creative decline, and his own attempt to write an all-encompassing memoir.

Yet what the neatness of this or any other schematism leaves out are the ambiguities that attend the pivotal events of his life, especially his formative years and the period in which he wrote *One Hundred Years of Solitude*. So I want to indicate, however sketchily, the difficulties of examining the intricate relation between his life and craft, if only to help point the way toward the route future biographers might follow.

The very first mystery to address is his elusive date of origin. According to some accounts, Gabriel García Márquez—or simply Gabo, as his friends like to call him—was born on March 6, 1928, in Aracataca, a small forgotten town on Colombia's Caribbean coast, but a lack of official documents makes it hard to confirm this information. The writer himself claims he is not sure of the precise birth year, and his father, Gabriel Eligio García, known as Dr. García by friends and acquaintances, maintains that it was 1927, before a famous banana workers' strike that agitated the entire region. What is certain is that he came to this world a couple of decades after his country, once part of a region called New Granada, which included Panama and most of Venezuela, had undergone the far-reaching and thoroughly exhaustive War of a Thousand Days (1899–1902), which resulted in the deaths of more than 100,000 people.

He was an opinionated, intelligent, highly imaginative boy. Legends and myths, ubiquitous in his childhood, are the stuff Latin America's collective past is made of, a region where History is malleable—always adjusted to the needs of the regime in power. During García Márquez's early years, numerous stories about brave army men still circulated, including one about the liberal Colonel Rafael Uribe Uribe—a model for Aureliano Buendía, one of the main protagonists of *One Hundred Years of Solitude*—who had lost a total of thirty-six battles and still remained quite popular. The colonel's pair of identical last names recalls the endogamous marriages that plague the Buendías chronology, where cousins marry each other and have children with pig tails. Indeed, what García Márquez did was to transmute the fictions that surrounded him into literature: his originality is based on the artful redeployment of the flamboyant creations that inhabit Hispanic America's popular imagination. Everything he saw and heard was eventually recorded in his early literary works, given its most crystalline shape in his 1967 masterpiece, and then revamped in subsequent works.

Throughout the nineteenth century, Colombia, which became a republic in 1886, has been filled with political unrest; partisan division along conservative-centrist and liberal-federalist lines would not infrequently erupt into civil war. After the War of the Thousand Days, when the conservatives emerged victorious, the regime of General Rafael Reyes (1904–10) ushered in a boom of banana plantations along the Magdalena River, the place where *The General in His Labyrinth* and other titles are set. Many foreign companies settled down in the region, including the United Fruit Company, which had 3,000 employees in 1908, more than a fourth of the whole banana work force.

Flush with new-found prosperity, Aracataca was a place where, it was remarked, prostitutes danced *cumbias* at the side of arrogant tycoons. "With the banana boom," the writer would later recollect, "people from all over the world began to arrive at Aracataca and it was very strange because in this little town in Colombia's Atlantic coast, for a moment all languages were spoken." A couple of decades later, with the growth and expansion of organized unions from Mexico to Argentina, and after the creation of Colombia's Socialist Revolutionary Party, a bloody massacre took place in Ciénaga. The army used machine guns to disperse striking banana laborers near a train station. Hundreds died, perhaps thousands. The event was retold through stories and folksongs time and again while García Márquez was still young. It took hold in his memory and would eventually make for a powerful scene in *One Hundred Years of Solitude*: scores of bodies of United Fruit toilers lie motionless on the battlefield after an unsuccessful strike and are then piled in a train. The next day, nobody in Macondo acknowledges the tragedy and many even insist that it never happened.

Dr. García, the novelist's father, had a total of fifteen children, three the result of extramarital affairs. One of these three, a daughter, was raised by his wife, Luisa Santiaga Márquez Iguarán, much in the way Ursula Iguarán, the matron at the heart of Macondo, takes upon herself the raising of the vast bastard descendents of Colonel Aureliano Buendía. Gabriel was oldest of the legitimate branch, most of whom share his left-wing politics, although a few of his siblings, like their dad, are *gordos*, or conservatives. As García Márquez has said in public statements, *Love in the Time of Cholera*, his 1986 romance in which an old couple reunites after persistent passion and decades of separation, is based on his parents' relationship. Before getting married, Dr. García was a telegrapher. (Indeed, telegraphs and other forms of pre–Second World War wire communication are ubiquitous in his son's oeuvre.) After strong opposition from Luisa Santiaga's family—her parents, probably the most aristocratic couple in Aracataca, were first cousins—they married, and Dr. García and his wife left their then only son Gabriel to the care of the child's paternal grandparents because the father wanted to improve his economic situation. The newlywed couple lived in numerous towns throughout the Caribbean coast. Dr. García eventually received a degree in homeopathic medicine in Barranquilla. Afterwards, while studying for four years at the medical school of the Universidad de Cartagena, he became a pharmacist.

After ten years of separation, Gabriel was reunited with his parents, and during 1939–50, the family, already numerous, settled in Sucre, a port town in Bolívar Province, a place where several of his novels would be set, including *No One Writes to the Colonel*. But soon they had to move again because another doctor had settled in the same town and taken most of Dr. García's clientele. Around 1951 (some say it was 1950), the family moved to Cartagena, where the father, in spite of his unfinished course in clinical medicine, finally received an M.D. and maintained his own practice for decades. Luisa Santiaga, the novelist's mother, a spirited, strong-willed woman with a liberal upbringing—her father, Nicolás Márquez Iguarán, an army man, fought on General Rafael Uribe Uribe's side—is said to have been quite intuitive. She won the lottery several times based on information she claimed to have gotten in dreams.

In interviews and autobiographical pieces, García Márquez has said that his first eight years of life were the most crucial and memorable. At twelve months of age, when his parents left Aracataca, he went to live in his grandparents' home, a place, he says, full of ghosts. In Luis Harss's volume of narrative portraits *Into the Mainstream*, the novelist describes his new tutors as superstitious and impressionable people.

> In every corner [of the house] there were skeletons and memories, and after six in the evening you didn't dare leave your room. It was a world of fantastic terror [in which] there were coded conversations. . . . There was an empty room where Aunt Petra had died. And another one where Uncle Lázaro passed away. Thus, at night you couldn't walk because there were more people dead than alive. I remember [an] episode well, one that captures the atmosphere of the house. I had an aunt. . . . She was very active: she was doing something else at home all the time and one day she sat down to sew a shroud. I then asked her: "Why are you sewing a shroud?" "Because I'm going to die, my boy," she answered. When she finished sewing her shroud, she lay down and died.

In 1969, a Bogotá journalist who traveled to Aracataca discovered that García Márquez's childhood house was being devoured by ants and covered with dust. Just like the Buendiá mansion, and, for that matter, all of Macondo, it was condemned to perish.

Death, a common, banal fact in Latin America, was a preoccupation of the novelist. Aunt Petra's end and others sharply more violent color his work: colonels agonizing before firing squads, corpses found in a huge palace, a killing solved by a private eye. Memory, in García Márquez's view, is synonymous with redemption: to remember is to overcome, to defeat the forces of evil. Lust, illusion, corruption, and the recalcitrance of barbarism are also at the core of his work. These themes, openly or otherwise, are frequently intertwined with another pressing subject: a sharp critique of institutionalized religion. His attack on the Catholic church is not surprising when one considers the fact that García Márquez completed primary and high school in a private Jesuit institution in Zipaquirá, near Bogotá, a place where his mother's liberal views and his own frequently clashed with institutional dogmas. Priests and clerical acolytes are often portrayed by him as distant, corrupt, ill-informed, or simply lazy. In the story "Tuesday's Siesta" (La siesta del martes), a woman and her daughter arrive in a small town to pay last respects to Carlos Centeno, the woman's only son, who became a thief in order to support the family. The response she gets from the local priest is not only cold but offensive: he refuses to help her; when he finally agrees to give her the keys to the cemetery, it is only after asking her for charity.

Such a jaundiced view of matters ecclesiastical is, of course, unsurprising from a leftist. And yet García Márquez, it should be made clear, does not attack God or human spirituality; his target is the clerical hierarchy. In his universe the Almighty is alive and well, and, one senses, possessed of literary talents. After all, couldn't *One Hundred Years of Solitude* be read as a daring rewriting of the Bible? Floods, prophesies, sin and condemnation, epic wars and the abuse of power, hero worship and romance—the elements are all there, and so are the theological and teleological undertones. Both the Bible and the Colombian's master-piece intertwine the individual and the collective in a concrete, urgent fashion with images that seem tangible, real.

Indeed, García Márquez's imagination, since early on, has been graphic: scenes, however surrealistic, always have an incredible imme-diacy. This fact is important when one considers García Márquez's life-long passion for the movies. He is founder and executive director of Cuba's Film Institute in Havana, to which he often donates the profits of his films. His interest in the silver screen dates back to when he worked for Mexico's J. Walter Thompson advertising agency. He wrote com-mercials and was enchanted with the filmmaking process. "To write for the movies," the Colombian once reflected, "one needs great humility. That distinguishes it from the literary endeavor. While the novelist sit-ting at the typewriter is totally free and in control, the screenwriter is only a piece in a complex machinery and thus the target of contradic-tory special interests." Aside from his youthful work as a film reviewer for newspapers in Barranquilla and Bogotá, his numerous film projects began when he collaborated with Carlos Fuentes and others in adapting Juan Rulfo's *El gallo de oro* (The golden rooster), and include such titles as *Time to Die,* directed by Arturo Ripstein; *Patty My Love*; Alberto Isaac's *No Thieves in This Town*; and Rulfo's *Pedro Páramo*. Later he would also shape the screenplays of *Difficult Loves*, a series made for Spanish TV, as well as *Chronicle of a Death Foretold* and *Eréndira*. Nor can I forbear mention of *Clandestine in Chile: The Adventures of Miguel Littín*, a journalistic piece on his friend the filmmaker Littín and his secretive journey to Augusto Pinochet's Chile in the mid-eighties. (After the downfall of Salvador Allende, García Márquez publicly swore he would not write again until Pinochet gave up power. As it turns out, the dictator had more endurance than the author.)

Many of his adaptations and screenplays originated in short stories and vice versa; a few, in prose form, are collected in *Strange Pilgrims*, conceived as "mere entertainments," to use Graham Greene's fashionable term, and unified by the common theme of investigating the lives of Latin Americans transplanted to Europe—the New World inhabiting the Old. One of them is "The Summer of Miss Forbes" (El verano de la Señora Forbes), directed by Jaime Humberto Hermosillo, about a German nanny who, in taking care of a pair of children in Sicily, kills herself in an apocalyptic act of unresolved sexual passion; another is "I Only Came to Use the Phone" (Sólo vine a usar el teléfono), about a young wife mistaken as a lunatic and imprisoned in a psychiatric home.

But García Márquez's vivid imagination reaches beyond the screen. Consider the extraordinary metafictional imagery in *One Hundred Years of Solitude*. In the last few pages, Aureliano Babilonia, the last in the Buendía lineage, whose first member is found tied to a tree and whose last is eaten by ants, discovers the lost manuscripts of the gypsy Melquíades. Like *Hamlet*'s play-within-a-play and Cervantes's novel-within-a-novel, García Márquez introduces a text that can be read "as if it had been written in Spanish," in which the very novel the reader holds in hand is included. What follows is Gregory Rabassa's superb translation:

> It was the history of the family, written by Melquíades, down to the most trivial details, one hundred years ahead of time. He had written it in Sanskrit, which was his mother tongue, and he had encoded the even lines in the private cipher of the Emperor Augustus and the odd ones in the Lacedemonian military code. The final protection,

which Aureliano had begun to glimpse when he let himself be confused by the love of Amaranta Ursula, was based on the fact that Melquíalades had not put events in the order of man's conventional time, but had concentrated a century of daily episodes in such a way that they coexisted in one instant.

It's a passage that recalls Borges's tale "The Aleph," in which the Argentine narrator discovers, hidden in a Buenos Aires basement, a magical object capable of turning past, present, and future into one single unifying moment. But García Márquez's passage, although intertwining spiritual elements, also has a concrete, visual, cinematographic texture: the act of reading, the sudden discovery of death, the past as a bewitchment. Perhaps that's why García Márquez has stated he will never sell the movie rights to *One Hundred Years of Solitude,* for the novel is already a film. By contrast, Isabel Allende's 1982 best-selling genealogical novel *The House of the Spirits*—a novel that suspiciously resembles the Colombian's masterpiece and could almost be considered a trivialization of his trademark style—is, after a highly competitive auction, being directed by the Danish filmmaker Bille August, a concession to the imposing ways of mass culture.

Of course, one could argue that although *Don Quixote* has been adapted to the screen time and again, its sheer literary force remains intact, as enchanting as when first written half a millennium ago. Could Anthony Hopkins play the role of Aureliano Buendía and Vanessa Redgrave that of Ursula Iguarán on location somewhere in the Amazon? Can actual vistas of the jungle do justice to García Márquez's colorful, baroque style? Most devoted fans hope it will never happen, but sooner or later they are likely to be betrayed. It won't matter, though. In keeping with the metaphysical transmutation any literary classic undergoes with time, the book's mesmerizing Biblical images are somehow already no longer the property of the author but of language and tradition.

To return to his formative years, García Márquez was still twenty years old in 1948 when another tragic clash between conservative and liberal parties took place, again costing hundreds of thousands of lives. On April 9, Jorge Eliécer Gaitán, ex-mayor of Bogotá and the Liberal Party's populist presidential candidate, who had defended the workers in the strike of 1928, was assassinated. The event, known as *el bogotazo,* inaugurated a decade-long period generally referred to by Colombians as *la violencia,* chaos and disorder prevailing in rural areas. The year before, García Márquez had enrolled as a law student at the National University, and it was around that time that he met Plinio Apuleyo Mendoza, a strong supporter of his talent, whom he would reencounter in Paris in the late fifties. At age nineteen, García Márquez wrote, in the fashion of Maupassant's "Le Horla," his first short story, to my knowledge still untranslated into English, "La tercera resignación" (The third resignation), published in *El Espectador.* The violence that surrounded him at the time left a profound scar. The National University was temporarily closed, and he had to move to Cartagena, where his family had resettled. He entered the local university and, in order to support himself, began his career as a journalist in *El Universal.*

Not much else is known about his beginnings, making the job of a biographer all the more urgent: to dig—to recover, uncover, and discover; to trace lost steps on the map of the subject's existence. Why did García Márquez select law as a profession? Why not a medical career, like the novelist's father, Dr. García? (The doctors in his plots are, in the Flaubertian manner, always representatives of science and modernity.) The relationship between oral storytelling and literature is at the core of his craft. When did he decide to sit down and write? Was he politically active as a student? Did he perceive literature as an instrument to educate and enlighten the masses and to further a process of social revaluation and reconstruction? (This view of literature's purpose is in fashion at the time and was later debated by Jean-Paul Sartre and Albert Camus in a controversy with far-reaching effects in Latin America during the late fifties and early sixties.) Did he have any direct confrontations with the government and the armed forces, a rite of passage decisive for most intellectuals in the region?

What is sure is that around 1948 he began reading Faulkner, a turning point in his career. Literature would become his sole passion. His goal now was to build an architecturally perfect, fictional universe that most of his ghosts and fears could inhabit, a mirror of the reality that daily overwhelmed him. Faulkner immediately became his secret personal tutor. For Faulkner had, in one novel after another, devoted all his creative energy to investigating the historical wounds of the Deep South—and those wounds are not unlike Latin America's: the acceptance of collective defeat and the adjustment to external colonizing forces and the phantoms of history. At the same time, Faulkner's fictional constellation seemed autonomous and self-sufficient. Besides, his introspective, experimental, Rashomon-like style appealed greatly to the Colombian fabulist.

He started by reading *A Rose for Emily*, which had recently been published in a poor Spanish translation. (García Márquez's English is weak.) Based on a July 1949 newspaper review by the author, critics like Jacques Gilard and Raymond L. Williams claim it was the Colombian's first encounter with the southern U.S. writer, an interest that would evolve into a lifelong fascination. Today, out of saturation perhaps, the Colombian claims he is no longer able to read good old Faulkner. Still, the encounter with the Yoknapatawpha saga changed his view of literature forever. "When I first read [him]," he would later say, "I thought: I must become a writer." A similar Faulknerian impact, by the way, transformed the Uruguayan Juan Carlos Onetti and the Peruvian Vargas Llosa, to name only a few Latin Americans with a Faulkernian drive. More than a decade later, around 1961, García Márquez, married and with a son (he has two, one of them a writer in his own right), traveled by bus from New York to Mexico through the Deep South "in homage to Faulkner." Segregation reigned, and the family encountered signs that read "No Dogs and Mexicans Allowed" and were frequently not allowed to stay at hotels.

Two other U.S. authors commanded an overwhelming influence across the Rio Grande in the fifties: Hemingway and John Dos Passos. With respect to the latter, one can point to García Márquez's interest in cruel realism; but it was the former who truly influenced him by teaching precision, objectivity, and directness in style. Literature and journalism, he understood, were brothers. Indeed, as was the case with the author of *The Sun Also Rises,* the impact of the Colombian's journalistic writing on his future artistic development was enormous. He learned to write in short, clear sentences. But unlike Hemingway, who claimed journalism could kill a writer's career, García Márquez not only saw the trade as essential in the shaping of a novelist's style but also needed it as a source of income until book royalties began to come in, well into his forties.

In 1952 he began writing for *El Heraldo* in Barranquilla and became part of the so-called Barranquilla Group, a gathering of intellectuals who read and discussed Hemingway, Virginia Woolf, Faulkner, Erskine Caldwell, and Dos Passos. (The group included two aspiring writers who would eventually leave a mark on Colombian letters, although never with the impact of García Márquez: Alvaro Cepeda Samudio and Germán Vargas.) Already in his mid-twenties, García Márquez began to take himself seriously as a writer. He was constantly publishing short stories in newspapers and magazines, and even finished a first novel, *La casa* (The house), which Buenos Aires's Losada, the prestigious imprint responsible for the works of the River Plate luminaries Borges and Adolfo Bioy Casares, rejected after one of its editors told García Márquez he had no talent as a writer and should devote himself to something else. The novel, known today as *La hojarasca*, has an unquestionably Faulknerian style: its plot is told from three different viewpoints—that of a father, his daughter, and his grandchild—and circles around the funeral of a doctor who had been hated by everybody in town and who, at the end of his life, had become a recluse. As William Kennedy has argued, the protagonist's personality recalls Rev. Gail Hightower of *Light in August.*

It is an interesting fact about the world of letters into which García Márquez emerged that, with very few exceptions, Colombian literature was, and remains, largely undistinguished. When García Márquez was born, José Eustasio Rivera, author of the country's heretofore most famous work *The Vortex,* was dying. Besides his, few names are worthy of notice: Jorge Isaac, author of the best-seller *María,* the *modernista* poet José Asunción Silva; the eccentric Porfirio Barba Jacob; Eduardo Caballero Calderón, author of *The Noble Savage*; and that's about all. Recently, however, another name has emerged: Alvaro Mutis, who, as it turns out, is a key figure in García Márquez's artistic progress. He invited García Márquez to return from Cartagena to Bogotá to write for *El Espectador,* and, after his acceptance, they became good friends. In the early sixties, García Márquez sent Mutis, who was in a Mexican prison, two of his short stories, which his friend in turn showed to the journalist Elena Poniatowska. Later, after a few mishaps, she and Mutis managed to convince the Universidad Veracruzana Press to publish them, alongside other tales, as *Big Mama's Funerals*, for which the author got an advance of a thousand pesos. Published in 1962, the book's first printing of 2,000 copies took years to sell.

As a belated expression of deeply felt gratitude, García Márquez dedicated *The General in His Labyrinth* to Mutis, for having given "me the idea for writing this book." The novel, to my mind one of the writer's most sophisticated and accomplished, studies the last few days of Simón Bolívar, who, on December 10, 1930, soon after he had dictated his last will and testament and a physician had insisted that he confess and receive the sacraments, said: "What does this mean? . . . Can I be so ill that you talk to me of wills and confessions? . . . How will I ever get out of this labyrinth!" In the section "My Thanks," García Márquez writes:

> For years I listened to Alvaro Mutis discussing his plan to write about Simón Bolívar's final voyage along the Magdalena River. When he published "El último rostro" [The last face], a fragment of the projected book, the story seemed so ripe, and its style and tone so polished, that I expected to read it in its complete form very soon afterwards. Nevertheless, two years later I had the impression that he had regarded it to oblivion, as so many writers do with our best-loved dreams, and only then did I dare ask for his permission to write it myself. It was a direct hit after a ten-year ambush.

The Bolívar novel, rather poorly received in the United States because of its abundance of historical data and a period setting that many Anglo-Saxons found unappealing, created a huge controversy in South America. There Venezuelan and Colombian politicians attacked it as "profane," claiming García Márquez was defaming the larger-than-life reputation of a historical figure who, during the nineteenth century, struggled to unite the vast Hispanic world. But Mutis, the author's ideal reader, is known to be very fond of the book. That alone made García Márquez happy.

While working for *El Espectador*, García Márquez wrote a series of fourteen semijournalistic pieces, composed in the first-person voice of a twenty-two-year-old mariner, that chronicled the episode of a shipwreck in which eight crew members were left alone at sea. Only one,

Luis Alejandro Velasco, survived, and he became a national hero. According to the official version, bad weather had caused the tragedy, but when assigned to investigate the details, the novelist discovered the boat was carrying *contrabando*—smuggled items: television sets, refrigerators, and laundry machines brought from the United States. Dictator Rojas Pinilla had allowed only progovernment newspapers to cover the event. Although the Velasco celebration had diminished by the time García Márquez published his articles, they became a public sensation and an embarrassment to the government in power. A Barcelona publishing house reprinted the serial in book form in 1970 as *The Story of a Shipwrecked Sailor,* a volume that, had readers never seen the Colombian's name on the cover, would frankly have passed without pomp and glory as a forgettable and poorly structured report.

The year 1955 was among the most decisive in the novelist's life. When he was twenty-seven, a small Bogotá house, Ediciones Sipa, finally decided to publish his first novel under the title *La hojarasca.* Reports of the early critical and commercial reaction are ambiguous, and García Márquez has only added to the uncertainty. In an interview, he claimed it sold some 30,000 copies, but some sources, including Vargas Llosa in *History of a Deicide,* claim it elicited very small interest and passed largely unnoticed.

An indication of the book's poor reception was the writer's reaction: as often happens to South American first-time novelists, García Márquez felt depressed and swore never to write again. Ironically, this wasn't another of his histrionic gestures. His trust in literature actually diminished as he became increasingly conscious of his personal needs in the future: he would have to support himself and a family, and writing novels didn't seem like a money-making venture, at least not at the time. Fortunately, fate managed to stimulate him by other means. That same year he was awarded a prize by Bogotá's Association of Artists and Writers for his story "Un día después del Sábado" (A day after Saturday), and while the amount of money he received was small, his name and photograph circulated in newspapers. To add to the excitement, his editor at *El Espectador* had earlier decided to send him to Geneva as a foreign correspondent. He would leave his native town for Europe, where the literary careers of those from south of the Rio Grande have always been forged.

Things at Colombia changed drastically the moment he left. The overall reach of *la violencia* was omnipresent, and soon the military regime of Gustavo Rojas Pinilla, a merciless *caudillo*, closed down *El Espectador*. The old battle between federalists and centralists took a high toll, and nobody was immune from the violence. García Márquez arrived in Europe excited to be an independent young man in a strange and glamorous place, and ready to seize the opportunity to perfect his craft as a novelist. But now, suddenly, he was left out in the cold. He had been staying at Hôtel de Flandre in the Latin Quarter, where he waited for a check from the newspaper to come in the mail. For obvious reasons, none arrived. In time he would owe the management some 123,000 francs. Since he was on good terms with the hotel administration, he was allowed to stay for a little while, in spite of some clients' complaints of his typing after midnight. He then managed to travel to Rome, where he participated as a student at the Centro Sperimentale di Cinematografia—where Manuel Puig would later enroll—and finally moved to Paris. The legends about his Parisian stay conform to the stereotype of the down-and-out litterateur: he had a hard time making ends meet, and in one instance was seen collecting empty bottles at garbage cans to exchange for extra centimes to buy food.

And yet the European years proved to be very fruitful, in part because he finished *No One Writes to the Colonel* and *In Evil Hour,* published, respectively, in Medellín by Aguirre Editor in 1961 and in Madrid by Talleres de Gráficas Luis Pérez the year after. These titles, together with *Big Mama's Funeral,* form a unified whole. "I tried to put in them everything I knew," he said later. But after a painful artistic struggle, he gave up the encyclopedic approach to narrative: "It was too much accumulation." He thus cut sections, expanded chapters, and turned ideas into short stories. (Robert Coover believes the conflict between "the realistic" and "the fantastic" is never adequately worked out in these works.) Away from Latin America, his imagination had begun to metamorphosize his past, his native culture, into the stuff of myth. Distance distorted the actual size and value of things, misforming them into pieces of a personal puzzle. Through literature, he could revisit the ghosts of his grandparents' home. He could recreate the violence he had witnessed by invoking plots where brave military soldiers are forgotten by their army peers. Years later, when a journalist asked him to summarize the region's idiosyncratic nature, he answered with the following tale set in a small rural town in Colombia: At around ten o'clock, two men parked a truck outside a boarding school and said, "We've come to pick up the furniture." No one knew if they were supposed to come, but the principal allowed them in, the furniture was placed in the truck, and the two men left. "Only later people found out they were thieves."

García Márquez returned to South America in 1956. He made a quick stop in Colombia to marry Mercedes Barcha, then moved to Caracas, Venezuela, where he worked for *Momentos* and *Elite.* Together with Apuleyo Mendoza, García Márquez traveled back and forth through Eastern Europe and the Soviet Union in 1957 and produced a report in ten installments, more anecdotal than political, for the magazines *Elite* in Venezuela and *Cromos* in Bogotá, under the general title of *Noventa días en la cortina de hierro* (Ninety days on tour through the Eastern Block). Among other places, he visited East Germany, Czechoslovakia, Poland, and Russia.

Upon his return, he went to London to learn English, then to Venezuela, and finally to Mexico. At thirty-one, he was enchanted by the Cuban Revolution and began working for Cuba's press agency, Prensa Latina, a job he performed for two years. He was stationed in New York to cover the United Nations General Assembly, but after a while his relationship with the news agency deteriorated and he quit. García Márquez's role in modern politics is evident in his left-wing views, his solid friendship with Fidel Castro, and his defense of Latin America. "I have firm political beliefs," he once told Luis Harss, "but my views of literature change with every digestion." In his Nobel acceptance speech to the Swedish Academy in 1982, he said: "Latin America neither wants, nor has any reason, to be a pawn without a will of its own; nor is it merely wishful thinking that its quest for independence and originality should become a Western aspiration." Often he has acted as intermediary between human rights commissions and the Havana regime, as in the celebrated Heberto Padilla affair, in which a Cuban poet, imprisoned for betraying his country's national security, was freed after many pleas from, among others, Susan Sontag and Robert Silver, editor of the *New York Review of Books,* thanks in part to García Márquez, who persuaded a reluctant Castro to let him go.

Some have criticized García Márquez for at once being a devoted Fidelista and having two mansions, one in Havana and the other in Mexico City, in the exclusive southern San Angel section. Don't his material circumstances contradict his ideological beliefs? García Márquez turns to another subject every time the question is asked. But this apparent tension between life-style and politics is prevalent among famous Latin American intellectuals of the seventies: to act as the voice of people, to attack the government, to promulgate left-wing views has never required that one's daily domestic life be reduced to the bare essentials. It's an irony that becomes all the more evident among exiled scholars and writers who for decades have portrayed the United States as an imperialist aggressor but who, when the time comes to escape from a repressive regime, avail themselves of the safe haven offered by the U.S. academy: a comfortable salary at a college or university. García Márquez, in many ways, epitomitzes this outrageous behavior. While he never stayed at an American campus for a long period of time because of immigration problems with the Immigration and Naturalization Service, he is a symbol of lavish life-style and anachronistic Franciscan principles: the revolutionary struggle amid champagne glasses.

After his stay in New York, García Márquez settled in Mexico and was largely inactive as a writer, devoting himself exclusively to gestating Macondo in his own mind. His novella *In Evil Hour* had won an obscure prize, sponsored by Esso in Colombia. Through an ambassador, he was sent word that the award would be his if he agreed to eliminate a couple of "nasty" words: "prophylactic" and "masturbate." In reply, he agreed to censor only one, whichever the ambassador wished. The transcript was sent to Spain to be printed, and a copy editor, to make the style Iberian, changed the wording of his sentences. When García Márquez saw the final product, he was furious. In the Mexican edition of 1966 and the one he considered "official," he added an author's note stating that the text had been restored to its original form.

The mythical Macondo acquired its structure in the stories of *Big Mama's Funeral*. Critics mistakenly claim *No One Writes to the Colonel* and *In Evil Hour* take place in it, when, in fact, as George R. McMurray has shown, their setting is a town, probably Sucre, farther inland in the coastal region. In their exuberant *Dictionary of Imaginary Places,* Alberto

Manguel and Gianni Guadalupi describe Macondo "as a Colombian village founded in ancient times by José Arcadio Buendía, whose boundless imagination always stretched farther than the inventiveness of nature." Its apex occurs between 1915 and 1918, during the height of the banana plantations. Toward the east, as Manguel and Guadalupi have mapped it, the town is protected by a high and forbidding range of hills and, toward the south, by marshes covered with a kind of vegetable soup. Toward the west the marshes give way to a large body of water in which cetaceans of delicate skin, with the face and torso of a woman, lure sailors with their firm and tempting breasts. To the north, many days' march away through a dangerous jungle, lies the sea. Among Macondo's most notable events is the unusual insomnia epidemic that strikes the entire population: the most terrible effect isn't the impossibility of sleep—because the body does not tire either—but the gradual loss of memory. When a sick person becomes accustomed to staying awake, memories of his childhood start to vanish, followed by names and concepts of things. With self-reflecting mirrors and all, the novel's self-reflecting ending is simply remarkable:

> Macondo was already a fearful whirlwind of dust
> rubble being spun about by the wrath of the biblical
> hurricane when Aureliano shipped eleven pages so as
> not to lose time with facts he knew only too well, and he
> began to decipher the instant that he was living, deci-
> phering it as he lived it, prophesying himself in the act of
> deciphering the last page of the parchments, as if he
> were looking into a speaking mirror. Then he skipped
> again to anticipate the predictions and ascertain the date
> and circumstances of his death. Before reaching the final
> line, however, he had already understood that he would
> never leave that room, for it was foreseen that the city of
> mirrors would be wiped out by the wind and exiled
> from the memory of men at the precise moment when
> Aureliano Babilionia would finish deciphering the
> parchments, and that everything written on them was
> unrepeatable since time immemorial and forever more,
> because race condemned to one hundred years of soli-
> tude did not have a second opportunity on earth.

The legend behind the final shaping of Macondo has come to be referred to, by García Márquez and others who know him, simply as "the miracle." It took place in 1965, on the road from Mexico City to Acapulco in the family's Opel. Suddenly, as the writer puts it, the entire first chapter appeared to him, and he immediately felt he was prepared to write the rest of the story. Afterwards he told an Argentine friend that if he had had a tape-recorder in the car, he would have dictated the chapter right then and there. Instead of continuing on to Acapulco, he decided to turn around and seclude himself completely for a year. He asked Mercedes, his wife, not to interrupt him for any reason, especially where bills were concerned, and indeed she protected him fully. When the novel was finished, the García Márquezes were $12,000 in debt; to tide themselves over, Mercedes had asked their friends for loans (according to Vargas Llosa, it was around $10,000). Soon rumors of the book's qualities began to circulate: Carlos Fuentes and Julio Cortázar, who had read pieces of the manuscript before it was finished, were so excited they praised it highly in articles and reviews. And so, by the time *One Hundred Years of Solitude* was published in May 1967 by Editorial Sudamericana, it ignited the literary world, and García Márquez, at thirty-nine, became an instant international celebrity. The first edition sold out in a few days, and the novel sold half a million copies in three and a half years, a huge sum for any Spanish book anywhere in the Hispanic world. He immediately began to receive honorary degrees and prizes: the Rómulo Gallegos award; the Prix du Meilleur Livre Etranger in France; the Italian Chianchiano Prize; the Neustadt Prize by the magazine *Book Abroad* (now *World Literarure Today*); the National Book Award to Gregory Rabassa for the English translation; and, a bit more than a decade later, the Nobel Prize. (Five Latin Americans have now received it: before him, Gabriela Mistral, Pablo Neruda, and Miguel Angel Asturias; after, Octavio Paz.)

Does someone capable of creating a book of such caliber have a second such opportunity on earth? Having set the standard sky-high, he has written nothing since 1967 that seems fully satisfying. While some maintain that a bad García Márquez is extraordinary by other people's standards, it is clear that the Colombian has always been haunted by his masterpiece's overwhelming success. His method of writing has also changed over the decades. He can spend long seasons without putting a word on paper, and then, during creative periods, write eight to ten pages each day from sunrise to noon. His paragraphs are extremely polished, the opposite of André Breton's idea of automatic writing, which Jack Kerouac and the Beat Generation took to an extreme. The dialogue is infrequent but crisp and full of parables and metaphors. In the age of mechanical typewriters and liquid corrector, he claims to have rewritten *No One Writes to the Colonel* a total of nine times. "I had the impression I was writing it in French," he once said, as if after so many rewritings his native tongue had become alien to him, and pure technique ended up shaping the book. He took a similar approach with future books, until the late seventies, when he bought a word processor. Considered by many his second best title—a distant second, though—*Love in the Time of Cholera* was published in 1985. It is a romance of sorts (according to Salman Rushdie, "a masterful revamping of the genre") encapsulating the affair of García Márquez's parents from their youth to their eighties. Written with the help of a computer, the book retains his typically labyrinthine paths of fantasy, but the texture seems a bit removed, less immediate than that in *One Hundred Years of Solitude.* The protagonists are Fermina Daza, who is married to Doctor Juvenal Urbino de la Calle, and Florentino Ariza, who has a crush on her that lasts, in one of the novelist's typical phrases, "fifty three years, seven months, and eleven days." Many biographical elements are included: the telegraph, a Flaubertian doctor who functions as a voice of reason, a critique of religion, and an unrelenting love beyond all odds.

A succession of repetitive, structurally overdone narratives has steadily issued from the Colombian's pen since 1967. Predictably, their reception nevertheless has been enthusiastic, as if anything produced by García Márquez, no matter the quality, is to be applauded. The truth is, his magnum opus had satisfied and engrossed so many readers that each new narrative became legendary even before it could reach the bookstores.

The novelist's lifelong interest in continental history is apparent in his 1975 experimental novel *Autumn of the Patriarch,* a favorite of such postcolonial critics as Edward Said but, to my mind, too allegorical, too boring. The book was also a disappointment to those expecting another installment of the Buendía saga. One of about a half a dozen Latin American narratives about dictators (others include Alejo Carpentier's *Reasons of State*, Augusto Roa Bastos's *I, the Supreme*, Tomás Eloy Martínez's *The Perón Nobel*, and Miguel Angel Asturias's *El Señor Presidente*), the novel deals with a tyrant's relentless desire to accumulate power and narrates his obsessive love affair with Manuela Sanchez, the status of "civil sanctity" given to his ailing mother, and his final demise. Already close to his hundredth birthday, he marries Nazareno Leticia and has a child with her, only to find mother and child assassinated, their bodies ripped apart by dogs at a public plaza. Contrary to common belief, García Márquez did not base the story and its protagonist solely on Gustuvo Rojas Pinilla and his military regime in Colombia but also on the Venezuelan *caudillo* Juan Vicente Gómez. "My intention," he once said, "was always to make a synthesis of all the Latin American dictators, but especially those from the Caribbean."

Another unbalanced text is *Chronicle of a Death Foretold*, published in 1981, shortly before the announcement of the Nobel Prize. Built as a detective story in reverse, it describes the assassination of Santiago Nasar, accused of deflowering Angela Vicario, who is hence unable to marry Bayardo San Román. Everybody in town knows Nasar will be killed, but nobody does a thing. The story is told from the point of view of a journalist, a chronicler who years later returns to the place to unveil the truth. As Raymond L. Williams has shown, the novella is based on real events reported by *El Día* in Bogotá in 1981:

> In the municipality of Sucre . . . the elders still remember with horror the rainy morning of January 22, 1951, in which a young man . . . Cayetano Gentile Chimento, twenty-
> two years old, medical student at the Javeriana University in Bogotá and heir of the town's largest fortune, fell butchered by machete, innocent victim of a confused duel of honor, and without knowing for sure why he was dying. Cayetano was killed by Víctor and Joaquín Chica Salas, whose sister Margarita, married the previous day with Miguel Reyes Palencia and returned to her family by her husband the same night of the marriage, accused Cayetano of being the author of the disgrace that had prevented her being a

virgin at her marriage.

García Márquez recreates the events by mixing sex and exoticism, and filtering it all through the surreal prism of his imagination. According to William H. Gass, the novel is not told but pieced together like a jigsaw. The result, although entertaining, is another minor work in the novelist's corpus.

In some ways a remarkably ordinary man by all accounts, the Colombian is, and will always be, an object of rumors. According to Roger Straus, when to celebrate the centennial of the world's most important awards, the Nobel committee decided to invite every awardee from around the globe (paying handsomely for everybody's room and board), García Márquez alone refused the invitation—unless he received a payment of $10,000, which was not forthcoming. But perhaps the most convoluted of the legends surrounding him is his friendship with Mario Vargas Llosa. They met in Caracas and moved together to Bogotá and Lima, where they participated in a symposium on the novel (published as *The Latin American Novel: A Dialogue* [1968]). Alongside José Donoso, Fuentes, and Cortázar, they are part of the so-called Latin American boom of the sixties. The Peruvian, of course, wrote the previously mentioned *History of a Deicide,* a 667-page literary study of the Colombian's life and oeuvre, submitted originally as a doctoral dissertation at Madrid's Universidad Central. They shared a room in Mexico's capital, but then, some time in the seventies, a fight erupted at Cine Lido, in which Vargas Llosa punched García Márquez for circulating tales about an (unconfirmed) extramarital affair with a Nordic model. Since then, they have not spoken to each other. Others claim it was their politics that created a rupture: after the 1959 Cuban Revolution, Vargas Llosa, like Octavio Paz, slowly grew disenchanted with Fidel Castro's worldview and soon became an enemy, his ideology today being center-right.

As the leading voice of the Latin American narrative boom of the sixties, García Márquez is the decisive force and influence behind Salman Rushdie, Anton Shammas, Isabel Allende, Oscar Hijuelos, Laura Esquivel, and scores of other writers who came to prominence from the seventies onward. His craft so uniquely mixes magic, hyperrealism, and exotic dreamlike images, that one could thank him for having finally put Latin

America, long a forgotten part of the world, back on the map. Of course, by the same token, one could also accuse the Colombian of having distorted the hemisphere's reality by reducing it to a theater of clairvoyant prostitutes, opinionated matrons, and corrupt generals. He turned Latin America into a distraction—a chimera, a magical creation.

Today, unfortunately, his decline is not only creative but physical. Around 1991 news began to circulate that García Márquez was sick with cancer. In spite of his reclusiveness, the Associated Press announced a serious medical operation in Colombia. How serious the illness was is anybody's guess. In fact, when *Strange Pilgrims,* an unremarkable compilation of tales written from 1974 on, appeared a year later, people talked about a hidden desire on his part to sum up, to leave the desk clean. His next project, his American editor claims, is a memoir. Although in photographs and public appearances the writer looks healthy, what is unquestionable is his exhaustion. Since *Love in the Time of Cholera* and perhaps even before, he has not seemed at the peak of his power; his creativity seems diminished by an exhausted imagination.

And yet, anybody ready to count him out makes a big mistake. In early 1994, for instance, in a renewed display of stamina, he published a short novel: *Del amor y otros demonios.* Set on the Caribbean coast during the colonial period, it describes a passionate affair, under the shadow of the Church, between a young girl, Sierva María de Todos los Angeles, a saint adored for her many miracles but who supposedly was possessed by the devil, and her exorcist. While García Márquez's story is engaging and well-crafted, it ultimately becomes a showcase of his recent excesses: an overly compressed style that creates a sense of suffocation in the reader, a plot that seems flat, and a lack of spontaneity in the prose that ends up undermining any kind of suspense.

The rumor that he is writing a memoir, which he once claimed in an *El País* interview, would be structured theatrically and not chronologically, raises the expectation of his turning his personal odyssey into literature; and it is obvious that the Colombian himself understands now the imminence of his fate. The closeness of death provides an opportunity for him to wrap up and reshape reminiscences, to translate the past into a historical record. He is ready to consummate his act of fabricating his own heroic destiny by stamping his signature on everything he did and did not do, or preferred never to have done. But most important, he, the person and the persona, knows he has already entered the pantheon of literary giants and wants full control, in death as in life, of everything that has to do with his life and craft. The Hispanic world keeps a double standard regarding biographies and autobiographies. As is the way with confessional genres, they do what Hispanic society otherwise wholeheartedly discourages: to make public what is private, to forsake intimacy for extroversion. And yet, the extraordinary attention that the narrative boom of the sixties received has persuaded many to control memory, to stop cultural thieves from dismantling the mythical aura with which experiences were lived: José Donoso has written a personal recollection of the boom years, originally published in English in *TriQuarterty*; Heberto Padilla did his part in *Self-Portrait of the Other*; in 1993, Mario Vargas Llosa wrote *The Fish in the Water,* a self-serving study of his first twenty-two years, including a detailed recollection of his campaign as a presidential candidate in 1990; Borges, in collaboration with Norman Thomas Di Giovanni, wrote his "Autobiographical Essay" for the *New Yorker,* and Reinaldo Arenas, the talented Cuban exile who died in New York City, denounced every one of his enemies in *Before Night Fall.* As a fiesta of intellectual rebirth, the sixties and seventies in Latin America are emerging as one of the most exciting periods in the region's cultural history. And García Márquez's authoritative voice is probably destined to become the chronicle against which everything else is to be judged. Yet biographical accounts revisiting the period, in Spanish or for that matter any language, are almost nonexistent: Emir Rodríguez Monegal wrote *Jorge Luis Borges: A Literary Biography* for Dutton in 1978, but that's about it. While Norman Mailer, a lover of scandals, has already been written about in several biographies, official and unauthorized—as have Paul Bowles, Saul Bellow, and J. D. Salinger— south of the Rio Grande, little, if anything, has been written about Julio Cortázar, an experimentalist who wrote "Blow-Up" and died in 1984, Manuel Puig, and Juan Rulfo, not to mention Fuentes, Vargas Llosa, and, of course, the creator of Macondo himself.

Physical or creative decadence aside, *One Hundred Years of Solitude,* which, in John Barth's words, is "as impressive a novel as has been written so far in the second half of our century and one of the splendid specimens of that splendid genre," will no doubt remain resplendent with prestige. Its existence alone more than justifies the Colombian's days and nights. John Leonard once wrote that "with a single bound García Márquez leaps onto the stage with Günter Grass and Vladimir Nabokov, his appetite as enormous as his imagination, his fatalism greater than either." If it weren't for this larger-than-life novel, Latin America's prominence on the literary map would be much diminished. And if he has often failed to live up to the supernal standards he set himself, that achievement alone ought to keep García Márquez on the bookshelves of humankind for a long time to come. Redemption through a single artistic stroke, the overcoming of death through memory: What else can a writer desire?

[1994]

6 / THE VERBAL QUEST

"We will build our Temple here," said they,
simultaneously, and with an indescribable conviction that
they had at last found the very spot.
　　　　　　　　　　　　　—Nathaniel Hawthorne,
　　　　　　　　　　　　　　　Twice-Told Tales

For quite some time I have been interested in the link between language and religion—more specifically, in the search of a primal tongue that precedes all others, one whose virtue is not lessened by time. Can such a proto-language be at once divine and secular? Can its meaning and interpretation be standardized? My interest is also targeted toward translation: Would such a proto-language symbolize, once and for all, the abolition of the act of translation? Such miscellaneous questions rumbled in my mind not long ago, as I was reading two thought-provoking essays, one by the Mexican poet and essayist, Octavio Paz: "Edith Piaf Among the Pygmies"; the other: "The Ephemerality of Translation" by Ray Harris, an Oxford professor. While both share a common theme—the reaches and limitations of translation—their asymmetrical relationship is fascinating. Paz argues that the job of translating a text from one language to another is simply impossible. He offers as an example a television documentary he once saw about several Pygmies who heard Edith Piaf's voice magically reproduced by a phonograph an ethnologist had turned on for them to hear. Whereas the ethnologists could identify with the song by the French pop singer, a song about jealousy and violent love, the Pygmies immediately became quite frightened: they covered their ears and ran away. They fled because they were unable to recognize such passionate groans. What seemed to be an aesthetic experience for the scientists was horrifying to the Pygmies. Inspired by Claude Lévi-Strauss's book *Tristes Tropiques,* Paz explains that, had the ethnologists tried to translate the song, surely the Pygmies would have felt even more repulsed. The Petrarchian concepts of courtly and passionate love in Piaf's lyrics were totally alien to them: unrecognizable, unapproachable. One could argue, of course, that the Pygmies indeed understood Piaf's message; otherwise they would have made it clear, through a subtle gesture of annoyance, that they disapproved of her groans. Precisely because both the content of the lyrics and the musical form in which these were expressed were so aggressive, so passionate, there was a misunderstanding, a loss in the act of translation. They probably could not picture a woman screaming vehemently without knowledge of the context from which such suffering was born. Perhaps they could not understand why the fragile threads that make a relationship between a Western man and a woman become the source of such misery. In short, they simply could not understand. Paz concludes that translating moral, aesthetic, scientific, or magical concepts from one language to another, from one culture to another, is a hopeless task; it requires that the recipient in the translation process stop being himself—which means that each translation, by its very nature, creates an insurmountable abyss between civilizations, one impossible to bridge.

At first sight, Paz's argument might seem too emphatic, a statement against translation, but it isn't. Without translations our world would be even more chaotic than it already is. Translations result from dialogue, communication, encounters between disparate entities. Although much can be, and in fact is, lost in translations, they ultimately emerge as an attempt to unite, a desire to reach out. In other words, the translation act, in spite of cultural abysses, cannot so easily be discharged: it is a necessity the modern world cannot afford to live without; it provides an essential taste our intellectual life has become accustomed to, the seasoning that keeps our cosmopolitan spirit afloat. And yet, translation is framed by time and space. Before beginning the task, each translator knows, consciously or otherwise, who his reader will be. If *The Iliad*, in its original language, can overcome the passing of numerous generations of readers and still be accessible, with translations we tend to have little patience: when a translation loses vitality, when it becomes obscure, impenetrable, we replace it with a new one; that is, whereas the original text is treated as invaluable and of primary importance, translations are disposable.

This is where Harris's thesis becomes relevant. More and more new translations of literary classics are required, he claims, because mass culture, in love with disposable products, is always in need of new commodities, always involved in prefabricating past goods. From 1947 to 1972, at least eleven translations into German of Wilde's *Portrait of a Dorian Gray* were made; and betwen 1949 and 1969, at least eight translations of Flaubert's *Madame Bovary* were cast into English. To make a new translation is to recycle an already appealing product, to commercialize it once again in order to make it accessible to a new readership. Publishers and the academy have found a logic to justify such a multiplication of items on library shelves: modern translations are needed because the language of the original becomes outdated with the passing of time. History wears language down and erases formal structures. It invents new meanings for old words, it introduces neologisms, it reshapes syntax. Since our present civilization is in the process of eternal renovation, retranslating a text is a form of renewal, a strategy for rediscovering who we are, for once again posing old questions in search of meaningful answers. For obvious reasons, marketing plays a crucial role here: each translation entering the literary market promises to be even more "perfect," even more faithful to the original—even more accurate. But accuracy is a tricky word: an accurate depiction is one in which a reader fully believes the portrait a writer delivers; that is, his social model is reflected in the literary model. History is made up of a never-ending drive to reinterpret old models, to reevaluate ancient epochs. The fall of the Aztec city of Tenochtitlán, for instance, has been understood quite differently in the seventeenth, nineteenth, and late twentieth centuries: The fall of Tenochtitlán is constant but the implications of the disaster vary. The same applies to translation. As consumers, we get trapped in the uncontrollable torpedoing of new translations, texts that reproduce old texts, texts that revise well-known texts—which, at the end, do nothing but annihilate the utopian dream of ultimate perfection.

Of course, no translation can ever be perfect: as a human endeavor, each attempt is doomed to fail before it was ever begun; it will be useful to a generation of readers and then, when language changes, a new translation will become necessary and available. Like everything else around us, new translations add up to the never-ending flow of life-and-death cycles generated by nature. Volumes pile up, shelves are constantly expanded, and our poor, disorganized, incoherent, and illegible Western culture remains imperfect despite our strivings for coherence.

Clearly, Paz's and Harris's arguments are two facets of one ample, irresolvable matter: Do translations serve a purpose? Are we only falsifying the original message? I use the verb "to falsify" with some uncertainty and awe; translators, not without reason, thoroughly dislike it. After all, no one proud of his career would want to perceive his livelihood as the treason the famous adage urges: *traduttore, traditore.** An act of betrayal involves dishonesty and deception; a falsification implies fakery, infidelity, and even misrepresentation. The dedicated translator spends hours, days, perhaps months and years finding *le mot juste,* the perfect equivalent for a simple word, only to be accused later on of betraying the original—no doubt in a display of ingratitude by readers who were expected to respond positively. But translations do carry in themselves a measure of distance from the original text and although, at times, a writer might confess that his text in a certain translation reads better than in the original, the natural flavor has magically disappeared. Hence, by the verb "to falsify" I mean to distance, to pervert, to switch words and meanings so as to make a specific message accessible to a foreign culture. I want to be cautious enough not to inject the translation with negative powers, however. Although translations are falsifications, we desperately need them to communicate, to find each other across borders.

In translations one frequently gets the feeling that while the taste of the translated text is legitimate and even acceptable, it carries in itself a form of removal, a distancing from the source. Cervantes thought that reading a translation was the same as seeing a Turkish tapestry from behind: as a silhouette, a shadow, not the real object. Robert Frost used to say that poetry is what gets lost in translation. And Isaac Leibush Peretz, a Yiddish master from the turn of the century, author of *Into the Marketplace* and the memorable short story "The Kabbalists," felt that approaching a translation is like kissing a bride through the wedding veil: the physical contact is indeed experienced but only through a degree of separation. Paz begins his article in an interesting way. He tells us that the search for a common language, one that could transcend all

* I first wrote about translation in "Octavio Paz and the Kabbalists," published in 1985. The essay appeared under a different title in my book *Prontuario* (Mexico: Joaquín Mortiz, 1992), pp. 19–24.

languages, is a way to resolve the opposition between unity and multiplicity which does not cease to intrigue the human spirit: he posits one language of languages *vis-à-vis* a multiplicity of idioms and dialects, the one and the many. I suggest that that original tongue could be approached in at least a couple of ways: as silence, the absence of language, which, of course, is also a form of language; and as music, which, according to Plotinus, is the natural rhythm of the celestial spheres. Music, dance, and pictorial art are enviable forms of creativity because they are never in need of translation: the original message can never be lost. But music, what Hegel considered the true language of the soul, has an even more nearly unique quality: its ceaseless, ephemeral, innate, abstract nature makes it universal. Anywhere, at any time, music seems to contain a religious ingredient: it links the earthly and the heavenly terrain, it elevates nature to a supernatural level. Spoken language, on the other hand, precludes an education: it depends on context, and thus, it carries an equivocal message. As a result, the longing for a universal language reflects a need as ancient as humankind: to eliminate error, to make words indefinite, unconfined, open to everybody. Latin, Sanskrit, Hebrew are tongues injected with sacred universality: in spite of their imperfect metabolism, they are the closest we can get to the musicality of the original proto-language. Music and silence are what human languages long for.

Another way to resolve the conflict between unity and multiplicity, Paz says, is through translations. Before the erection of the Tower of Babel, the Old Testament myth claims that all nations on earth spoke the same sacred tongue, a human version of God's proto-language. Everyone understood each other. Words were less equivocal and thus less poetic. Meanings were standardized. As humans we will always long for that primal language. We will look for it in the dark corners of our creativity. Shelley once wrote, for instance, that all the poems of the past, present, and future are episodes or fragments of a single infinite poem, written by all the poets on earth—a proto-poem in a proto-language. Borges thought that "every man should be capable of all ideas." And in "Poetry and Imagination," Ralph Waldo Emerson wrote:

> Poetry is the perpetual endeavor to express the
> spirit of the thing, to pass the brute body and search

the life and reason which cause it to exist—to see that
the object is always flowing away, whilst the spirit or
necessity which causes it subsists. Its essential mark is
that it betrays in every word instant activity of mind,
shows in new uses of every fact and image, in preter-
natural quickness or perception of relations. All its
words are poems.

And we are attached to poetry, with its plurality of meanings, because,
as George Steiner has claimed, after Babel human communication became a casualty: it was lost—irrevocably lost in the chaos of translation.

The interpretation given by rabbinical Judaism to the causes and echoes of Babel can be easily summarized: The desire to unravel the enigmas of the universe and the desire to understand (e.g., explain) God's
mysteries made the Almighty angry. He exploded by creating a majestic
idiomatic rupture in the universe: the resulting fragmentation was His
revenge against man's daring to understand the impossible. Consequently, today everyone speaks a different language and no one understands anything at the same time. Unity has given way to multiplicity
and interpretation has become a sort of religion: to interpret is to understand and vice versa. Our human temples are built on multiplicity.
We inhabit a world where meaning is relative, equivocal, malleable.
Which means that we are always in search of a completely meaningful
language but will never be able to find it. Interpretations are hence often
for sale. After the oceanic confusion at Babel, man's presumptions have
been in the open, and human communication has been ruled by our
lack of understanding. Since early on, the search for a universal language, a *lingua franca*, a tongue meaningful to all, was a dream dreamt
by prophets, necromancers, and apocryphal messiahs: the abolition of
interpretation, the unificational meaning, a return to the source. Classical Latin of the Middle Ages, unlike its vulgar counterpart, upheld this
inspiration. In the modern era, two attempts can be noted: Esperanto,
invented by the Polish linguist Ludovic Zamenhof in 1887; and the so-
called International Auxiliary Language Association, which originated
in 1951. Paz did not quite develop the theme of universal language; instead, he chose to develop the concept of the art of translation. Nevertheless, the drive for a language of languages has always led us to a dead

end: while we long for unity, we will always be surrounded by multiplicity—our religiosity, our most profound philosophical questions emerge from such a fracture of the many from the ultimate one. But his logic also leads Paz to discredit the phenomenon of translation: Edith Piaf will never be understood by the Pygmies, who will always run away from her groans.

When talking about language, meaning, and communication, what Paz leaves out, and what Harris does not attempt to address, is a third aspect, as important as a universal language and translation, polyglotism. In a sense, polyglotism, the plurality of fluency in languages in a single speaker, unity *in* multiplicity, is the only possible human triumph of a universal tongue: a speaker capable of many tongues—a multifaceted entity; or better, a speaker, the source of many speeches. Polyglotism, it goes without saying, also carries within itself a high dose of imperfection: it is self-centered and solipsistic; but it is an option that manages to eliminate needless obstacles in the search of an entirely meaningful act of communication—and as such it is a metaphor of God's stream of consciousness—in which speaker and listener are one.

At this juncture, I need to center on the nature of the Hebrew language and to bring to my readers' attention the linguistic plight underscored in the theory and practice of Kabbalah, a system of thought which I studied under Moshe Idel (a successor of Gershom Scholem) at the Jewish Theological Seminary in New York City. Among Jewish mystics in medieval and Renaissance times, and above all in the esoteric texts *Ra'ya mehemmá* and *Ticuné Zohar,* written between 1295 and 1305 by a certain disciple of Moisés de León, the principle author of *Sefer ha-Zohar,* we see the idea that the Law that Moses received at Mount Sinai had been thought out and even written in its entirety in advance by the Almighty; that is, that Moses served only as a confidant, a vehicle through whom God dictated the past, present, and future history. Nothing resulting is random; everything has been predetermined. We are only actors in a multicast epic saga that began on the first day of Genesis, in the first chapter of the Hebrew Bible, and will end when God's text reaches its final line. Divine language, the Kabbalah suggests, is different from human language (*lashon adoni* and *lashon beni adam*). They are as incompatible as oil and water. Yet in order to make himself understood, the Almighty had to translate Himself, to make His message comprehensive, accessible to earthly creatures, almost mundane. Thus, He communicated with the people of Israel in a human tongue: that is to say, in Hebrew—the sacred language, the universal tongue, the language of the synagogue and holy scriptures and the vehicle that unites heaven and earth—which does not imply that God spoke Hebrew to Himself. The Almighty is most likely beyond words. He chose Hebrew, *lashon bnei adam,* to find a channel of communication with His chosen people. Consequently, to speak biblical Hebrew is to elevate oneself to the linguistic code of heaven, to sanctify oneself. Understandably, Jewish literati in the diaspora who spend their lives creating in pagan languages—the cases of Kafka, Scholem, Walter Benjamin, Cynthia Ozick, to name a few—often crave a return to the origin, an ascendance to paradise, a desire to master the Hebrew language.

Translation, then, is a synonym of transformation, of alteration and movement. It is not an aftermath of the Babel confusion: it actually precedes the event. It is not simply a human act, it is also a divine activity. But translation does not preclude interpretation; on the contrary, it incorporates the original in its womb: to understand a text, one has to uncover its secret truths, those truths God carefully hides from us: the mysteries and enigmas of the universe. To translate the Bible into Yiddish or into English does not imply simplifying God's word: it implies an interpretation. It serves to disseminate the divine teachings in a partial manner. Whoever would like to learn the original significance should read the Hebrew. Was the communication between God and Israel in Hebrew mutually understood? Probably not. Probably something was lost in translation . . . with a bit of conceit, says the *Sefer ha-Zohar* as well as Maimonides in his mysterious *Guide for the Perplexed.* The meaning behind God's words and actions is, and will always be, hidden, unclear, mysterious. The fabric of the Divine Mind, the secrets of nature, cannot be completely understood by humans—but it can be interpreted. Interpretation is a way to clarify, to adapt, to make accessible to human ears. It is also often the case that Hebrew is spoken only by a handful of sages. During the Diaspora, the 2,000-year exile, Israel has come into contact with numerous nations and the need to learn new languages also has become an imperative: Russian, German, Ladino, Polish, Yiddish, Arabic, Czech, French, Latin, Greek, Italian, Spanish, English, Portuguese are secular, pagan tongues used to establish earthly communication. But through these languages the rabbis also want to explain the hidden meanings in the Bible. To speak many languages is to exist in different dimensions, to search in vain for the sole evasive meaning: it helps reduce the degree of misunderstanding although it does not solve the confusion that reigns in human affairs. Like translation, polyglotism is a desire to penetrate what is not ours; but it is a more authentic, less confusing attempt: after all, there is no third player in the game; the bridge, the intermediary between reader and author is the translator. In a multilingual existence, the translator and the receiver can be one and the same. Multilingualism, thus, is the journey to penetrate different cultures without accessories and without the necessity for change. What is written in Hebrew—the Bible above all—is original; everything else is vulgar reproduction. And yet, to attempt a translation, to make a life of interpreting texts, which is what rabbinical existence longs for, is an act worthy of the heavens.

While translation and interpretation are two very different activities, they are also part of the same linguistic process: to translate is to interpret; and simultaneously, to interpret is to translate. It is true that a diaphanous and integral translation of meanings between cultures is utterly impossible. It is an impossible feat stemming from our fallible and awkward human condition. To create a universal language, a tongue meaningful to all, is also impossible because it could imply the inversion of the Tower of Babel, a return from multiplicity back to unity, and such a fanciful return to the origin can happen only in mythology, not in the real world. The third solution is a polyglot existence necessary in our civilization: it is obviously the more difficult to accomplish simply because it requires an infinite amount of human energy. But it is the solution that transgresses the original meaning the least. Perhaps it is a solitary device, but the search for a perfectly meaningful language can be accomplished only when the one is inhabited by the many: when God and man are one.

Of course multilingualism has an extraordinary capacity to live in many words at once. Besides, scientists have shown that a polyglotic child must activate more brain cells and ultimately acquires a higher I.Q. than children exposed to a single tongue. Knowledge of many languages also allows one to understand the nuances that distinguish one culture from another. As for translation, I spend a good many hours of my day reading literature removed from its original source. I do so me-chanically, to the point where I, like millions of other readers, forget it is a translation I am reading. That, precisely, is the nature of technological communication in our mass culture: a reality where every encounter seems to contain a degree of separation. Encounters today come through sophisticated artifacts—phone, TV, radio, computers; direct human contact is becoming a casualty of modernity. Translations can thus be perceived as metaphors for our reluctant accessibility to dialogue: our original voice is often replaced by a secondary source. As for interpreta-tion, we are children of Einstein's relativity and pupils of Rashomon, thriving in finding multiple perspectives, multiple truths. Such multi-plicity pushes us to a bizarre form of idolatry: Truth, the Truth spelled with a capital *T,* becomes fragmented, departmentalized, broken into numerous pieces. Interpretation gives way to deception. But again, we cannot do without it: I interpret, thus I exist.

To return to my main interest, the bridge where language and reli-gion intertwine, the more I reflect on the subject, the more I am per-suaded to believe in a neo-Platonic structure linking the two: first comes the original language, a proto-language—be it silence or music—through which the Almighty communicates with Himself and, at the same time, narrates the history of the universe; second comes a sacred though im-perfect tongue—Hebrew for the Jews—a bridge between heaven and earth; and third comes the plurality of languages we use daily to com-municate with one another. Hence, the search for an original language can be understood as an impossible journey, an emanation process that craves a return to the Origin of origins through stops in many linguistic spheres. A proto-language, it seems to me, is a corpus in which every word is simultaneously reduced to one meaning and still keeps a dose of poetry; a vehicle of communication in which words contain within them-selves the ancestral memory of everything that once was and will ever be;* a tongue in all places at once; a set of infinite words impossible to misunderstand—a linguistic temple that reverses, once and for all, the idiomatic fracture that came after the destruction of the Tower of Babel.

---

*I have written about language and memory in my introduction to *Cuentistas judíos* (Mexico: Editorial Porrúa, 1994), pp. iii–xvi.

It is an abstraction made of smoke rings, of course. The closer we want to get to it, the more we burn the energy that enables us to travel in search of the original tongue. We waste it without any revenue. Some would, of course, suggest that the pilgrimage in search of the primal tongue can also be approached as an end in itself; that the object of the search is always in the searcher. But this opinion leads us nowhere, for nothing can replace the original proto-language: like paradise, its true worth is beyond human reach. We therefore must find satisfaction in dissatisfaction, happiness in multiplicity. As Borges wrote in "The Analytical Language of John Wilkins": "The impossibility of penetrating the divine scheme of the universe cannot dissuade us from outlining human schemes, even though we are aware that they are provisional." Unity, as a result, is but a dream: we shall always aspire to reach it but will inevitably fail to attain it. The human language thrives in alternatives to the unifying dream in translation, in polyglotism, even in Esperanto; but these are all self-consuming forms of confusion. I am reminded of Stéphane Mallarmé's poem equating the soul to a cigar:

> *Toute l'âme résumé*
> *Quand lente nous l'expirons*
> *Dans plusieurs ronds de fumée*
> *Abolis en autres ronds*
>
> *Atteste quelque cigare*
> *Brulant savamment pour peu*
> *Que le cendre se sépare*
> *De son clair blaiser de feu . . .*

[1994]

7 / ART AND ANGER

Alberto Manguel, the editor and translator, once divided writers into two groups: those who perceive a single corner of the world as their entire universe, and those who look everywhere in the universe for a place called home. Judith Ortíz Cofer and Cherríe Moraga, new American female voices with a Hispanic ancestry, exemplify the opposition between the particularists and the universalists—the one introspective and self-possessed; the other outspoken, her writing meant to unsettle.

Ortíz Cofer, born in 1952 in Hormigueros, Puerto Rico, writes delicate, carefully shaped poetry and prose. She believes that literature doesn't need to come to us as a shock. Instead, it should deliver its recreation of what Gershom Scholem once called "a plastic moment," an instant in life in which a single insight might provoke a whole re-evaluation of our worldview.

She assumes her writing life fully and without apology. In her essay "5:00 A.M.: Writing as Ritual," Ortíz Cofer says: "Since that first morning in 1978 when I rose in the dark to find myself in a room of my own— with two hours belonging only to me ahead of me, two prime hours when my mind was still filtering my dreams—I have not made or accepted too many excuses for not writing. This apparently ordinary choice, to get up early and to work every day, forced me to come to terms with the discipline of art." An unequivocal particularist, as well as a transcendentalist in the nineteenth-century sense of the term, she may well be the most important Hispanic writer in English today, the one who will happily leave behind ethnic writing to insert herself and her successors in a truly universal literature, one that is neither apologetic nor falsely "representative." She has no national or racial vanity. In that sense, Ortíz

Cofer is the most American of Latino writers. Like Thoreau, she is a writer intoxicated with the personal, enamored of a democracy that leaves the individual alone to struggle with internal demons. Like Emerson, her poetry is her faith.

Her novel, *The Line of the Sun,* chronicling the years from the depression to the sixties, is sweet and amorphous. Her autobiographical essays, particularly "Silent Dancing," about growing up in Paterson, N.J., are touching and impressive. Her Puerto Ricanness is neither intrusive nor exclusive. I once heard Ortíz Cofer address the questions most frequently put to her: If you consider yourself a Puerto Rican writer, why do you write in English? And, what are you doing living in Georgia? "This is what being a Puerto Rican means to me," she answered unequivocally.

> To claim my heritage, to drink the life-giving *aguas buenas*, to eat the mango fruit of the knowledge of good and evil that grows in the Borinquen of my grandmother's tales. And also, to claim the language of my education, English, as well as the culture and literature of the country my parents chose as home for me. To claim both places. And so I plant my little writer's flag on both shores. There are exclusivists that would try to coerce me to take sides. I do not find that I need to make such decision any more than Isaac Bashevis Singer needed to give up being Jewish when he wrote his universal stories. . . . My books are neither Puerto Rican immigrant history nor sociological case studies.

Moraga, on the other hand, understands literature as sister to politics. Born in Whittier, California (also in 1952), she puts art at the service of anger, "Sometimes when I write," she notes, "I feel I am drawing from the most silent place in myself—a place without image, word, shape, sound—to create a portrait of la Mechicana before the 'Fall,' before shame, before betrayal, before Eve, Malinche and Guadalupe; before the occupation of Aztlán, *la llegada de los españoles,* the Aztecs' War of Flowers." In her eyes, the writer's odyssey is a journey of social discovery and commitment, a text is a *j'accuse.* Moraga recognizes the cosmic forces constantly affecting our behavior. Our sexuality, our self, our schizo-phrenic identity—all have to be reclaimed, remastered, rearticulated, repossessed. Thus, to write is to recognize ourselves as ideological animals. She writes about herself and others in a February 1990 poem entitled "Ni for El Salvador":

> *I am a woman nearing forty without children.*
> *I am an artist nearing forty without community.*
> *I am a lesbian nearing forty without partner.*
> *I am a Chicana nearing forty without country.*
>
> *And if it were safe, I'd spread open my thighs*
> *and let the whole world in*
> *and birth and birth and birth life.*
> *The dissolution of self, the dissolution of borders.*
>
> *But it is not safe.*
> *Ni for me.*
> *Ni for El Salvador.*

For both Ortíz Cofer and Moraga, literature offers a kind of redemption—but Moraga sees redemption of the individual alone as suicide, whereas for Ortíz Cofer redemption has almost nothing to do with prescriptive virtue. Ortíz Cofer approaches words for memory's sake and perceives literature as the recognition of the particular. Moraga uses art to illuminate diversity and sees the pulse of literature as directly linked to the universal salvation of humanity.

Enlightening and always surprising, *The Latin Deli* can easily be recognized as vintage Ortíz Cofer. Dedicated to her daughter Tanya, the delicate volume opens with a symbolic poem, subtitled "Ars Poetica," which reduces the universe to a kind of curative store, a *bodega* in which customers look for a medicine for their disheartened spirit:

> *Presiding over a formica counter,*
> *plastic Mother and Child magnetized*
> *to the top of an ancient register,*
> *the heady mix of smells from the open bins*
> *of dried codfish, the green plantains*
> *hanging in stalks like votive offerings,*
> *she is the Patroness of Exiles,*

a woman of no-age who was never pretty,
who spends her days selling canned memories
while listening to the Puerto Rican complain
that it would be cheaper to fly to San Juan
than to buy a pound of Bustello coffee here,
and to Cubans perfecting their speech
of a "glorious return" to Havana—where no one
has been allowed to die and nothing to change until then;
to Mexicans who pass through, talking lyrically
of dólares to be made in El Norte—
all waiting the comfort
of spoken Spanish.

The store is made to represent ghetto life, a tiny corner in which the protagonist, a goddess with unlimited powers, is forced to live in exile. The rest of *The Latin Deli* is an exploration of various aspects of the corner: the relationship between mainland and island Puerto Ricans, the myth of the Latina woman, assimilation to the American Dream.

In the first half of the book, subtitled "From the Book of Dreams in Spanish," Ortíz Cofer returns to autobiography, remembering her father, the music of the Beatles, the day President Kennedy was shot. The pieces are carefully crafted, powerful in their inner feeling—oscillating between past and present, between Hormigueros and Paterson, between Spanish and English, between satisfaction and blessedness on the one hand and anxiety on the other. The writer sets out a memory, and then proceeds to analyze it. But the act of interpreting the past is not aggressive; on the contrary, lyrical evocation and interpretation go hand in hand. Politics are not on Ortíz Cofer's agenda.

The second part, "The Medium's Burden," while continuing the same preoccupation with the personal, is more focused on the act of writing. It contains one of the best autobiographical pieces by Ortíz Cofer, one often reprinted: "The Story of My Body." From the first sentence on it summarizes her intellectual and physical journey: "I was born a white girl in Puerto Rico but became a brown girl when I came to live in the United States."

The real secret of Ortíz Cofer's stories and poems is probably life itself. By rejecting the blur of universalism, she becomes fully universal: a writer talking about small things attractive to all. She refuses to adapt her writing to the current literary fashion, rejecting fancy and easy affirmation. Her art, like life, is painful, sudden, frustrating.

If anything, what links *The Latin Deli* to Moraga's *The Last Generation*—essentially different books by opposing and opposed artists—is the hybridization of literary genres. Both books refuse to separate poetry from prose. Instead, they offer what I would call "literary miscegenation," the intercourse between different narrative forms. But Moraga's objective in intertwining poetry and prose is unlike Ortíz Cofer's: while one is a militant speaker, a promoter of resistance and affirmation whose importance is not literary but historical, the other is an artist, a transcendent inventor.

In *The Last Generation*, Moraga's language is labored, ideologically charged: She perceives herself as a soldier in the culture and identity wars, and, not surprisingly, has been seized upon by feminists and multiculturalists as an emblem of America's "internal revolution." "I complete this book 500 years after the arrival of Cristóbal Colón," she writes. "Its publication reflects a minor Mexican moment in an otherwise indifferent world literary history. Colón's accidental arrival to these lands, on the other hand, was an event of catastrophic consequence to the world, literary and otherwise. Still, in my mind, the two events are somehow intimately connected—the violent collision between the European and the Indigenous, the birth of a *colon*ization that would give birth to me."

Moraga begins the volume, a sequel of sorts to her 1983 *Loving in the War Years*, by describing her role as a lesbian writer in her family and community. "My family is beginning to feel its disintegration," she writes. "Our Mexican grandmother of ninety-six years has been dead two years now and *la familia*'s beginning to go. Ignoring this, it increases in number. I am the only one who doesn't ignore this because I am the only one not contributing to the population. My line of family stops with me. There will be no one calling me *Mami, Mamá, Abuelita*. . . . " She continues by touching on topics as varied as the Nicaraguan Revolution; the "inconsequential" men in her life; sexual identity and repression; colonialism. Disregarding the reader's limited fluency, her language travels freely, effortlessly from English to Spanish. Her references are to Navajo Indians, to the Chicano movement of the sixties, to Malcolm X.

For Moraga, literature is a weapon. In her autobiographical pieces, characters aren't free; they don't act by themselves but are acted upon.

Not surprisingly, her opinionated work is highly predictable and often stale. It seems to me doomed because it is created to fulfill reader's expectations and because it fashions a literature that divides the world too neatly into victims and colonialists.

Clearly, the abyss that separates Judith Ortíz Cofer and Cherríe Moraga, one that ultimately and sadly splits American letters today across ethnic lines, is not only based on the need to perceive a single corner of the world as one's entire universe or the universe as our home. It's a far deeper, less bridgeable abyss that points to the value one gives to the act of writing: one sees writing as exploration, the other as explosion. The explosive writers may gain immediate attention, but only the explorers will win a place on the eternal shelf of classics.

[1994]

8 / PESSOA'S ECHOES

Portugal sits in the Iberian Peninsula as an eclipsed region in the heart of Europe, its culture commonly overshadowed in international circles. Few twentieth-century Portuguese writers, for example, have managed to find an audience beyond their national borders. Even the most notable poet, Fernando Pessoa (an extraordinary figure, roughly the equivalent of T. S. Eliot in the Iberian world), is still, sixty years after his death and in spite of homage paid by Octavio Paz, Susan Sontag, and other intellectuals this side of the Atlantic, the property of a relatively tiny elite.

Indeed, John Hollander is alleged to have said that if Pessoa had never existed, Jorge Luis Borges would have had to invent him. With a complex and fascinating personality, this early modernist, born in Lisbon in 1888 and deceased at age forty-seven, is today honored mostly for his extraordinary poetic style, elusive yet intimate, always concerned with the perils of identity and the human inability to grasp the meaning of life. But his triumph lies also in having created a set of many "heteronyms"—facets or variations of his own narrative self—each with a distinctive character and vitae (a messianic, a rationalist, a stoic, a Nietzschean, etc.). Ricardo Reis, one of his imaginary selves, was, for instance, a doctor and a neoclassicist poet born in 1912, who lived for many years in self-imposed exile in Rio de Janeiro, and died in 1936, a year after Pessoa himself. Alvaro de Campos came to being after an inspired night in which his creator wrote some thirty poems. Alexander Search, more than a mere heteronym, was a pseudonym used for many years while writing English poetry. And then came Alberto Caeiro, Bernardo Soares, as well as the Chevalier de Pas. This multiplicity of selves motivated Paz to remark in a now-famous study published in book form in 1965 (translated into English by Edwin Honing, and included as an introduction to the Portuguese's *Selected Poems*), that Pessoa was "a poetic generation in and unto himself." In a letter published in the magazine *Presença* in June 1973, the poet himself explains this phenomenon of psychological and literary dislocation:

> How can I write in the name of these three? . . . Caeiro, out of pure and unexpected inspiration, without knowing or even calculating what I'd write. Ricardo Reis, after abstract deliberation, which quickly takes on concrete form in odes. Campos, when I feel a sudden impulse to write and I don't know what. My semiheteronym Bernardo Soares, who in many ways resembles Alvaro de Campos, appears whenever I'm tired or sleepy, when my power of ratiocination and my inhibitions are slightly suspended; that prose is a constant daydreaming. He's a semiheteronym because while he doesn't actually have my personality, his personality is not different than mine, rather a simple mutilation of it. Me minus ratiocination and affection. The prose, except for the tenuous quality ratiocination gives me, is the same as his, and his Portuguese is exactly the same; on the other hand, Caeiro writes bad Portuguese. Campos writes tolerably, but with lapses like "it's me" instead of "it's I," etc. Reis writes better Portuguese than I, but with a purism I consider exaggerated.

Was Pessoa a neurotic? Perhaps, but since one of the attributes of the artist is his vulnerable identity, the fact tells little about his poetic gestations. João Gaspar Simões (b. 1903), a personal friend, a novelist in his own right, and the author of some illuminating studies on Eça de Queiroz, wrote a monumental biography: *Vida e Obra de Fernando Pessoa: História duma Geração*. It's such a beautifully described portrait of this somber, opaque, yet incredibly talented genius that one is tempted to place him alongside Franz Kafka, for while the Czech looked unsuccessfully for his personal redemption in an antinomian world, the Portuguese, a man of profound sorrow, multiplied himself in the world. However, outside the blank piece of paper, he remained troubled and ultimately failed to see the light. For both men, the act of writing seemed to be the only door to temporal salvation, an escape from daily miseries. Kafka was a craftsman in a godless universe; Pessoa, a man of many faces in an individualistic society.

Simoes claims that the writer was possessed by an undefeatable sense of solitude due to his boyhood: first and foremost, the early and sudden death of his father, Joaquim de Seabra Pessoa, followed by those of a younger brother and two half sisters; the internment of his paternal grandmother, Dionisia Estrela de Seabra Pessoa, in a sanatorium; and the distress he suffered when he moved, in 1896, from Lisbon to Durban, South Africa, to follow his mother's second husband. Thus, he created his numerous personalities, all male, all about his age, to accompany him. In a sense, Pessoa—a word that, as Paz points out, means "person" in Portuguese and comes from *persona,* the mask worn by Roman actors—is a perfect Dr. Jekyll/ Mr. Hyde type of character: many selves in only one body. Yet in him, the division is far from moralistic. The heteronyms were echoes, mirages of his own soul. Each possessed a unique sensibility that appreciated the world in a distinct way and offered insights from a peculiar perspective.

But one also needs to remember that the labyrinthine twists of his ego didn't finish with his heteronyms. After a crisis in middle-age, searching for clues to human existence, Pessoa found them in astrology and esoteric knowledge. He attempted to explain his destiny and depressive moods by advocating cabalistic secrets and the wisdom of alchemy. Never approaching these fields from a scholar's point of view, he trusted that our reality has a hidden facet, unseen by the naked eye, only available to mediums and inspired poets. All of these puzzling elements make him an intriguing enigma, a question mark, a symbol of modern man with his many shadows.

Unfortunately, North American readers have had little exposure to Pessoa's writing. While most of his work has long been available in Spanish and French, only his poetry has been translated into English and published by small presses in Great Britain or by university presses in the United States. Things might change one day, as indeed they are beginning to: For one thing, his semi-diary, *The Book of Disquiet,* a marvel made of entries that Pessoa wrote during the last twenty years of his life, is now available. The text recalls Rainer Maria Rilke's *Notebooks of Malte Laurids Brigge,* and even Paul Valéry's *Monsieur Teste.* It's a disturbing spiritual confession, a search for identity, a desire to understand things divine and earthly. Yet this is not quite as intimate a diary as one might expect from a mere adolescent writer. After all, Pessoa was in his late thirties when he wrote its most substantial passages, giving to it a tone of maturity, self-effacing candor, of struggle with his own solitude, defects, and talents. According to Simões, at nineteen he kept a record of his juvenile years, and if one compares it to the self behind *The Book of Disquiet,* it is obvious the adult one is but a literary product; that is, even in his most desolate moments, Pessoa meant the text to become literature, as if constantly thinking of posterity.

Some of the puzzles surrounding Pessoa's character are quite apparent here. One of the questions a curious reader may ask is why he decided to attribute its content to Bernardo Soares, who, according to the cover, was "assistant bookkeeper of Lisbon," instead of writing it under his own name. Soares is different from all other heteronyms in that he is a prose writer, not a poet. Yet there may be another factor: Pessoa, so deeply submerged in his own intimate worlds, wanted to provide a distance, to see things from afar. By choosing a particular heteronym, he was capable of examining himself with a degree of separation.

In 1935, at the time of Pessoa's death, *The Book of Disquiet* was left unfinished. Here and there, some instructions explain how the poet wanted it to be edited, yet the organization is so chaotic that it's quite hard to envision an ad hoc final product. Although in this beautifully rendered English translation every entry is organized by date, it's obvious there is little development or progression. Actually, at times, the book as a whole seems a collection of excellent quotations. These are some examples: "To live is to be somebody else. Feeling is impossible if we feel today as we felt yesterday: to feel today the same thing we felt yesterday is not to feel at all—it's merely to remember what we felt yesterday, since today we are the living cadaver of yesterday's lost life."

> After a bad night's sleep, no one likes us. The lost
> sleep took with it whatever it is that makes us human.
> There is a latent irritation, it seems, in the very
> inorganic air that surrounds us. It is we, in the last
> analysis, who reproach ourselves, and it is between us
> and ourselves that the diplomacy of our silent battle is
> torn asunder.

A solitary bachelor, semi-alcoholic, and a dreamer always in search, Pessoa appears to have been writing these brief, passionate narratives when defeated, overwhelmed by depression, and in a metaphysical state of mind. Yet every single segment is full of light, a gem of insight into the human soul. The conclusion is that life is banal, mediocre, unsurprising, the daily routine turning people into automatons. As Pessoa puts it at the end, "The world belongs to he who doesn't feel." In his mind, much better universes than ours can be envisioned. As published by Pantheon in the United States, the book's structure has a scholarly tone: notes on the text and translation, a chronology, an introduction. Although it will always remains an esoteric volume, a wider audience will be able to digest, and be moved by, its compassionate, stylized pages.

But his overall eclipse is unlikely to change, a fact that stands in contrast to the the internationalization of José Saramago, Portugal's most prominent contemporary man of letters, an extraordinarily talented artist, the type of playwright, novelist, essayist, and occasional poet irresistible to lovers of literature. Born in 1922, he published his first book in the forties, a juvenile novel he now disowns. As a young Communist he found it virtually impossible to publish under the Antonio de Oliveira Salazar dictatorship of 1932–68, but after the bloodless coup of 1974 brought a modicum of press freedom, he exploded into Portugal's intellectual arena. Since then, with his pen, Saramago has over the past few decades publicly re-evaluated Iberian history, offering insightful, at times uncomfortable reflections on Portugal's religiosity and daily behavior. His artistic vision and his powerful style, which appears increasingly influenced by Gabriel García Márquez in its realist and magicalist tension, have made him a perennial Nobel Prize contender, an award he richly deserves. (No Portuguese writer, by the way, has ever been anointed by the Stockholm committee.)

Although too slowly, readers in the United States are getting to share in the excitement surrounding Saramago. *Memorial do Convento,* his dense 1982 narrative about a one-handed soldier in love with the slender daughter of a witch, whose romance plays to the ethereal music of Domenico Scarlatti, was rendered into English as *Baltasar and Blimunda* in 1987; Irving Howe praised its texture and lauded it as "a lyric fantasy about a company of free spirits escaping for a moment into freedom."

The novel's unique polyphonic feel of orchestrated voices and plots was indicative of what was yet to come. *The Year of the Death of Ricardo Reis,* Saramago's second book translated into English, is a bridge between his world and Pessoa's. I rank it among the best novels I've ever read, a sweet masterpiece set in Lisbon in 1936. It's about one of Pessoa's literary heteronyms who returns to life after Pessoa's final expiration, as a heavy ideological fog is descending over the Old Continent. Saramago pays tribute to his most famous literary predecessor, linking himself to a national tradition that values baroque self-reflection and self-referentiality. As in *Hamlet* and *Don Quixote,* Saramago builds a universe that is a hall of mirrors; Ricardo Reis, a doctor, returns to Portugal after a long stay in Brazil; rather than keeping a private practice, he wanders Lisbon's labyrinthine streets reciting poetry and is often visited by his creator, Pessoa, with whom he discusses current affairs at a cafe. The influence of Borges and Miguel de Unamuno is undeniable in Saramago's approach to the universe as a huge book written by a self-centered, larger-than-life novelist. Aren't we all trapped in someone else's dream? he wonders.

Still in top shape, the writer delivers *The Gospel According to Jesus Christ,* expertly translated, as were the two previous titles, by Giovanni Pontiero. Here, Saramago works wonders with the Passion story. His goal, clear from the outset, is to humanize the son of Joseph and Mary, to make His odyssey immediate, to shape Him as a perfect novelistic creature, one suitable to our *fin de siècle.* As Saramago puts it, his novel "was never meant to dismiss what others have written about Jesus or to contradict their accounts." And yet, although the plot has been repeated ad infinitum, much still comes as a surprise to the reader, mainly because Saramago has seasoned it with imaginative details full of mystery and gothic twists. For instance, after Jesus, Mary's oldest son, is born in a pool of blood, the mother gives birth to many more children with whom He, the wise brother, will keep in close touch. Joseph, Mary's husband, is portrayed as a relentless skeptic, constantly suffering from a sense of guilt, a hunted man ultimately crucified by the Romans. Jesus grows up to become an uncompromising, questioning, moody adolescent with sexual urges and a troublesome attitude. Even though His dialogue with God becomes a permanent feature toward the second third of the novel, the adolescent's ordeal is very much an affair of this world:

He excretes the usual bodily fluids and enjoys physical pleasure with Mary Magdalene; a doubting Jesus is pushed into the role of Messiah not only by friends and acquaintances but also by an ambivalent God ready to change His mind as circumstances arise.

The vertebrae of Saramago's novel are to be found in the recurrent dreams and nightmares, omens about death and resurrection, as well as in a mystical García Márquez–like character, a visitor sometimes posing as angel and other times as devil who foretells the future and establishes a communication line between the celestial and earthly spheres. Of course, others, from Nikos Kazantzakis in *The Last Temptation of Christ* to Paul Claudel in his oratorios with Catholic motifs, have been in the same theological terrain, but Saramago creates room of his own. Like Hermann Broch and Milan Kundera (the latter has also dealt with Christ's defecations in his fiction), the Portuguese has reinvented the novel as literary genre by making dogma and Holy Scripture fundamental narrative components. His crystalline prose ponders the weight of human existence, meditates directly rather than elliptically on cosmic questions, and dares to travel the fragile frontier where faith and the intellect intertwine.

Perhaps what's most memorable about *The Gospel According to Jesus Christ* is the role played by God. (Again, Borges's sensibility comes to mind.) Saramago makes Him simultaneously a witness and a puppeteer; at times He is late in receiving news of His child's pilgrimage; at other points He reluctantly participates in the tragedy unfolding before His eyes. The book has been injected with a sense of awe and spirituality that the novel as genre supposedly dismantled long ago. Saramago incorporates scriptural quotes to create a reinvigorating hybrid, one oscillating between a secular and a religious tone. In an outstanding scene, one recalling Dostoyevski's segment on the Grand Inquisitor in *The Brothers Karamazov*, Jesus encounters God not as a cloud or a column of smoke but as an elderly man with a great beard flowing over his chest, head uncovered, hair hanging loose, and with fleshy lips that barely move when he speaks. For over thirty pages Saramago's protagonist sustains a discussion in which the Almighty tells Him the consequences His death will have on Europe (and Portugal) while Jesus ponders His desire to go on. Immediately after this seductive encounter, a touching end to the narrative is precipitated over the reader's mind, one in which Jesus's individual will is actively questioned.

While other outstanding Saramago novels await an English translation, *The Gospel According to Jesus Christ*—part of an important religious facet of Saramago's career in which Catholicism is examined in the context of contemporary theological ambivalence—is enough to assure him a place in the universal library and in human memory. He has delivered a poignant reinterpretation of the Passion, one sensitive to the needs of our dissenting era. Not surprisingly, when the book was first published in Lisbon in 1991 it caused an uproar, felt soon after in the whole Iberian Peninsula, thanks to the Spanish edition that quickly followed. Those accusing Saramago of blasphemy for portraying Jesus as a Communist (a questionable attack), a vulnerable and lascivious person, forgot something altogether crucial: As a literary genre, the novel retains a loyalty to the secularist and even cynical views it was born with during Erasmus's age; any historical figure metamorphosed into a novelistic character thus becomes an expression, a mirror of the container it inhabits.

Fernando Pessoa may not figure literally in Saramago's account of Jesus, but his influence can be felt everywhere. Pessoa's poetic journey, let's remember, focused on deciphering the mysteries of individual identity in the modern world. Poetry was his means and vehicle. Saramago, on the other hand, seems involved in a quest to re-evaluate European history and sense of the collective using another tool: the novel, an instrument once thought exhausted after Joyce's, Musil's, and Proust's contributions, later reinvigorated by so-called Third World writers during the sixties. While Pessoa directed his attention to the enigmas of the self, Saramago centers his energy in deciphering the foundation of Iberian civilization in general, and Portugal's past and present in particular. No doubt the best pens to emerge out of Portugal since Eça de Queiroz, the two writers represent differing aspects of a depressed nation pushed into introspection and doubt. Nowhere else in Europe would the milieu allow for such uniquely contemplative approaches to man and the divine. In Saramago's portrait of Jesus and the Holy Family, Pessoa plays a fundamental role: The Messiah, the owner of a divided self, lives in a fractured world where reality and fiction are thoroughly commingled, heteronyms of each other.

[1991, 1994]

9 / OF ARMS AND THE ESSAYIST

Is the despot a knight of Utopia? . . . Everything has to do
with him—and his favorite word is *everything*. . . . The rest
ridiculous.

—Norman Manea, *On Clowns:*
The Dictator and the Artist

Nature, said Ralph Waldo Emerson in the prologue to *Representative Men,* seems to exist for the excellent. The world is upheld by
the veracity of extraordinary individuals who make the earth whole-
some. Octavio Paz, Mexico's foremost essayist and poet, appears to hold
this stature in his native country and in the vast Hispanic world: a renaissance *hommes de lettres,* an intellectual ambassador who personifies
Latin America's wholehearted embrace of European culture—in sum, a
cultural demigod. But much like one of his idols, T. S. Eliot, who commanded an overwhelming influence over English and American literary
aesthetics during the 1940s and 1950s and was later condemned for his
reactionary politics, Paz, once greeted with unmixed applause, now faces
an increasingly critical readership.

To be sure, his photo as a wise, tranquil old man is still ubiquitous,
and his work collected in his native Spanish in thirty-plus volumes is
seen in practically every bookstore from Barcelona to Buenos Aires to
Bogotá. And yet among much of the Hispanic intelligentsia, Paz is now
considered the pompous property of a conservative elite identified with
the status quo. Of course, not all express their misgivings with candor.

This fatherly figure, as he often seems, is at once revered and feared.
He projects the kind of anxious exercise of power that recalls the Stalinist
era: he requires loyalty and love from each of his free-spirited young
followers while his closeness to the Mexican government makes him an
almost forbidden target of criticism among his compatriots. And for
two decades now his prolific pen has been devoted to poetic essays that
rewrite national and international history where he is a character in decisive scenes and at the side of crucial personalities.

In the United States and Europe his public image as the 1990 winner of the Nobel Prize for literature is colored by his overwhelming erudition and a sense almost of sanctity that he projects. Should the counterview be made available? Thomas Carlyle used to argue that literature is the product of an abstract force and each individual writer only a dispensable medium. Should we dismiss Paz's ideology as we appreciate the beauty and insight of his oeuvre? Is the *homo politicus* less important than his work?

Encompassing some fifty years, Paz's career as essayist has been an extraordinary one. He loved the role of critic. Criticism, he once said, "is the apprenticeship of the revising imagination—imagination cured of fantasy and resolved to confront the world's reality. Even when his subject matter is abstract, his ideological views remain crystalline. A true dilettante, he began reviewing books in his early twenties in, among other places, the Argentine magazine *Sur,* where Borges published his most memorable works. Paz's interests then were never abandoned: poetry, language, politics, and pictorial art—in short just about everything. Ultimately he developed a theory of literature as a container of society's collective fears and its desire for the absolute.

His studies in poetry and aesthetics eventually resulted in *Children of the Mire: Poetry from Romanticism to the Avant-Garde,* the Eliot Norton Lectures delivered at Harvard University in 1982–83. In them he investigates the power and presence of poetry in the modern world, its impact and function. His research was expanded in his 1991 collection *The Other Voice: Essays on Modern Poetry,* where he focuses on Walt Whitman, Rimbaud, Eliot, and the Cuban poet and activist José Martí. His claim is that poetry, although elitist and apparently unimportant when it comes to historical and scientific progress, is the only true habitation of the human soul—that one can measure the sensibility of an epoch through its most mature verses even if they are unread by the masses.

Since early in his career, Paz has nurtured the idea of the poet as the only hero of modern times, a visionary with a complex understanding of things earthly (sexual, social, political, scientific) who nevertheless prefers to surround himself with muses. He once said, "Poetry, which yesterday was required to breathe the free air of universal communion, continues to be an exorcism for protecting us from the sorcery of force and of numbers. It has been said that poetry is one of the means by which modern man can say *No* to all those powers which, not content with disposing of our lives, also want to rule our consciousness. But this negation carries within it a *Yes* which is greater than itself." Indeed, Paz's magisterial oeuvre is a guided tour through the intellectual debacles of the twentieth century and a representation of the poet as a sort of clock of humankind. In "Nocturne of San Ildefonso," one of his finest poems, he claims, "Poetry, the bridge suspended between history and truth, is not a way toward this or that: it is to see the stillness within movement."

Octavio Paz was born in 1914 as the peasant revolution of Emiliano Zapata and Pancho Villa was under way. Modernism was bubbling in Europe and *modernismo* in Spanish poetry—a romantic literary movement that started in 1885 and included authors like Rubén Darío and Julián del Casal—had reached its peak. A couple of years before, Marcel Duchamp, about whom Paz would write a slim theoretical volume in 1968, shocked the world with *Nude Descending a Staircase.* Igor Stravinsky had just finished *The Rite of Spring,* and D. W. Griffith was about to release *The Birth of a Nation.* For over three decades, Mexico had lived under the dictatorship of Porfirio Díaz, considered until very recently a tyrant who nonetheless brought prosperity and foreign investment into the nation and helped transform it from a rural landscape to a vibrant republic by building a complex railroad network (contemporary assessments are less forgiving). Paz's grandfather fought against the French and supported Díaz, but his father, a journalist and lawyer, defended Zapata in New York, and helped introduce agrarian reform after the revolution. Decades later, Paz would describe Zapata's project as an attempt to return to origins. The paradox of Zapatismo, he would argue, "was that it was a profoundly traditionalist movement; and precisely in that traditionalism its revolutionary might resides." As poet, he would turn Zapata into an inspiration, mainly because, like the guerrilla hero, Paz's verse has a redemptive component—the emergence of certain hidden and repressed realities.

The woman Paz's father married was a pious, uncultivated Catholic, affectionate and supportive, who was descended from Spanish immigrants. The child would come to describe his mother as "a love letter with grammatical errors." Later the father became an alcoholic and died in a train crash in 1935. The family owned a substantial library similar to the one of Borges's childhood. It was a place where young Octavio found escape and early inspiration, a place that for a while he perceived as a map of the universe. His birthplace is Mixcoac, a southern suburb of the nation's capital, which during the colonial time included the Carmelite convent where Sor Juana Inés de La Cruz, another one of Paz's idols, lived from youth until her early death in 1695. Sor Juana was a proto-feminist nun and Latin American's foremost pre-Independence intellectual, who wrote the celebrated poem "First Dream." This geographical link between Paz and Sor Juana nurtured his view of Mexican history as a pyramid: each person, each epoch, he believes, established its own identity by finding its place on top of preceding generations. The present, then, is a sum of pasts eternally recycled, and every contemporary citizen a continuation, a reincarnation of those alive before. And so Sor Juana lives *in* and *through* Paz.

The adolescent Paz was a passionate student who would fervently discuss politics in the streets, loved Dostoyevski, and, together with his schoolmates joined a student strike in 1929. French culture, too, was essential in his upbringing. During the late nineteenth century, Parisian culture, glamorous and romantic, was glorified from the Rio Grande to the Argentine pampa. *Modernistas* like Darío and Casal emulated the decadent romanticism of J. K. Huysmans. Latin American poets and painters imitated the rhyme and tastes of art nouveau, while the bourgeois saw the tongue of Victor Hugo and Flaubert as a sign of sophistication. This trans-Atlantic influence left an indelible mark on Paz. As a young man, he dreamed of visiting France's capital, and he would eventually live there for three years (between 1959 and 1962) becoming a devotee of Baudelaire and Rimbaud.

What was the nature of political and cultural authenticity in the Americas? The question would overwhelm his later years. And yet he would always view the European impact on Mexican culture as a necessary evil. Despite the many attacks on his position, Paz would always seek to rehabilitate the image of the conquerors. He saw little point to a one-sided portrayal of Spaniards and other trans-Atlantic newcomers as "abusers." After all, their impact on native culture was ubiquitous, undeniable, and impossible to erase. (Joseph Brodsky, the Russian poet and Nobel laureate and once one of Paz's close friends, develops this view in a 1975 poem "To Yevgeny," written during a trip to Mexico).

In 1937 Paz discovered his native Mexico during a visit to the Yucatán peninsula where he had been assigned the task of setting up a pedagogical center for poor campesinos. Ironically just as Paz fell in love with the aboriginal aspects of his country's culture, his literary vision began to be tarnished by surrealism. An unusually precocious writer, he had published his first book of poetry at age nineteen, one he later criticized as inflammatory and too rhetorical. He would not consider himself an essayist until after reaching thirty-three when he began shaping *The Labyrinth of Solitude,* the book that made him an instant celebrity. Again, this so-called return to the sources ought not to be seen as an identification of young Paz with the lower classes. In fact, his experience in Yucatán and elsewhere in the southern states of Mexico brought a good deal of physical discomfort and intellectual puzzlement. His individual identity emerged as divided: Was his "Mexicanness" a denial of things European? Could he balance the two—become a bridge across the ocean where the New and the Old Worlds could communicate? The dilemma, it goes without saying, is at the core of Hispanic America's collective soul, and Paz resolved it in an estimable, if highly debatable fashion.

Besides Paris, his early career took him to the Spanish Civil War in Barcelona and Valencia. He went to the Iberian peninsula penniless, in search of adventure—much like young Hemingway but for rather different reasons: he came less as a man of courage than as a man of ideas, and he sought less to prove and promote his manhood than to acquaint himself with left-wing utopias. Invited by the militant poet Pablo Neruda to participate in the Second Congress of the Alliance of Intellectuals in Defense of Culture, Paz arrived in 1937, the same year he visited the Yucatán. He had been married the year before to Elena Garro, who would later become an important writer in her own right, the author of the classic Mexican novel *Recollection of Things to Come,* and with whom he had a daughter.

Europe provided an excellent opportunity for a would-be Mexican writer to witness the revolutionary artistic atmosphere that would eventually change our global perception of reality. In his pilgrimage he was befriended by the Peruvian poet César Vallejo, the filmmaker Luis Buñuel ("whose work," he would write, "tends to stimulate the release of something secret and precious, terrible and pure, hidden by our reality"), the poet and dramatist Miguel Hernández, and a number of other artists and writers. And yet his tender age (he was twenty-two) made him some-

thing of an outsider. Many years later, Paz, with his typical grandilo-
quence and absence of humility, would describe his voyage to Spain as a
rite of passage not only for him but for the Hispanic world as a whole.
Looking back, he would criticize Neruda's Marxist dogmatism. He would
also embellish, perhaps even falsify, his personal experience in the battlefield. Such a refurbishing of the past was not unusual for him. History,
in Paz's eyes, is a grand stage, "a ghostly procession without meaning or
end," where he is the leading actor and sole protagonist, every instant of
his life enlightening to others. For him, historical knowledge is
nonchronological. He often mixes autobiographical insights and fac-
tual information, thus becoming his own sole object of worship.

Despite Paz's bitterness toward the crossroad between politics and
letters, between the pen and the sword, the two have always been his
obsession. He wrote:

> The history of modern literature, from the German
> and English romantics to our own days, is the history
> of a long, unhappy passion for politics. From Cole-
> ridge to Mayakowski, Revolution has been the Great
> Goddess, the eternal beloved and the great whore to
> poets and novelists. Politics filled Malraux's head
> with smoke, poisoned the sleepless nights of César
> Vallejo, killed Garcia Lorca, abandoned the old poet
> Antonio Machado in a village in the Pyrenees, locked
> Pound in an asylum, dishonored Neruda and Aragón,
> has made Sartre a figure of ridicule, and has acknowl-
> edged Breton all too late.

Politics also blinded the Mexican. To equate Marxism with a higher
spirituality was young Paz's primary goal. His concern with man's lone-
liness in the world—a state he believes can be transcended only through
faith, compassion, and sexual love—emerges from his antireligious sen-
timents, his courage to rebel and experiment, but also and more con-
cretely, his desire to find solutions to social problems.

In this respect, André Breton, the French surrealist, was his role model.
"In my adolescence," he wrote in his 1967 book *Alternating Current,*
"during a period of isolation and exaltation, I read by chance some pages
which, I learned later, form chapters of *L'amour fou.* In them Breton

describes his climb to the summit of the Teides, in Tenerife. That text, read at almost the same time as Blake's *The Marriage of Heaven and Hell*, opened the doors to modern poetry to me." He admired Breton, himself a dictatorial figure among surrealists, not as a thinker but as a poet. "It is impossible to write about [him] with unimpassioned language," he would expand in *On Poets and Others*, a collection of essays published in 1986. "What's more, it would be wrong to do so. For him, the powers of the word were undistinguishable from those of passion, and this, in its highest and tensest form, was nothing but language in a state of savage purity: poetry." In the Frenchman's eyes "nature is language. The attraction between syllables and words is not different from that of the stars and bodies."

Enchanted by Breton's method of automatic literature, by the magic of his style, Paz stood at the intellectual crossroad where Leon Trotsky and Breton collide: a point where the writer is both activist and soul-searcher. He saw himself as an antagonist of the state—a voice for the repressed and oppressed. Yet the Mexican was more contemplative than belligerent. He adapted the surrealist technique to his own personal needs; his passion for Blake and a slow process of disenchantment with Marxism-Leninism would finally make him a Satan in a continent where, for decades the only respectable path to salvation was through bloody insurrection. Breton, Trotsky, Blake—an intriguing combination behind the portrait of Paz as a young man.

As time went by, and he began to move away from the spell of left-wing politics, many of his colleagues were compelled to re-evaluate their own ideological stand. His change became more apparent on his return to Mexico, when even anarchism seemed to fit him better. In the meantime, the country had become a safe haven for artists and political refugees, including Trotsky, who lived his last years in Coyoacán, where he was assassinated. Paz continued writing verse and dealing with the affective realm, and although an atheist and anticlericalist, he began finding inspiration in medieval Christian poets from the Iberian peninsula like Santa Teresa de Jesús and San Juan de La Cruz, who were concerned with a higher plane of understanding. With Leonora Carrington, Benjamin Péret, Remedios Varo, Wolfgang Paalen, and other European surrealists stationed south of the Rio Grande, Paz participated in a number of poetic and theatrical projects.

His ideological running point, an authentic rite of passage, occurred as a result of the triumph of Fidel Castro's insurgency in Cuba in 1958–59. It developed in the next decade or so shaping his new vision. At first, his position, like that of scores of other Latin Americans, including Carlos Fuentes, Julio Cortázar, and Mario Vargas Llosa, was unconditional support. In spite of his innate skepticism, Paz believed another direction had to be taken to solve the problems of Hispanic society—poverty, lack of collective self-respect, and governmental corruption. And when, in 1966, the Argentine Ernesto "Ché" Guevara gave up his high-ranking status in the new Havana regime to continue his struggle on behalf of the peasants and the working class in Bolivia and elsewhere in South America, the euphoria was overpowering: a new era had begun. But Paz's applause was not from the heart. He had doubts. During the next few years, just as Jean-Paul Sartre and Albert Camus held their well-publicized debate on the role of the writer in "an age of change," just as, from Lima to Santiago, some like Roque Dalton and Ernesto Cardenal were hoping to destabilize the rigid governmental structure, Paz shifted to a more center-left position and eventually supported the right wing.

A few years before, he had published an essay documenting Stalin's concentration camps (included in *On Poets and Others*). It infuriated many Marxist believers, and Paz was accused of treason. And when Castro finally confessed his loyalty to Moscow's Politburo, Paz's criticism became even louder and more insistent. Attacking the apologists for the Soviet influence in Central America in 1975, he eulogized the dissident Aleksandr Solzhenitsyn as a symbol of antitotalitarianism who "passed the test of history." His political coming of age is also tangible in other occasional pieces, reviews and essays on major historical events and personalties where he ridiculed left-wingers and portrayed himself as champion of democracy. The equation of transformation with revolution now seemed to him preposterous. He discovered he was in favor of dialogue, of peaceful change, and against any form of destructiveness. In his collection entitled *Convergences,* and even before, probably dating back to the 1940s, his object of worship was Charles Fourier, a Frenchman of Bretonian lineage who celebrated the body and stood as a challenger to industrialism and consumerism, a man committed to the twin goals of erotic freedom and sexual equality. It was the late 1960s and early 1970s, and the climate of rebellion and hippie life put him in touch with Buddhism and Oriental mysticism. The body, not the world, captured his attention.

Paz's metamorphosis from inspired young activist to representative man is largely due to the epoch-making work he produced after the Second World War. As a Guggenheim fellow, he lived in the United States between 1943 and 1945, primarily in California. He used his time and money to work on what would be his most outstanding accomplishment, an unequaled nonfiction masterpiece that investigates the Mexican psyche: *The Labyrinth of Solitude.* Paz's goal was fully to explain the nation's inferiority complex and what he viewed as its ambiguous relationship with death. And his method was to examine the folklore, religion, cosmology, and psychology that had surrounded him since childhood. Completed in Paris, serialized in a Mexican magazine, and published in book form in 1950 and in an expanded edition nine years later (he has a Whitmanesque obsession for updating his books in order to correct typos and, in a Gargantuan fashion, to eat up his critics' arguments by including their comments in the form of appendixes), the book was intended to be in the tradition of José Ortega y Gasset's philosophical inquiries, an exploration of what it means to be Mexican. Paz injects a solemn, erudite tone that has helped to monumentalize his opinions and promote an almost Olympian sense of his literary authority.

Comprising eight chapters and an epilogue, his argument is governed by two insights: the view of his countrymen as reticent, introverted, and alienated from Western civilization; and the conception of history as a trauma difficult to overcome. Similar to W. E. B. Du Bois's perception of Africans in the United States, Paz's claim is that Mexicans have a dual personality, a split soul, half Iberian and half aboriginal—no doubt the same division that prevails in Paz's character.

When Hernán Cortés and his conquistadors colonized Tenochtitlán in 1523–25 instead of eliminating the native Aztec culture to build on its ruins, they mixed, combined, and syncretized themselves with the environment—that is they used the existent infrastructure to build a totally different architecture. Then too, instead of battling the Spanish intruders, Moctezuma II and Cuauthémoc, the last two native emperors, welcomed them with precious gifts. Their unexpected attitude (studied among others by Barbara Tuchman in *The March of Folly*) was based on the certainty that Quetzalcóatl, their god, would one day return by sea as a bearded white male. The bloody clash between the European dream of conquest and the aboriginal festivity dedicated to the Almighty's second coming, in Paz's view, marks the birth of the dark-skinned mestizo race that populates Mexico. Christopher Columbus and his successors could thus be seen as incubators of a new people. Add to the story the fact that Cortés used a female Aztec interpreter, La Malinche, to communicate with his enemies, took her as lover, impregnated her, and left without acknowledging his descendants, and a clear picture emerges of the male and female archetypes presiding over the country's conflicted identity: macho and virgin villain and prostitute.

It is that identity, dissonant and unstable, that Paz sets out to explore, from various angles of approach, in *Labyrinth of Solitude*. "The Pachuco and Other Extremes," the volume's first chapter, discusses the topic very much in fashion today: the Chicano community in Los Angeles—and in particular, its rebellious youth, the Pochos, whose spiritual homelessness, lack of definition, and exotic styles of dress are a basic feature of the contemporary multicultural climate in the United States. "Mexican Masks," perhaps the most remarkable chapter in his book, describes the popular soul as nothing but a sum of theatrical props useful to hide the nation's true self. Collectively seen as either prostitutes or celestial creatures, women south of the border are, he claims, crucial in the shaping of everyday life, while men, often absent and evasive, have merely a supporting role. In a country piously Catholic, not Jesus Christ but the Virgin of Guadalupe, Mexico's equivalent to the Virgin Mary, is the one and only national savior—mother earth acting as God. The energy-consuming corruption of politicians can be related to the lack of trust and honesty Paz finds in Mexico. The author's ideology is clear: the whole Mexican bureaucratic system, in his diagnosis, is a result of a traumatic history. Left and right, good and evil—no regime can really solve the fracture at the nation's heart. Politics is the country's sickness.

No masterpiece stands on its own. *The Labyrinth of Solitude*, which has been translated into twenty-five languages and withstood numerous revisions, is now an essential feature of Hispanic letters today, one that has acquired the status of a classic and has been written about mercilessly by academics. But a number of precursors, some immediate and others more remote, helped determine its content, structure, and reception. These include the political writings of José Vasconcelos and Samuel

Ramos, two Mexican intellectuals (the first Mexico's minister of education in the early decades of the twentieth century, the second a college philosopher), as well as the psychoanalytic theories of Alfred Adler and Otto Rank dealing with the inferiority complex. The image of its title, a metaphorical reference to the baroque structure of the endless doors and forking paths Hispanics call home, is now frequently invoked when referring to the reality south of the Rio Grande. (The labyrinth, by the way, a feature in the art of Borges and Franz Kafka alike, seems to be a bridge linking Eastern Europe to the Americas.) The book acquired a major book-long appendix in 1970. *The Other Mexico: Critique of the Pyramid,* discussing the violent student massacre in Tlatelolco Plaza in the late 1960s among other epoch-making events.

However unrealistic, Paz's ultimate political message in these and other essays is that society will return to its original freedom and men to their primordial purity. Then history will cease. Are we, he asks, living at the end of time? His answer is staunchly in the affirmative. He thinks that modern time, linear time, the homologue of the ideas of progress and history, ever propelled into the future, is coming to an end: "I believe that we are entering another time, a time that has not revealed its form and about which we can say nothing except that it will be neither a linear nor a cyclical time. Neither history nor myth. The time that's coming, if we really are living a change of times, a general revolt and not a linear revolution, will be neither a future nor a past, but a present." The sources of this idealistic view are not only Rousseau and Nietzsche but mysticism and Hindu religion. When he can, he criticizes (although in a reverent tone) European rationality for imprisoning man; he considers the dreams of reason to be horrendous. In the tradition of Buddhism and even early Christianity, what is left is to search for the inner world— to dream with the eyes closed, to look for the eternal present. It's quite obvious that, at this point, Paz has moved from Marxism to anarchy to a view of society characterized by a form of solipsism. Contemporary problems are a result of man's anomie. The burden of the past is too oppressive. What is needed is a regression, a search for new beginnings.

Since the Second World War eclipsed Europe's glamour, Paz would argue that the so-called Third World, including, of course, Mexico, has ceased to be foreign. Instead it has become a contemporary of the rest of humankind—alienated and full of anguish just like everybody else.

Hence, the purpose of *The Labyrinth of Solitude*, like *The Other Mexico*, is to awaken Mexico's collective consciousness to historical forces, to make a nation preoccupied with the past fully aware of the present. To the larger world, however, it seeks to show the world how Mexico is anxious to revisit its past and reformulate its present.

Some three decades after the publication of *The Labyrinth of Solitude*, Paz would produce another masterpiece. At the age of sixty-eight, he published *Sor Juana: or, the Traps of Faith*, an outstanding biography of the Mixcoac-born nun. Published in 1982, after he had won the Olin Yoliztli Prize given by the Mexican government, the Cervantes prize by Spain, and many honorary degrees from major U.S. institutions, it is at once a product of a man at peace with the world and a mystifying game of mirrors: a contemporary poet looking into the past to explain his own intellectual journey. Masterfully mixing historical research, anthropological insights, personal speculation, and autobiographical allusions, the thick volume analyzes Sor Juana Inés de La Cruz's sophisticated style through a wide range of topics like church activities, Neoplatonism, courtly love, medieval Spanish poetry, and the political and social foundation of the Americas.

Its most exemplary segment is devoted to the poem "First Dream," published in 1692, where the protagonist is the human mind traveling in a night's jurney through heaven and earth to decipher the terrestrial and spiritual enigmas of life. For a long time, this puzzling text has left a rich trail of contradictory interpretations; Paz's own interpretation centers on Sor Juana's religiosity and her implicit conflict of interests: as a Catholic living in a Carmelite convent, the Mexican nun could neither question God's role in the creation of the universe nor attempt to clarify those doubts left to faith. At the same time, her intelligence could not consent to reduce the human mind to a timid, paralyzed entity without the courage to question its surroundings. Thus—much like the explanation of Maimonides's *Guide for the Perplexed* offered by Leo Strauss, an influential conservative professor at the University of Chicago and Allan Bloom's mentor—Paz's argument holds that the nun positioned a number of crucial clues throughout the text to enable astute readers to discover her hidden intention. From his perspective, the poem is not only a night-long journey into religious certainty, it is also a defense of poetry.

This interpretation applies to Sor Juana's *Response to Sor Filotea de La*

Cruz, a 1691 letter the nun wrote after her confessor accused her of being too bold a woman, a threat to the male-oriented milieu. After careful reflection, she renounced her personal library and literary career. Paz shows how, as society first protected then attacked her talents, her final action held a double meaning: it is simultaneously a renunciation and a triumph of the literary will, a sign of her knowledge that posterity is her only true judge.

Because of a long-standing resistance toward the public confessional mode, toward the communication of inner fears, the literary genre of (auto)biography is not well regarded in the Hispanic world. That is why the urgent message in Paz's book is such a refreshing treat: finding the particular in the universal, it unravels the enigma of Mexico's collective psyche by explaining Sor Juana's existential plight. One can hardly ask anything more of a book. Before its publication, Sor Juana was but a mere shadow, an academic delicacy—today she is a key to the collective identity. Paz's political motivation for such an enterprise is once again clear: anxious to be fully technologized, contemporary Mexico runs the risk of losing itself in the labyrinth of modernity. The solution is to look into the mirror of the past, to be loyal to the nation's foundation. Sor Juana's struggle to make faith and intellect compatible, to be recognized as a half-native and half-Iberian hybrid and respected as a woman in a dogmatic male-dominated universe, is not unlike Paz's desire to retain the poet's power to understand and decipher a world easily corrupted by consumerism and idolatry, his hope to perpetuate highbrow culture and his dream to be a Europeanized Mexican.

The style and content of *The Traps of Faith,* and Paz's other essays of the time, are in debt to his passion for structuralism, a school of thought with which he identified in the 1960s because of its interest in "primitive" modes of thought. His intellectual curiosity led him to write a booklet on Claude Lévi-Strauss and, as well, to attempt, with little success, an explanation of his own poetic oeuvre in structural categories. After that, he became enchanted with a handful of other stars in the French constellation: George Bataille, Marquis de Sade ("after whom no one has dared to discover an atheist society"), and other Parisian writers interested in exploiting sexuality and intrigued by the bodily signs and metaphors.

Again the language of the body, its "rebellion," became a bewitchment. In one of his most difficult but rewarding volumes, *Conjunctions and Disjunctions,* a tour de force published in 1969, he applied Lévi-Strauss's categories to distinguish between *cara* and *culo*—"face" and "backside"—as metaphorical oppositions present in Francisco de Quevedo's poetry and in the cartoons of José Guadalupe Posada, a famous Mexican lampooner during the 1910 revolution. The work recalls *The Unbearable Lightness of Being,* in which the narator discusses Jesus Christ's excrement as divine object. Ranging among such topics as Taoism, Goya's pictorial art, the inflammatory essays by Jonathan Swift, and the eschatological poetry of Juan Ramón Jiménez, Paz pursues his objective of understanding the duality in man: heaven and earth, love and hate, the bodily and the spiritual. The volume, full of energy, curiosity, and intelligence, is, in Irving Howe's words, the product of "an intellectual one-man band who performs everything from five-finger sonatas to full-scale symphonies and even electronic music"—an extraordinary analysis of the many contradictions that make us human and of how the body is represented in Western pictorial art and letters.

From the 1950s to the 1980s, in terms of politics, Paz traveled light years. He became a literary lion. And his vanity, his need for adulation, have certainly influenced his oeuvre. His later essays show a deep sense of intransigence toward other viewpoints. He has become a demigod—the orchestrator of history. To be sure, this summoning of authority wasn't an overnight phenomenon. On the contrary, it took shape slowly and steadily while Paz published one book after another. And the aura was sustained by a devoted intelligentsia that saw him as a compass.

An indirect sign of his self-promotion and global sense of ambition can be found in his passion for polyglotism and translation. Translating gems of foreign cultures into his own might seem like an act of literary self-abnegation. And yet translation is also appropriation: here is Paz exercising a will to power unconfined by cultural and linguistic boundaries. By representing important works of other cultures, he annexes and introjects everything non-Mexican.

Paz has produced his own versions of poems by Charles Tomlinson, Elizabeth Bishop (her work during her Brazilian period), and the Swedish Artur Lundkvist, as well as a number of Chinese (including Li Po, Wang Wei, and Su Shih) and Japanese poets (Kakinomoto Hitomaro, Matsuo Basho, and Kobayashi Issa). He has translated verses by Fernando

Pessoa, Mallarmé, Apollinaire, Gerard de Nerval, John Donne, E. E. Cummings, William Carlos Williams, and Ezra Pound. (His best translations into Spanish are included in *Versiones y diversiones*; his views on the art of translation are part of *Confrontaciones,* known today as *El signo y el garabato.*) These exercises in translation have a unique structure: with the help of appendixes and personal commentary at the end of the text, Paz shows how wise and incomparable he really is.

His career as translator also includes a curious anthology, at least in the eyes of English-speaking and French readers, entitled *Mexican Poetry.* Compiled in 1958 under the sponsorship of UNESCO and originally published by Indiana University Press the book dates to a time when Paz was submerging himself as researcher in the nation's colonial and independent periods. It includes verses by Bernardo to Balbuena, Ramón López Velarde, and other national poets—all serviceably, if somewhat quirkily translated by Samuel Beckett. (As far as I know, this is Beckett's only translation from the Spanish.) For Paz, the anthology provided an opportunity to set forth his aesthetic views of how literature developed within Mexican borders. Indeed, the anthology, which is accompanied in the American edition by a preface by the Oxford classical scholar C. M. Bowra, and in French by an essay by Paul Claudel, features Paz as the ultimate interpreter of Mexican culture, the entrance door to its secret codes and bizarre manifestations. He ponders the impact of the Iberian poets Quevedo, Lope de Vega, and Luis de Góngora in colonial letters; studies the impact of Latin America's *modernista* movement on late nineteenth- and early twentieth-century versifiers like Rubén Darío, Amado Nervo, Enrique González Martínez, and José Juan Tablada; and reaches across the Pacific and Atlantic to link Mexican letters to Japanese, Arabic, European, and Hindu art. In a spectacular display of knowledge and lucidity, he finds a way to make the poetry in his native country a showcase of the best and worst in world literature, which is a daunting task indeed. Again the objective here is to turn the universal into a particular or vice versa, all with the effect of showing how Paz is the embodiment of absolute truth.

Even if Paz's intellectual reach and essayistic ambition can seem inexhaustible, and his pen ubiquitous, there are silences. He has, for example, never written an essay on Latin America's literary boom of the 1960s. For a man constantly rewriting history, this particular absence is intriguing, especially when one thinks how the works of Gabriel García Márquez and his colleagues have been compared to the renewal of Russian letters in the second half of the nineteenth century, in the writings of Tolstoy, Dostoyevski, Chekhov, and Turgenev. Occasionally, Paz does publish an obituary, as when Julio Cortázar died in 1984 (although, not surprisingly, he devoted most of the space to recollecting his Paris years and only in passing mentioned the Argentine's life and work). This silence, nevertheless, is just on paper. In real life, Paz has had a long list of well-publicized quarrels with Carlos Fuentes, Mario Vargas Llosa, and other writers from the region with whom friendship has always been a difficult affair.

Take the Peruvian, for example. His own intellectual pilgrimage, similar to Paz's, has brought him from active support of the Cuban Revolution to enthusiastic promotion of a free-market pluralistic approach to Latin America. Invited to a conference entitled "The Freedom Experience" and organized by Paz's monthly magazine *Vuelta* in 1989, Vargas Llosa took the opportunity to portray Mexico as a perfect dictatorship, thus embarrassing President Carlos Salinas de Gortari who travels the world selling his country as a democracy and hates to be compared to Augusto Pinochet or Juan Domingo Perón. After his remarks, the Peruvian was forced to leave the country right away while Paz apologized. For months Paz stopped speaking to Vargas Llosa and ceased publishing him in his magazine. But then an armistice was reached. Love, hate, love, hate. . . .

His companionship with Carlos Fuentes has been marked by the same ambivalence and volatility. For instance, in an essay written in New Delhi in 1967, Paz hailed Fuentes as an extraordinary prose writer, singling out such books as *Los días enmascarados* (Masked days), *Where the Air Is Clear, The Death of Artemio Cruz,* and *Aura.* Paz celebrated Fuentes again in 1972. But things went sour, and they have been enemies since, in the 1980s, the historian Enrique Krauze—Paz's loyal follower and managing editor at *Vuelta*—published, with Paz's blessing, a strongly negative review in the *New Republic* of Fuentes's *Myself with Others, Old Gringo,* and other titles. Gabriel García Márquez and other major Latin American intellectuals have also been involved in similarly volatile relationships.

From antagonism to consent, today Paz is even portrayed by some as a sell-out, one with suspicious ties to the oligarchy. In any event, his complaisant attitude toward the current Mexican regime is the result of a long and perhaps extenuating process. At first, two decisive events made Paz a critic of the Mexican status quo, a nonconformist observer forced to action. In 1968, while he was ambassador in India and the Olympic Games were about to begin in Mexico, a massive civil and student demonstration took place against Mexico's dictatorial Revolutionary Institutional Party (PRI). The demonstration ended in a massacre in Tlatelolco Plaza in which numerous young men and women were killed by the army. As a sign of solidarity, he resigned his diplomatic post. The second event took place eight years later, while Paz was editing *Plural*, a literary magazine (the precursor of *Vuelta*) whose parent company was one of the nation's most important dailies critical of then-president Luis Echeverría Alvarez. It was 1976. An angered government ordered a takeover of the media emporium, invading its offices with soldiers and stopped the presses—an obvious aggression against free speech.

At both junctures Paz voiced dissent, but time would soften his attitude. Today, he is a personal friend of President Salinas de Gortari. Even more important he has the support of Emilio Azcárraga, the Hispanic Ted Turner who owns Latin America's most far-reaching private television station (called Televisa in Mexico), with tentacles in Europe and the United States.

To such a degree has Paz become the government's marionette that when he was awarded the Nobel Prize, the nationwide newspaper headlines claimed the award was a present from his two closest friends, Salinas and Azcárraga. Suspicions were fortified by the fact that the award coincided with the multi-million-dollar exhibit "Mexico: Splendors of Thirty Centuries" at the Metropolitan Museum of Art in New York, sponsored by the Mexican president and a close group of rich businessmen. Since Paz happened to be in Manhattan when he received the phone call from Stockholm, some conjectured about an illicit monetary dealing timed with the Nobel selection by the Swedish Academy.

Paz's close association with the centers of power has had an inhibiting effect on his literary and political writings. In essence, his critical eye can no longer be taken seriously. He is seen as a tentacle of the state, a conformist who traded his dreams for institutional recognition. Ambrose Bierce defines a dictator, in *The Devil's Dictionary,* as the head of a nation that prefers the pestilence of despotism to the plague of anarchy. From antiestablishment poet to guardian of democratic values, Paz's current standing as Mexico's foremost man of letters, is, at least in part, the result of his courting state officials and international benefactors. In the 1970s and 1980s, his face would constantly appear on state and private television (for his seventieth birthday, Azcárraga's Televisa devoted a series of programs to his life and work), and diplomats and academics sought his advice and favor. His home was a required stop for overseas celebrities visiting the country. Yet, in becoming the government's favorite citizen, he also, in the eyes of many, lost his freedom. Many Mexicans saw him as handcuffed. His youthful views of government as implicit offender were reshaped to portray authority as a necessary evil. Paz had become a conservative, a right-wing supporter of the Mexican establishment.

His present politics mirror those of Mexico's ruling party: his tyrannical self, with personal stakes in everything cultural within the national borders, dislikes chaos; championing democracy and free enterprise, it in essence remains dictatorial. (The long-standing tradition of intellectual dictators in Mexico, and for that matter the entire Hispanic world, is seldom discussed overseas. Before Paz, Alfonso Reyes, an essayist and scholar of Greek studies born in 1889 and dead at the age of seventy, was a similar cult figure. Neruda and Borges were also revered as larger-than-life entities by the Latin American intelligentsia.) A spectator of Mexico's profound transformation during the twentieth century from rural society to technologized modern nation, Paz seems out of touch with the young today. The new generation, dislocated, uneasy with itself, looks to the United States and Canada for a shared future, perceiving the Rio Grande as a wound separating two distinct, although not totally incompatible cultures. Yet Paz knows very little about their collective angst. And his cultural significance for this generation is that of a historical figure, not a contemporary consciousness.

Since an early age Paz recognized his role models and set out his objectives clearly: to write erotic poetry, to examine the labyrinthine paths of the Hispanic soul, and to investigate the impact of modernism on

society. He fulfilled his dream with fanfare, even if his multiple contradictions have increased the attacks of his critics, which he often prefers
to ignore. Paz has kept his work free of the exoticism and stereotypes
easily attached to the literary legacy from south of the Rio Grande: the
political prisoners victimized by the state police, immortalized in the
novels of Isabel Allende and Manuel Puig; the corrupt colonels and clairvoyant prostitutes that populate the fiction of Gabriel García Márquez
and Mario Vargas Llosa. Consequently, his work hardly fits the image of
Latin American letters to which foreign readers are accustomed, full of
those two indispensable ingredients—magic and exoticism. Paz believes
that even if for centuries Western civilization was the legacy of Europe,
its unrecognized roots are found in India, China, and the Middle East:
that the study of pre-Columbian cultures in the Americas is crucial to
understanding today's world; and that after the Second World War, the
ostensibly peripheral Third World has as much a claim to high art as the
Old World. Thus, his essays attempt to legitimate the value of Hispanic
sophistication.

One can say of him what he said of Sartre: He lives the ideas, the
battles and tragedies of our age, with the intensity with which others
live out their private dramas. He represents both consciousness and passion. The two terms do not contradict each other. A Europeanized Mexican and a cultural dictator undergoing his final eclipse, Paz is an
authoritative and authoritarian consciousness of our time. Like T. S.
Eliot, himself an astute witness of history, Paz goes into the dying light
as an old-fashioned aesthete without a clear role in the future.

In the end, his closeness to the status quo, his relentless need to be
worshiped and applauded, his arrogant, imperious manners, and his
depiction of European civilization as the ticket to Latin America's im-
provement make him an unlikely hero for a new generation. While Paz
is a representative man in the Emersonian sense of the term, through
whose talent and achievements Mexico is upheld, the theater in which
he acted no longer commands attention. His time has come and gone.
Other intellectual, ideological, and cultural needs are being felt. A new
Mexico is being born. As Paz himself once put it, liberty is other people.

[1993]

10 / *VUELTA:* A SUCCINCT APPRAISAL

Literary supplements and journals of opinion have always played a major role in the shaping of Hispanic culture. They have served as gathering points to catalyze transnational artistic moods, crystallize current political opinions, and promote intellectual trends which would otherwise never reach the largest segment of the population. They also function as ideological galaxies in which secondary voices endlessly rotate around an imperious dictatorial figure, making them temples of adoration and sacrifice in which to pay tribute to a *caudillo* and, simultaneously, from which to orchestrate fanciful battles to debunk the enemy. By the same token, their autocratic editors use them as springboards for their own personal and artistic purposes.

The prestigious Cuban magazine *Orígenes* launched an esthetic renewal promoting seriousness and artistic commitment regardless of political affiliation. Initiated by high-caliber figures such as Virgilio Piñera and Cintio Vitier, and controlled by José Lezama Lima, the periodical, active between 1944 and 1956, while mapping out Cuban culture, pretty much behaved as a centralized, undemocratic, self-generating system. Similarly, José Ortega y Gasset's long-running *Revista de Occidente,* interested in natural and human sciences, as well as in literature and pictorial art, from 1923 on promoted German philosophy (Oswald Spengler, Max Scheler, Ludwig Klages) in the Iberian peninsula and throughout Latin America. The magazine served Ortega y Gasset as a springboard to project his own ideas and make them extremely influential. And *Sur,* the Buenos Aires monthly founded by Victoria Ocampo, where Borges published his most enduring and dazzling essays and stories, for decades exerted an incredible influence on Argentine culture, welcoming Europeanized literary fashions and accusing pro-Soviet, pro-aboriginal writers of obscurantism.

As a result of the insularity and peculiar metabolism of the Hispanic intelligentsia, commanding journals of this stature can only flourish in cosmopolitan centers like Buenos Aires, Havana, Mexico City, Madrid, and Barcelona. But their impact reaches far beyond urban and national borders, as is the case of *Vuelta*, a monthly magazine of enormous influence, controlled by a small group of writers. Since its troublesome birth, in 1976, it has gravitated around the colossal figure of Octavio Paz, the Mexican poet and essayist of imposing power. Published in a southern suburb of Mexico City and sold in major Spanish-speaking capitals, as well as in select bookstores throughout Europe and the United States, its handsome, refined pages regularly feature works by an international cast of contributors, from Milan Kundera and Daniel Bell to Susan Sontag and Hans Magnus Ensenzberger, from Leszek Kolakowski to George Steiner, from Irving Howe to Joseph Brodsky, from Derek Walcott to Charles Tomlinson. But they also include a vast number of Spanish-speaking counterparts (Mario Vargas Llosa, Jorge Edwards, Javier Marías, Guillermo Cabrera Infante, Fernando Savater, et al.), thus promoting the Bolivarian view of the hemisphere and the Iberian peninsula as a rich mosaic of dreams and ideas. Paz's primary interests, coloring the journal from the beginning, are politics and literature, both separate and together. An average of eight of the twelve monthly issues contain a text written by him. The topics: his own life, the 1994 *campesino* uprising in Chiapas, the Berlin Wall, the pictorial art of Wolfgang Paalen, Sor Juana Inés de la Cruz's intricate intellectual universe, Anglo-Saxon poetry, and so on. Or he'll publish a new poem or a translation of Chinese, French, or English classics. His writing is invariably lucid and insightful. A renaissance *homme de lettres* in full command of a vast array of knowledge, Paz, through powerful arguments, allows the reader to see the world anew.*

* A number of studies on literary magazines in Latin America have appeared recently, but unfortunately none devoted to *Vuelta*. See John King's *Sur: A Study of the Argentine Literary Journal and Its Role in the Development of a Culture, 1931-1970* (Cambridge University Press, 1986); and Jesús J. Barquet's *Consagración de La Habana: Las peculiaridades del grupo Orígenes en el proceso cultural cubano* (University of Miami-North South Center, 1992).

Allergic to any form of dogmatism and isolationism, he champions a view of Hispanic culture as deeply rooted in its pre-Columbian past but fully devoted to inserting itself in the banquet of Western civilization. Not surprisingly, *Vuelta* has served to open up Mexican literature to outside forces and to promote Pan-Americanism among the region's intelligentsia. Much like its predecessor *Sur,* its implicit dream has always been to become a sideboard of Latin America's collective search for democracy and against dictatorship, *un lugar abierto,* an "open place," and a site of intellectual and artistic convocation, as evidence that the Hispanics are not part of the so-called Second or Third World but, in Paz's own words, "contemporaries of the rest of humankind." But the magazine and its environment aren't without major contradictions, and the content of its pages cannot but reflect the fractured Mexican literary scene, divided, since the early days of our century, into opposing crowds unified by a political stand and dancing around a leading luminary. Indeed, others before Paz have functioned as the nation's literary *caudillos,* including Alfonso Reyes, an essayist and Hellenistic scholar once described by Borges as "the greatest prose writer in Spanish in any era."

In spite of its universalistic, antiprovincial stand, *Vuelta* is more receptive than projective. At least a third of the essays and reviews in every issue are translations from European and U.S. contributors. As for its original Latin American material, aside from Paz's own, very infrequently does it get translated and reprinted elsewhere. In an environment long known for pirating text from international periodicals, the magazine is a pioneer in fulfilling its copyright obligations: it regularly requests permission to reprint articles from, say, *The New York Review of Books* and *Nouvelle Revue Française,* and, unlike its competitors in Mexico and elsewhere in the Hispanic world, it pays its monetary dues. But its honesty doesn't compensate for its dependence on other languages and cultures. *Vuelta* always takes considerably more than what it gives. That is, although Paz's hope is to bring the Hispanic intelligentsia to Western civilization, it often looks the other way around.

As any living organism, the monthly is always in constant change. It consistently reflects Paz's rotating political beliefs. In its almost twenty years of life, it has crystallized his anti-Communism and his animosity toward the Mexican government in 1976 (he used to address it "the philanthropic ogre"), his subsequent partnership with top national politicians of the ruling Partido Revolucionario Institucional, and his current concern with the country's fragile civil and financial stability. Overall, what unifies the magazine's pages is a passive, dilettantish philosophy: to observe, to contemplate, to reflect and meditate seems to be *Vuelta*'s uniform attitude, never to act, to participate actively in order to change the way things are. Its young staff (the average age is thirty-five) isn't known for encouraging hard-writing journalism or debate about national and continental affairs; instead, it often sponsors discursive literary essays about abstract esthetic issues and literary subjects, which assume a high-level of sophistication among readers. Rather than debating the crisis of confidence of Mexico's population in its untrustworthy politicians and its repressive government system, for example, it sponsored global conferences on transcendental subjects such as "the experience of freedom," inviting international specialists. This contradiction ends up delivering a portrait of the periodical as uninvolved in local issues, isolated and inhabiting a self-contained bubble.

Of course one could argue that just because *Vuelta*'s offices are south of the Rio Grande, the magazine is not obligated to reflect solely on national and Third World issues. After all, the Latin American intelligentsia, like all others, is allowed a dose of dilettantism. Besides, it isn't the first to turn its back to regional problems: Ortega y Gasset and Victoria Ocampo often endorsed similar platforms in *Revista de Occidente* and *Sur*. Paz's pages no doubt fulfill an escapist function, vis-à-vis other Mexican monthlies (*Epoca, Proceso, Nexos*), where hard-writing journalism and antigovernment views are often expressed. Whenever its editorial policy does opt for a more active involvement in local affairs, it comes as a result of Mexico undergoing a deep crisis, like the one in 1982 involving the nationalization of the bank industry, or else every six years, as presidential elections are held. Recently, for example, as the nation lacked confidence in its politicians and in reaction to the assassinations of Luis Donaldo Colosio and Ernesto Ruíz Massieu, the magazine reevaluated its principles and took a more decisive, participatory attitude. And during the decisive 1994 presidential elections in which Ernesto Zedillo Ponce de León was declared winner, it published occasional news analysis and opinion pieces on Mexico's need for democracy. It also included a special supplement, "Chiapas: Days of Challenge," dealing with the Ejército Zapatista de Liberación Nacional. But if previous outbursts of commitment are any sign, this editorial direction is likely to fade away the moment the crisis is resolved.

Paz's old-time co-editor and right-hand, Enrique Krauze, is an iconoclastic historian interested in revolutionary heroes and in Mexico's monolithic political structure. While concerned with national and international matters, he is careful enough to have a cordial relationship with Mexico's government. It's a well-known fact that while the country has undergone an abrupt modernization process since the end of World War II, it has also experienced impossible corruption, guerrilla warfare, and urban unrest, and Latin America in general has been torn apart by foreign invasions and military coups. But readers browsing through *Vuelta*'s past issues would know very little about it. In a region where leftist intellectuals are in the pay of petty tyrants, the journal often discusses diplomatic issues in an obnoxiously abstract philosophical fashion. Krauze's pieces approach long-dead historical personalities like Humboldt, Hernán Cortés, Cuauhtémoc, Emiliano Zapata, Porfirio Díaz, and Pancho Villa with a critical eye, but his comments on present-day government matters, unless a crisis makes them urgent and unavoidable, are comparatively shy and without edge. Rather than inviting opposing parties to discuss their differences, the magazine frequently preaches universal values.

On the other hand, *Vuelta* ought to be commended for its independent spirit—and here again, its pages mirror the contradictions of its environment. Since the paper industry is government-run, and because a considerable segment of the advertisement of every single Mexican periodical comes from state institutions, freedom and integrity of opinion are often at stake. With a circulation of 15,000, it depends on national and international subscriptions as well as publicity, but only some 30 percent of its ads come from the government. Nevertheless, private corporations such as Televisa, a television consortium, the largest in the southern hemisphere, with close ties to the ruling party, is a strong advertising supporter, and in the eyes of the average Mexico reader, that amounts to having one's hands handcuffed. In the past, whenever periodicals have proven too critical of the state, the government has threatened to interrupt their ads and boycott paper supplies. But *Vuelta*, in spite of its condescending politics and as a result of its financial autonomy, has not been involved in a head-on confrontation with the authorities.

That is, aside from its very conception. It's birth was the result of a brutal government takeover. Its predecessor was a magazine called *Plural,* published under the aegis of *Excélsior,* one of Mexico's leading dailies. At Paz's return in 1971 from a long stay abroad, Julio Scherer García, then the newspaper's editor-in-chief and a Paz acquaintance, invited him to take charge of a publishing project devoted to literature and debate. Paz had finished his tenure as ambassador in India with a resignation used to protest the student massacre in Tlatelolco Square, made by President Gustavo Díaz Ordaz's regime, to control the population's growing unhappiness with corruption and rapid modernization. The student revolt coincided with uproars in Paris, Czechoslovakia, and Berkeley, among other places, and threatened to jeopardize Mexico's international reputation at a time when the Olympic Games were about to take place in the country. The Tlatelolco incident angered many intellectuals and was a turning point in their dubious, long-standing liaison with the State. Like Carlos Fuentes in Paris, Paz quit his diplomatic job as a sign of solidarity. He spent time at U.S. and European universities, and his return to his native home plagued him with doubts and uncertainty. Scherer's invitation was an excellent opportunity to air out his anger, to discuss critically the prospects of Mexico's democracy and, more than anything, to open up the nation's culture to international influences. Although accepting the offer meant giving up, in part at least, his most precious treasures (time and solitude), it was also a chance to solidify his position as dean of Mexican letters. He envisioned a publication with a universalistic standpoint, pro-debate, against any form of tyranny, appealing to an ideal ethical standard, much like *Sur* (where Paz began contributing in 1938) and *Nouvelle Revue Française,* a publication that conceived literature "as a self-sufficient world—neither apart, nor in front of other worlds—but never at their service." Its name, *Plural,* was its banner.

Paz had more than enough experience dealing with literary magazines. In his adolescence, between 1931 and 1943, he had edited the exciting and short-lived *Barandal, Cuadernos del Valle de México,* and *El Hijo Pródigo,* through which he had introduced dozens of foreign voices into Mexican circles and where he had forged his essayistic style. Later, after a brief incubating period, he helped to make *Plural* into an exquisite periodical. It had high editorial standards and its contributors did indeed inject a refreshing new life into Mexican letters. Paz quickly invited a number of major figures to write and promoted Mexico as a meeting point for discussing critical thought and inspiring good writing. As time went by, however, *Excélsior* as a whole came to be recognized as a focus of antigovernment feeling. Moreover, its views often clashed with Paz's. Expectedly, in July 1976, angry with its staff and having exhausted other venues to quiet the criticism targeted at him at home and abroad, Luis Echeverría Alvarez, then Mexico's president, ordered the army to intervene. The newspaper's offices were taken over, its employees dismissed. The scandal turned out to have positive consequences. While both the newspaper and *Plural* continued under new stewardship, Scherer and Paz, each supported by private funds, launched separate monthly magazines: *Proceso,* edited by the former, was devoted to "accurate, honest journalism that is ready to denounce corruption wherever it might be found"; Paz, on the other hand, orchestrated a reorganization of his editorial staff and began *Vuelta.* He was sixty-two—a totem, a T. S. Eliot-like figure in Hispanic American letters. Anything he touched he quickly turned into gold.

Eventually, like *Les Temps Moderns* in its relation to Jean-Paul Sartre, *Vuelta,* even more than *Plural,* came to be known as Paz's instrument of cultural control—his extremity, a permanent source of congratulation, a compass signaling the many influences of his fascinating mind. From its first issue its editorial principles were clear: to leave behind any form of provincialism, to reflect on international events from a philosophical perspective. In its first issue, Paz argued that *Vuelta* was not a beginning but, as its words imply in Spanish, "a return." In 1981, in a commemorative essay on its fifth anniversary, he described the magazine as borne out of a desire to oppose state power and Marxism as an ideological doctrine. He reinstated the magazine's utopian objective to create a platform where one could simultaneously find the writer's imagination and modern critical thinking. But Paz's democratic wishes could not fight against the well-known, essentially dictatorial facet of his personality. Consequently, the magazine never includes a correspondence section where ideas can be freely exchanged and left-wing writers such as Gabriel García Márquez, Julio Cortázar, José Agustín, and Paco Ignacio Taibo II, although their books might be reviewed, are generally excluded from its content. Paradoxically, dogmatism isn't only attacked but practiced in its pages: views differing from Paz's and the staff are pushed aside and ridiculed, never debated. As a result, readers interested in the whole spectrum of contemporary trends in Latin American thought and literature hardly get a comprehensive, uncensored view. *Vuelta* routinely ignores Hispanic pulp fiction, and either looks down at or handles with unusual care the work of regional celebrities with whom Paz is at odds, personally and politically—particularly his nemesis, Fuentes.

To read its pages is to suppose that most people in Mexico, and for that matter in the whole southern hemisphere, are comfortably tolerant of diverse views, not much concerned with local politics, highly literate, and metaphysically driven, which is far from true in a nation where 75 percent of the population live in poverty and 49 percent are still illiterate. This helps explains why, as counterpoint to *Vuelta,* left-wing Mexican intellectuals launched *Nexos,* a monthly, currently edited by the well-known journalist Miguel Aguilar Camín, skeptical of abstract cosmopolitanism, devoted to *realpolitik* and trendy literary movements. Unlike those of Argentina and Cuba, the Mexican intelligentsia is polarized, zealously moving around these two major periodicals, which often waste their energy discrediting the enemy.

To understand why throughout Latin America the journal is largely considered today a conservative publication, one needs to follow Paz's own ideological journey, from the Spanish Civil War to the fall of the Berlin Wall. At first a fervent supporter of Socialism and an enthusiast of Castro's Cuban Revolution, he grew disappointed in the late sixties with naive Utopian thought and turned against the Havana regime when he learned of its alignment with the Soviet Union. At a time when the Latin American left was still stuck in its dogmatic Stalinism, he denounced the Gulag, supported Aleksandr Solzhenitsyn, and in the pages of *Plural* was in favor of democratic change, not abrupt revolutions. His intellectual development, and that of *Vuelta,* pushed him more to the center: he declared himself in favor of an open-market of ideas in the Hispanic world and, while still viewing dictatorship as the region's major evil, he grew more complacent with the ruling party. By 1984, his seventieth birthday, and then again a decade later, in 1994, his eightieth, were jointly celebrated, with great fanfare, with TV programs, conferences, and museum exhibits, by the ruling party and by Televisa. Paz was seen by a large segment of Mexico's population as disconnected from the nation's new artistic, anti-establishment trends, as a close friend of the status quo and as an ally of the United States, his magazine as a reactionary organ of Mexico's intellectual right. Anybody critical of Paz as *caudillo* was either excluded from or viciously attacked in *Vuelta,* as was the case of José Emilio Pacheco, an internationally renowned poet targeted as enemy by some of Paz's supporters. And yet, when Pacheco's house in Mexico City was the target of a shoot-out, Paz's journal quickly published a manifesto denouncing the violence.

Although each issue, when compared to similar periodicals in the United States, sells a small number of copies, its impact on Latin American intellectual life cannot be minimized. Young writers dream of having manuscripts accepted and their books reviewed. By the late eighties the ownership opened an ultimately ill-fated branch in Buenos Aires, called *Vuelta Sudamericana,* and it also expanded to the book business, launching, in 1987, Editorial Vuelta, a publishing house largely devoted to translations and to promote the oeuvre of its contributors. Its efforts were crowned in 1993, when Paz and his staff were awarded Spain's Príncipe the Asturias Prize for their major contribution of the development of Hispanic culture.

It's a known secret that Paz, already in his eighties, often found at home alone writing or abroad lecturing, only occasionally comes to the offices of *Vuelta.* Whatever business he conducts, he does it mainly by phone. And yet, his shadow casts an incredible challenge to the magazine's future. To be honest, dilettantism in Latin America has always had a healthy life, particularly since the late nineteenth century, when the so-called *Modernistas,* led by José Martí and Rubén Darío, championed a literature obsessed with French Symbolism and Parnassianism. Indeed, Paz's magazine is an embodiment of the Hispanic intellectual contradiction between commitment and withdrawal: it supports an image of the intellectual as a creature devoted to producing high-quality writing, concerned with world affairs, but too individualistic to participate in making history. So make no mistake about it: issue after issue, *Vuelta* is indeed a pleasure to read: it's carefully edited, and most of its contributors, native Spanish writers and otherwise, are consummate stylists. But it's also a temple of adoration with Paz in its supreme altar and a map to his intricate, extraordinary mind.

[1995]

11 / DISCOVERIES

Ricardo Piglia

Detective thrillers—"beach reading" to many North Americans—have been serious staples of Latin American literature for better than a half-century. And more than anywhere else in the Southern Hemisphere, Argentina is known as the crib of first-rate armchair private eyes who, stylistically and verbally Europeanized, have devoted themselves to deciphering labyrinthine adventures in contexts that are psychologically ambiguous and politically corrupt. As the author of classic tales like "Death and the Compass" and "The Garden of Forking Paths," Jorge Luis Borges was almost single-handedly responsible for granting crime fiction a highbrow, nearly metaphysical status. Alone and in collaboration with his friend Adolfo Bioy Casares, he imagined bookish detectives such as Erik Lönnrot and Don Isidro Parodi, who, often from an insulated cell or while playing intellectual tricks, resolve unlikely mysteries through deductive logic. Aside from Borges, Julio Cortázar, who translated Edgar Allan Poe's entire oeuvre into Spanish, was also a practitioner of sorts. His brief "Continuation of the Parks" is a postmodern tale in which the searcher is also the object of his own search.

The stock character of such refined, deceptive sleuths was eclipsed in the Hispanic world in general and in Argentina in particular in the sweep of the late sixties and early seventies, however, which saw among other traumas the 1968 student uprising and massacre at the hands of the state in Mexico's Tlatelolco Square, and the murder of Salvador Allende in Santiago in 1973. The littérateur sleuth began giving way to the sort of dirty realist private eye who wore his political commitment on the sleeve of his tattered jacket: the detective as rebel ideologue, as found in the works of Brazil's Rubem Fonseca (whose novel *High Art* introduced his famous protagonist Mandrake to an English-speaking audience a few years ago) or Mexico's Paco Ignacio Taibo II, or Spaniards Manuel Vázquez Montalbán and Andreu Martín. Whereas the Borges whodunit was based on plausible (even while surreal) mental gimmickry, the detective a Nabokovian master with a unique memory, the new generation of detective writers came of age parodying the genre.

Fortunately, Borges's influence has not vanished altogether: Self-referentiality and a type of literary criticism that doubles as fiction have become permanent features in Hispanic detective narratives. For instance, one of the most inventive Latin American whodunits I know, typically baroque and reminiscent of Miguel de Unamuno, appears in the Uruguayan writer Hiber Conteris's *Ten Percent of Life,* a novel published in English in 1987. Set in Los Angeles against the backdrop of the powerful Hollywood studios of the McCarthy era, the plot brings Philip Marlowe back in 1956 to investigate the apparent suicide of Raymond Chandler's literary agent; in a baroque twist, Chandler himself, Marlowe's creator, becomes a primary murder suspect. A thriller about a thriller about a thriller. And now, from Argentina and stepping very smartly from Borges's shadow, we have an extraordinary detective novel, *Artificial Respiration,* by Ricardo Piglia.

Intellectually explosive, artistically refreshing, and aesthetically ambitious, *Artificial Respiration* appears after what seems to me a period of creative stagnation marked by repetitive narratives that are chockablock with incoherence and interjections. The book sold moderately when first published in Buenos Aires in 1980, shortly before Gen. Leopoldo Galtieri, the country's president, decided to occupy the Falkland Islands, pushing Argentina to war with Britain. Months later, it caught on with critics and readers, becoming one of the most talked-about works of fiction published during the 1976–83 dictatorial regime. In Daniel Balderston's remarkable English translation, Piglia's narrative, built as a subtle, hard-boiled detective story, is the kind of breathtaking read capable of delivering a complete re-evaluation of a nation's literary and artistic canon. Not since Cortázar's *Hopscotch* has a book from south of the border offered such shocking reassessment of Hispanic history and collective identity.

Detective fiction is never without a plot and a denouement, of course, but Piglia's fictional universe is intellectually sophisticated and joyfully self-referential. His novel begins with the sentences, "Is there a story? If there is a story it begins three years ago." The double plot, involving two different searches for information, circles around an old photograph found days after the military coup d'état of March 24, 1976. The suspense pertains to a *desaparecido,* less in the political sense than in the physical, an engimatic figure later identified as Professor Maggi. The narrator and protagonist, a writer called Emilio Renzi, is Maggi's nephew. After Renzi's first novel is published, he receives a letter from Maggi, from whom no one in the family has heard in ages. Renzi investigates his elusive uncle's whereabouts through correspondence and unlikely family stories. He discovers that Maggi had once devoted his energy to researching the life of Enrique Ossorio, secretary of the nineteenth-century dictator Juan Manuel de Rosas, who dominated Argentine political life for more than two decades, serving as governor of the province of Buenos Aires. As it turns out, Ossorio was also a spy for Rosas's enemy.

After numerous stops and obstacles, Renzi travels to meet his uncle in Concordia, in the province of Entre Ríos, where a group of philosophers and dilettantes surrounding him spend long hours discussing metaphysical and aesthetic matters. Piglia's attempt, clear from the outset, is to establish a bridge linking crucial periods in Argentine history: the 1810–16 struggle for independence, the Rosas tyranny, and the *guerra sucia,* the dirty war of the late 1970s. Not coincidentally, the book's title is anagrammatic and its overall theme is the *Argentine Republic.* Archives, primary and secondary historical sources and quotations invade the narrative, and a few questions reappear incessantly: How is meaning assigned to history? How can one "read" history? And how is knowledge of the past obtained?

As it turns out, the act of reading—reading dramas, reading the universe—is Piglia's primary obsession. Commenting on his initiations as a writer, he once wrote about his career as a reader in an autobiographical essay:

> How is a writer made? It is difficult to know. Certainly there is always a deviation, an eccentric movement, walking through side streets. Because the first thing that changes when one begins to write is one's mode of reading. Now, one does not read in the same way. Someone who intends to be a writer does not

want to read *all* of literature but to discover the books
that interest him. When he finds them he is always
intrigued to know how they work and how he could
create something similar. It is as though a book were a
mechanical object, with screws and gears that he could
take apart.

And indeed, *Artificial Respiration,* just like Borges's "Pierre Menard,
author of the *Quixote,*" is a masterful exercise in relativistic re-reading.
"To read," says one of Piglia's characters, "one must know how to associate."

Piglia's attachment to thrillers and crime fiction harks back to his
twenties (he was born in 1941), when he read Hemingway, Himes,
Hammett, and Chandler. He helped establish series in Argentine publishing houses, such as the Serie Negra, devoted to disseminating American hard-boiled novels in Spanish translation. This passion has certainly
paid off: *Artificial Respiration* is the most accomplished Spanish-language detective novel I've seen, an aleph in which every single precursor
(and perhaps successor) is contained. The book is simultaneously an
admirable crime story and an ambitious encyclopedia of literary criticism. Almost the entire second half, over a hundred pages, is devoted to
re-evaluating Argentine literature: Domingo Faustino Sarmiento, Paul
Groussac, Leopoldo Lugones, Macedonio Fernández, Borges, the anarchist Roberto Arlt, and a plethora of other men of letters (women, a
fairly recent addition to the Argentine literary pantheon, are ignored by
Piglia), as well as some politicos, become an intense source of reflection.
(Balderston accompanies his translation with a brief explanatory introduction and a thirteen-page section of notes detailing references pre-
sumed to be beyond the U.S. reader's scope.)

Piglia penetrates the Argentine psyche only to conclude that every
idea, every act, is an imitation. Parody and mimicry of someone else's
style, holding it up to ridicule, is, in his provocative view, a national
signature. Isn't it ironic, asks *Artificial Respiration,* that Argentine letters
begin with Sarmiento's classic *Facundo: Civilization and Barbarism,* a
"nonfictional novel" that opens with a phrase written in French, one
memorized by every Argentine child at school (in its Spanish translation, of course): *On ne tue point les idées.* Not only can't ideas be killed,
but whole nations can construct their intricate collective identity out of

borrowed images. One can trace this message to *Nombre falso,* Piglia's 1975 collection of stories, which includes an ingenious novella, *Homage to Roberto Arlt,* that through critical commentary develops a fictional universe. I'm tempted to call this miscegenation of genres "literary promiscuity." Piglia didn't invent it, of course, but in *Artificial Respiration* he has brought it to unexpected heights: The novel is history cum fiction and fiction cum critical analysis—reality as a Warhol reproduction.

Piglia grew up outside Buenos Aires; the author of four novels, a collection of interviews and the above-mentioned volume of stories, which was awarded Cuba's Casa de las Américas Prize, he began writing at sixteen while also keeping a diary. His first literary model was Faulkner, an influence hard to detect in his art today. In *Artificial Respiration,* his prose is high caliber, meticulous, fond of repetition, and pays great attention to detail. A quote from Chapter II:

> "You can call me Senator," said the Senator. "Or former Senator. You can call me former Senator," said the former Senator. "I held the office from 1912 to 1916 and was elected under the Sáenz Peña law, and at the time the office was practically for life, so in fact you ought to call me Senator," said the Senator. "But given the present situation it would perhaps be preferable and not just preferable but, moreover, in closer accord with the facts and the general course of Argentine history if you would call me former Senator," said the former Senator.

The men to whom *Artificial Respiration* is dedicated, Elías and Rubén, were among the thousands of *desaparecidos* during the 1970s who, according to Piglia, "helped me to come to know the truth of history." Truth and fiction. While Renzi is waiting for his uncle in Concordia, a place recalling Ralph Waldo Emerson's habitat, he chats with Tardewski, a Polish émigré and intellectual genius. Tardewski was a doctoral student under Wittgenstein at Cambridge. Just as World War II broke out, he was pushed to a distant New World, but before that, while preparing his dissertation at the British Library in 1938, he read Hitler's *Mein Kampf.* He tells Renzi he concluded that Hitler and Kafka had met in

Prague's Café Arcos in 1909 and that, irreversibly, the genocidist-to-be influenced the writer and vice versa. "The word *Ungeziefer* . . . ," writes Piglia, "which the Nazis would use to designate prisoners in the concentration camps, is the same word that Kafka uses to describe what Gregor Samsa has turned into one morning, when he wakes up." This means that fiction and reality, partners in crime, are intertwined in ways at once inspiring and atrocious. Piglia's work is obsessed with this partnership. Not surprisingly, his thriller closes engimatically rather than conclusively: The reader has been invited to chart paths that twist and turn unexpectedly, but no happy end comes. (By the way, detective novels from Latin America commonly end the same way: with total obscurity, moral and historical.)

Introducing a foreign writer to a naïve, often cold, English-speaking audience, V. S. Pritchett, finding the most florid description possible to convey a wholehearted admiration, once hailed Gabriel García Márquez as "a master of a spoken prose that passes unmoved from scenes of animal disgust and horror to their lyrical evocation, opening up vistas of imagined or real sights which may be gentle or barbarous." Let me now introduce Ricardo Piglia, another Latin American master, in equally florid terms: He is a giant, the type of writer capable of imagining perfect imperfections for us. As it happens, one of his inventions is already easily recognizable: the Argentine Republic.

Alfredo Bryce Echenique

The United States has limited patience for Hispanic letters, compared with its French, Italian, and German counterparts, which emerge from geographically smaller habitats. There's a kind of literary I.N.S. that seems to establish quotas on how many south-of-the-border novels can be translated into English annually: around five at most, the vast majority of which have been secured by "boom" authors for the last three decades. (And with a new U.S.-Hispanic literature in the making, that number is likely to be reduced.) A few exceptions aside, writers born in the fifties and sixties remain largely unattended, as if the region were artistically fixed in the amber of the golden generation that came before. What's worse, a handful of first-rate narrators, marginalized by the boom's ideological stand and lacking a showman's personality, were left behind. Such was the case with Fernando del Paso, a Mexican of Rabelaisian lineage whose 1975 masterpiece *Palinuro of Mexico* awaits publication north of the Rio Grande; Alvaro Mutis, a Colombian who, according to García Márquez, is "one of the greatest writers of our time" and whose tantalizing *Maqroll,* three novellas in a single volume, was finally made available last year; and Alfredo Bryce Echenique, a Peruvian whose heart must palpitate whenever somebody invokes the name of Vargas Llosa.

With a total of six novels to his credit, Alfredo Bryce Echenique is a master storyteller born in Lima in 1939 into an oligarchic family of Scottish descent. Hoping to become a prominent *littérateur,* he left Peru by steamer in 1964 after simultaneously receiving law and letters degrees (his thesis was on the function of Hemingway's dialogues), first enrolling in the Sorbonne, then moving to Italy, Greece, and Germany before returning to France and settling in Montpellier, where for years he taught Latin American literature and civilization at the University Paul Valéry. Thus he shared the Parisian stage with the boom bunch without ever becoming a club member. While Vargas Llosa, immensely talented and energetic and only three years his senior, made his novelistic debut at the age of twenty-seven with *La ciudad y los perros,* awarded the prestigious Premio Biblioteca Breve in Barcelona and translated into English in 1966 as *The Time of the Hero,* Bryce Echenique was thirty-one when his first novel, *A World for Julius,* was published and became the recipient of Peru's top literary honor, the Premio Nacional de Literatura. But it has taken almost two dozen years for it to become available in the United States—too long for such an extraordinary book. Perhaps the delay can be explained by understanding the personalities of the writers: Bryce Echenique has little avowed interest in politics—he is an aesthete, not a polemicist.

The first novels of Vargas Llosa and Bryce Echenique, set in opposite neighborhoods, one aristocratic and the other lower-middle-class, are both about schooling and patriotism, about loss of innocence and the shaping of identity during childhood and adolescence. But an abyss lies between them: Vargas Llosa's deals with machismo in the now-infamous Leoncio Prado Military Academy, whereas Bryce Echenique's, seen through the eyes of an innocent boy, is about frivolity and excess among the very rich (a topic, by the way, dealt with in passing by Vargas Llosa in *Conversation in the Cathedral* and in more detail in *In Praise of the Stepmother*). Read together, they offer a fascinating mosaic of the tension in rigid Peruvian society.

An amalgam of featherbrained viewpoints, *A World for Julius,* in the tradition of Evelyn Waugh, is a semiautobiographical account of the inevitable decline of Lima's aristocracy in the forties and beyond, a bit over a decade after Augusto Bernardino Leguía's dictatorship promoted economic development by securing the interests of a wealthy minority and ignoring the Indian population. Indeed, this Proustian narrative is memorable less for its sophisticated structure and delicate sensibility—although at that level it is also enjoyable—than for what it chooses to ignore: Virtually no historical data are offered. Happiness inhabits a vacuum. Bryce Echenique's characters live in an oasis—isolated, uninvolved, unembarrassed, and obnoxiously unaware of the tragic implications of their silence. Julius, the child protagonist whom we accompany from age two to his eleventh birthday party, is left behind with cholo servants in a huge mansion while his mother, Susan, and his stepfather, Juan Lucas, play golf and travel to Europe. The silhouette of a suffering Peru haunts the background: Dissatisfaction among mestizos is high; a radical reform party, founded in 1924, is gaining influence; the ground for the Maoist guerrilla movement Shining Path is laid down. Not coincidentally, the 1970 publication of *A World for Julius* took place just after a crucial coup d'état in which a military junta, after deposing Fernando Belaúnde Terry, a moderate reformer, instituted a program of social reconstruction and seized U.S.-owned companies as well as huge landholdings belonging to the oligarchy.

Divided into five chapters of about eighty-five pages each, Bryce Echenique's novel, wonderfully translated by Dick Gerdes, a specialist in Peruvian letters at the University of New Mexico, has affection, in short supply in Julius's universe, as its unifying leitmotif. Since Julius receives love only from the servants in charge of his education (nannies, gardeners, cooks, maids, etc.), he grows up angry and irritated at the way his parents mistreat the lower class and confused about what is expected of him.

The people around Julius are preoccupied solely with leisure and the possession of foreign goods. (Items from the United States are seen as enviable treasure, an unfortunate ailment afflicting the entire Latin American bourgeoisie.) When Cinthia, Julius's beloved sister, dies in a Boston hospital at the beginning of the novel, the family mourns her with yacht cruises and spending rampages. Later on, in a touching scene in the book's powerful second chapter, a group of construction workers ridicule, abuse, and even put the protagonist's life in danger, a sign of barely repressed animosity among the poor—and a harbinger of the kind of hate that triggered Abimael Guzmán's Shining Path. At the center of *A World for Julius* is a mansion on luxurious Salaverry Avenue, right across from an old hippodrome. Houses, haunted and treacherous, are very much at the heart of modern Hispanic fiction, and while this one is meant to symbolize comfort and security, it is actually a cold, impersonal cell. To make matters worse, as the narrative develops and Julius becomes increasingly entangled in a labyrinthine universe of appearances and superficiality, leading toward psychological disaster, his parents (to whom money equals redemption) hire an architect to build an even more ostentatious palace.

Bryce Echenique doesn't see himself as a vociferous antigovernment activist, a flamboyant speaker of the truth. Unlike Vargas Llosa, his reading list would not include Sartre and Camus at the top, simply because in his eyes the writer should live in seclusion—a voyeur away from the mundane. Nevertheless, the impact of French culture on him has been tremendous. His complete baptized name is Alfredo Marcelo, after Marcel Proust, one of his mother's idols, whose influence is unquestionably felt throughout his work: the first chapter of *A World for Julius,* for instance, reads like an homage to Marcel's insatiable desire for his mother's goodnight kiss. The Proustian component is attenuated, though not erased, in the author's subsequent work. In more than one way, the character of Julius, reflecting Bryce Echenique's own difficult childhood, is a seed for his future protagonists, wealthy and disoriented architects and glitterati, alcoholic womanizers who waste their time wandering the globe—Peruvians who end up tourists in their native land.

Beyond the national borders, the current Peruvian novel is reduced to five names: The three other than Vargas Llosa and Bryce Echenique are the indigenists Manuel Scorza and José María Arguedas, both dead now, and Julio Ramón Ribeyro, whose oeuvre includes an interesting narrative about a native dictator. But Vargas Llosa, the only one with a huge following abroad, eclipses them all. Immortality in literature, of course, is a game of dice: Fortunes are turned upside down and artists once obscure become role models (the cases of Kafka and Zora Neale Hurston). Interestingly enough, Gregory Rabassa, the legendary translator of Cortázar's *Hopscotch* and other masterpieces and a professor at Queens College, not long ago referred to Bryce Echenique as "the best writer in Peru." Although the statement is obviously a personal attack against Vargas Llosa's merchandising ethos, he might be right (. . . or at least, the other best). In any event, those interested in Latin American literature have before them a chance to open another window, one unfairly shut to U.S. readers until now.

[1994, 1993]

12 / MEXICO: FOUR DISPATCHES

Nota bene: Written hastily, on deadline, the desideratum of these news bulletins was to chronicle Mexico's political drama. Together they are a record of a profound transformation and highlight, once again, the role of journalistic writing as "eyewitness to history."

8 March 1993

Mexico's electoral system is rotten to the core. Despite maintaining the illusion of democracy, the Partido Revolucionario Institucional (PRI) government has held on to its one-party rule, by hook or by crook, since 1929. And don't count on Carlos Salinas de Gortari, the current president, to allow truly free elections in 1994, when his six-year term comes to an end.

In 1988, at the age of thirty-nine, this Harvard graduate came into power in a highly contested vote in which he edged out challenger Cuauhtémoc Cárdenas. An engineer by training, Cárdenas, the former governor of the state of Michoacán, is the son of a national hero and a populist with huge appeal. He organized the vociferous Frente Democrático Nacional (FDN) before the 1988 election to demand respect for the constitution and to accuse the PRI of corruption and dictatorship.

When the initial electoral returns came in, mostly negative for Salinas, the computerized vote tabulation system mysteriously broke down. A short while later, Salinas claimed victory. He was inaugurated president with only 50.7 percent of the official national vote. The moment he took office, he promised to revise the electoral code and to invite small parties to participate actively in what appeared to be a new democratic spirit. A good act. A persuasive lie.

With Cárdenas announcing last month that he will again seek the presidency, the 1994 race is already under way. Salinas is barred by law from seeking re-election, and he has not yet selected a successor. But whoever is chosen will have history on his side.

From fiesta to funeral, Mexico's presidential terms always follow the same pattern. With a cast of refreshing faces and an infinite list of engaging promises, the first two years are presented as the remedy to a season of collective misconduct. The new leader, whose past the media never dares seriously to investigate, is promoted as an honest, well-behaved common man, the owner of a handful of seemingly "uncommon" attributes like patriotism and decency. He is to clean up the mess his precursors left behind by arresting the most renowned bandits and by punishing those that engaged in favor and patronage by abusing power. Corruption, it seems, is to be abolished.

Miguel de la Madrid, for example, in office from 1982 to 1988, began his term by threatening to put in jail his predecessor, José López Portillo, who by the time he stepped down had become one of Latin America's richest men. To show his power, de la Madrid did incarcerate a handful of politicos, such as Jorge Díaz Serrano, once the commander in chief of the national oil industry. He also assured the population that a revision of the national code of ethics was about to begin: *No más mordidas.* Thus, the incoming president establishes his reputation by ridiculing the past and by convincing the population to support his projects for a better future. It matters not that the system has never lived without corruption.

During the second third of the term—the middle two years—promises become policies. A new approach to the economy and foreign policy is established. Things are better simply because they are different. A mirage, of course.

During his third and fourth years, Salinas convinced his people that the long-held tradition of looking south—understanding Mexico as part of the Southern Hemisphere—was not the road to future development. Instead, the country had to look north, to stop approaching *Gringolandia* as the evil empire, to be part of North America by joining forces with

Canada and the United States. His solution was the North American Free Trade Agreement.

True to form, Mexico has been feeling different about itself: confident, self-assured, looking toward a bright future. This sense of closeness to *el coloso del norte* even permeates culture. I was invited to attend last year's Guadalajara International Book Fair, whose theme was "Mexico and the United States: A Dialogue." I was constantly reminded of Alan Riding's book, *Distant Neighbors,* on the proximity and idiosyncratic gap between the two nations. Writers from both sides of the Río Grande tried to discuss their own work "through the other's eye." Chicanos were obviously an essential component to the event: true frontier dwellers, they often speak the two languages, Spanish and English, and act as cultural bridges interpreting what is Mexican to the U.S., and vice versa. What was shocking is how close we felt to one another. A sense of partnership prevailed while Salinas's shadow loomed silently in the background. The event as a whole celebrated his hope for re-encounter. Down with stereotypes, down with an ancestral misunderstanding based on truths lost in translation.

And yet, and yet . . . As Salinas's last two years are about to begin, the pattern of every presidential term is once again apparent. Rumors, whispers, unconfirmed information—the last third of every regime is dominated by a lack of trust and sense of collective uncertainty. First the population hears about a possible coup. Then a photograph is circulated in which the leader's wife is seen buying expensive jewelry in a Paris boutique. Luis Echeverría and José López Portillo, it is a well-known fact, used their regimes' last "third" to empty the banks' reserve, to open accounts in Switzerland and elsewhere in Europe, to build mansions with Roman-style baths—in short, to enjoy an epicurean life.

In the next decade Mexico might turn into another Puerto Rico, a commonwealth of sorts where English and U.S.-style individualism is ubiquitous, but surely democracy will still be absent and corruption will prevail. In a couple of recent state elections declared "unclean" by opposition parties, Salinas supported a PRI candidate who was sworn into office amid massive protest. Rumors are beginning to circulate. In one, the president's sister is about to buy the corporation that owns important periodicals like *Artes de México,* a highly respected, profitable pictorial magazine edited by an Octavio Paz acolyte. In another, Salinas himself is using a fictitious name to become the owner of the newspaper *El Nacional* and the government TV channel *Imevisión,* which are mysteriously put up for sale. A third unconfirmed claim portrays Salinas as already extremely wealthy, the owner of huge businesses and industries at home and abroad. The well-orchestrated spirit of uncertainty makes it impossible to prove or disprove these rumors. If experience is to serve as proof, the only thing unquestionable is that the last third of past presidential terms has been disastrous.

Nothing indicates that the pattern will be broken this time. Dishonesty is as healthy as ever in Mexico. Democracy remains an ideal, which means that Salinas, seen as a doctor four years ago, shall soon be treated as a scoundrel. And his successor, a president once again appointed by the PRI, will be a refreshing redeemer—at least temporarily.

History, Friedrich Nietzsche and the Aztec priests of Tenochtitlán used to say, is a cycle, an eternal return.

24 January 1994

A handful of early conclusions can be drawn from the uprising in the southern Mexican state of Chiapas. First, the struggle is likely to continue for years, resembling the "low intensity" conflicts in Guatemala, El Salvador, and Nicaragua. The rebel military action was not a spontaneous one-time uprising, but the carefully orchestrated work of an apparently well-trained, well-armed force calling itself the Zapatista National Liberation Army. After long decades of superficial tranquility, violence may soon acquire frightening forms in other southern regions. The seed has been planted.

Second, Mexico's PRI will find it more difficult to leave the underclass behind in its rush down the road to a modern, industrialized Mexican economy. The rebels timed their attack to come just as the North American Free Trade Agreement (NAFTA)—the ultimate symbol of President Salinas de Gortari's modernization push—went into effect.

It's no wonder that the people of Chiapas, nearly half of whom are indigenous, feel left out of the "new Mexico." Although Chiapas's resources are central to the PRI's industrialization efforts, the state's impoverished people—hundreds of thousands of whom are landless—have been overlooked. For example, Chiapas and another southern state, Tabasco, produce 80 percent of Mexico's offshore oil, yet 60 percent of the people live below the poverty line, according to reports. Chiapas accounts for 50 percent of the country's hydroelectric power, yet half of the population has no access to drinking water or electricity. The state's dairy and beef industry make Chiapas the country's biggest provider of protein, yet residents have the largest protein deficiency. And NAFTA is only expected to make these disparities worse.

A third conclusion—the most important one—is that we are witnessing nothing less than a fracture in the nation's map. Northern Mexico, led by Monterrey, Chihuahua, and Hermosillo, is an advanced region, full of polluted cities controlled by technocrats. Its economy is quickly developing, thanks in part to foreign investment. The south, on the other hand, is a largely rural zone mainly populated by illiterate Indians and naive itinerant tourists, a region of ruins and pyramids never quite in touch with the present and the government's vision of the future. It's a tale of two Mexicos, a country divided, torn between its desire to move on and its ancient Zapotec, Mayan, and Aztec roots. The self-congratulatory PRI has never bothered to try to overcome this divide.

Salinas and his administration were so busy looking north, in fact, that they apparently failed to notice the dark clouds forming behind them. In truth, the Chiapas uprising should not have come as a surprise. Rumors of guerrilla training camps in Chiapas and on the Yucatán Peninsula had been circulating for years. And only six months before the actual violence began, the Mexican army made a thorough search in nearby towns, looking to confiscate weapons and to interrogate civilians.

Although local Indians have long expressed their unhappiness with the PRI's modernization push, they were repeatedly silenced by local bosses and their grievances were not addressed. Animosity soon turned into activism—and then armed revolt.

The government's immediate reaction to the uprising was absolute denial. The president did not address the Mexican people until several days after the original violence occurred, when it was obvious the crisis would not go away. While the rebel offensive seemed to be waning in Chiapas, other uprisings emerged in nearby areas. And just as Salinas and other officials finally were beginning to pay attention, several car bombs exploded in Mexico City and other urban centers. From Ciudad Juárez to Mérida, Mexicans were terrorized, and demanded accountability and action from their leader.

Ten days after the initial rebel actions, Salinas responded by sacking Interior Minister Patrocinio González. González had been governor of Chiapas from 1988 until 1993, during which time he had been widely condemned by human rights groups for turning a blind eye to the jailing and beating of Indian peasant organizers. He was replaced by Attorney General Jorge Carpizo, and Salinas named Foreign Minister Manuel Camacho Solís to head a new Commission for Peace and Reconciliation in Chiapas.

Salinas may be at least partly correct in his claim that the insurgency has been orchestrated by Central American rebels active on Mexico's borders with Guatemala and Belize. The government also put forth the theory that radical Catholic priests are aiding the rebels.

Links between the Zapatista National Liberation Army and south-of-the-border forces seem apparent—not only because of the Marxist tenor of the soldiers' proclamations, but because of the rebels' mention of light-skinned foreigners in their ranks. And ties between the church and left-wing militant groups are also nothing new. Around 1926, for example, a movement known as the Cristero Rebellion, which pitted priests against the state, flared in urban centers and the countryside.

The rebels' ties to the church and foreign forces, nevertheless, are beside the point. What's crucial about the emergence of the Zapatista National Liberation Army is that it demonstrates how few real democratic options now exist for disenfranchised Mexicans. After the dynamic fall of Nicolae Ceausescu in Romania, Mexico is now arguably the world's most sophisticated, self-contained dictatorship.

In recent decades, the PRI has consistently stolen elections from opposition factions and denied alternative parties a free democratic voice in the political debate. Salinas himself took office after a highly suspect election victory over Cuauhtémoc Cárdenas, which was widely denounced as a fraud at home and abroad. Forced to acknowledge its fragile status, the PRI has offered the gubernatorial seats of several states to followers of Cárdenas and his democratic front, as well as to supporters of the center-right National Action Party.

The next presidential elections are scheduled for August, and Luis Donaldo Colosio is already campaigning as the PRI's chosen successor to the outgoing Salinas. This time around, the election promises to be different, simply because the Zapatistas are on everyone's mind. Under increasing pressure at home and abroad, the government may finally be forced into holding fair elections. There's at least a chance that a presidential candidate of the ruling party could lose for the first time since 1929.

During the last couple of years, Salinas was so busy selling NAFTA that he obviously forgot to address urgent issues at home. In the end, he will probably go down in history as a leader of the middle class and bourgeoisie with no regard whatsoever for the underclass. I was in Mexico City the night when the American Senate finally voted in favor of a trade treaty with Mexico. A sense of renewal, of beginning a new era, could be felt throughout the nation's urban centers. In rural areas, however, the general opinion was essentially different.

The modern Zapatistas are accusing the government of selling the country's soul to the devil. While the rebels have yet to fully articulate their ideology, angry Indians in Chiapas are dreaming of socialism and hoping for a nonexclusionary tomorrow, in which the long-suppressed aboriginal population plays an active role.

18 April 1994

Graham Greene, the British author of *The Power and the Glory*, visited Mexico in the spring of 1938, a couple of decades after the socialist revolution of Pancho Villa and Emiliano Zapata, to find out the way ordinary people had reacted to the brutal anticlerical purges of President Plutarco Elías Calles. His journey took him to the states of Tabasco and Chiapas, where churches had been destroyed and priests shot to death or driven out of the region. Greene was appalled by what he saw. "How could a world like this end in anything but war?" he wrote at the time.

More than half a century later, Greene's views have become awkwardly prophetic. Mexico has become a time bomb. The leading presidential candidate has been killed. Political rivalries are insurmountable. Violence is rampant. Peasant guerrilla groups are active not only in the state of Chiapas but also in Oaxaca, Yucatán, and elsewhere in the southern and central regions. Terrorist acts have taken place in major cities, and a sense of pessimism reigns over the entire population.

Only a short time ago Mexico was an apparently stable nation dreaming of becoming a full partner in the industrialized world, one ready to sell its soul to the devil as part of NAFTA. Now the country is on the brink of total political collapse.

The PRI, which has dominated Mexican government for six and a half decades, seems no longer able to sustain its political balancing act. The stage seems set for a second revolution not unlike its counterpart in 1910, when Zapata fought for land and justice for the campesino population. It's anybody's guess if the animosity accumulated during years of repression and poverty can be restrained, if the country can opt for a peaceful path out of the current crisis.

Last month's assassination of Luis Donaldo Colosio, the presidential candidate of the ruling party, PRI, is only the latest addition to a complicated puzzle. Within hours of Colosio's death, Salinas de Gortari delivered a televised address to the nation, claiming that the country's fundamental principles—freedom, justice, and democracy—had been threatened by the assassination. But freedom, justice, and democracy have never been the rule in Mexico.

Now that he's buried, Colosio has become a larger-than-life figure, a martyr with a stature he never enjoyed in life. By the time of his death, his presidential campaign was out of focus and criticism of his chief campaign manager, Ernesto Zedillo Ponce de León, was common in the daily press. Zedillo, ironically, has now replaced Colosio as the PRI's candidate. The PRI's old guard likes Zedillo even less than it did Colosio. The American-educated Zedillo lacks political experience and has never run for public office. He has consistently alienated union leaders and has shown little patience for political maneuvering.

Not surprisingly, the old guard pushed for a more experienced alternative. But Salinas did not want to put the early success of his economic reforms, on which his place in history depends, on hold. Consequently, open opposition to Salinas is now being expressed even in the headquarters of the PRI, something unheard of only a few months ago.

Amid new evidence that Colosio's alleged murderer, Mario Aburto

Martínez, did not act alone, conspiracy theories about Colosio's death abound. People cannot refrain from comparing Colosio's assassination with that of John F. Kennedy.

Many believe Manuel Camacho Solís, who was immensely popular as Salinas's lead envoy to the peace talks in San Cristóbal de Las Casas with the Zapatista National Liberation Army, was behind Colosio's death. And if it wasn't Camacho, perhaps it was the Zapatistas themselves. Others go even further, suggesting that Salinas—having second thoughts about his selection of Colosio—himself should be included on the list of possible co-conspirators.

Shortly after Colosio's death, Camacho claimed he would not run for the presidency, and Mexico's Congress approved preliminary constitutional changes to make democracy a reality. But now the whole nation is in fear. Subcomandante Marcos, the mythical leader of the Zapatistas, has become a symbol of resistance for the lower class. And the riots that erupted in Mexico City as demonstrators supporting opposition leader Cuauhtémoc Cárdenas clashed with the police are further evidence of the growing impatience of the middle class, which is increasingly fed up with promises of freedom and justice. The army, accused of civil rights abuses during its Chiapas performance, is nervous.

The months between now and August, when presidential elections are scheduled, promise to be volatile ones. Mexico has no democratic tradition. Since colonial times, federal, state, and local institutions have been intrusive, tyrannical, dogmatic, and intransigent. Corruption and fraud, the law of the land, have proven impossible to eradicate. The PRI has perfected a dictatorial system in which dissent is welcomed only to be quickly erased from public debate. And so the 1994 transition will certainly be bumpy. Salinas and his party seem to be losing control of the situation.

Although a stable neighbor is obviously in Washington's best interest, the most sensitive approach the Clinton administration can take is to watch carefully while leaving Mexico's political fate to its citizens. An economic partner might be useful, but a stable neighbor is essential. And NAFTA, which was at first embraced by many Mexicans as a popular panacea, has now come to represent an evil emblem of foreign manipulation.

How could a world like this end in anything but war? Graham Greene's question remains unanswered. For now, Mexico's best hope is that democracy will prevail, even if liberty, freedom, and justice for all remain abstract ideas.

6 March 1995

I haven't been to the Chiapas jungle since the Zapatista rebels launched their uprising last January. Nor have I spoken to Subcomandante Marcos since his communiqués began streaming from the Lacandon rain forest. But even before the Mexican government identified Marcos as Rafael Sebastián Guillén Vicente, a thirty-seven-year-old former college professor—an identity Marcos has disputed—I easily recognized his rhetoric: it's a language I learned at the Xochimilco campus of Mexico City's Autonomous Metropolitan University (UAM), the decidedly radical school where Guillén taught.

Of course, I'm not sure Marcos *is* Guillén. And there is no good reason to believe the claims of the Mexican government, which "unmasked" Marcos as it sent tanks and artillery rolling into Zapatista-held territory last month. Nevertheless, in discussing Marcos's speeches with several old friends from college we've all been struck by the similarities between his postmodern language and the often hallucinatory rhetoric in vogue on the Xochimilco campus.

His communiqués, like the authors we studied at UAM, seamlessly mix fiction with reality. He enjoys quoting Gabriel García Márquez, Carlos Monsiváis, and Octavio Paz—all writers who profoundly influenced our generation. Marcos pens letters with a thousand addenda and postscripts, irreverently shows his buttocks to journalists, and knows his best soldiers have no weapons but rather carry TV cameras. Consequently, he has managed to turn the Chiapas uprising into a theatrical fiesta full of glare, sarcasm, and humor—an event that has enchanted the Mexican people and exasperated the political elite.

His unconventional style was commonplace at UAM in the early eighties, where I was a student at the time that Guillén, about five years my elder, was teaching. Although I never took a class with him, some of my friends did, remarking on his sharp intellect and infectious verbosity.

Crossing paths with him in hallways and cafeterias, I remember him as eloquent and savvy.

Well known as an incubator for Marxist, pro-Cuba, pro-Sandinista activity, UAM's Xochimilco campus was built in the early seventies by the Mexican government. The government constructed the UAM system—which included Xochimilco and two other campuses in far-flung corners of Mexico City—in an attempt to dilute the massive student population at Mexico City's National Autonomous University (UNAM), the oldest institution of higher learning in the country. It was UNAM's 30,000 students who led the protests of 1968, which were brutally crushed in the Tlatelolco Square massacre.

When Xochimilco opened, it immediately superseded UNAM in antigovernment militancy. It became a magnet for subversive artists, future guerrilla fighters, and sharp political thinkers. The place was known for its unorthodox educational methods, and fields of study often lost their boundaries. Professors not only sensitized us to the nation's poverty and injustice, they encouraged us to take action. Friends would often take trimesters off to travel to distant rural regions and live with the indigenous people. Most eventually returned, but many didn't; some simply vanished, apparently adopting different identities and new lives.

At UAM, finding links between political theory and activism was a sport. Those of us who studied psychology embraced the antipsychiatry movement and, during fieldwork, we were expelled from asylums for allowing patients to go free. I, for one, worked with an urban priest who had devoted his life to homeless children. He believed that to help the children he needed to live among them in Mexico City's garbage dumps—foraging with them for food, making and selling drugs for money, and even occasionally engaging in acts of vandalism.

Xochimilco was an exciting, if anarchic and contradictory, place. Our teachers were middle-class Mexican leftists, exiled Argentine intellectuals, and other Latin American émigrés. Our idols were Ernesto "Che" Guevara, Antonio Gramsci, and Herbert Marcuse. Wealthy professors urged us to agitate among peasants in the countryside. And, what's more, we were aware that the government perceived our radicalism, our animosity as productive. In fact, it wanted our hatred. The rationale was clear: if adolescents in the Third World are always full of antigovernment feeling, the government should provide a secluded space to let them vent their rage. They'll scream, they'll organize, but since their links to the outside world will be kept to a minimum, nothing will come of it.

In unmasking Marcos as just another college-educated radical, it is clear that President Ernesto Zedillo Ponce de León hopes to isolate the broadly popular Zapatistas by portraying them as ideologically extreme terrorists intent on destroying Mexican society. (More than one commentator has noted that the picture of Guillén/Marcos released to the media bears more than a passing resemblance to that of Abimael Guzmán, the former philosophy professor and now-imprisoned leader of Peru's Maoist Shining Path guerrillas.) Although the international press has largely overlooked this story, the Mexican media duly noted that as army troops were capturing Zapatista leaders in Chiapas, police in Mexico City were arresting Xochimilco faculty members for collaborating with the rebels. Other professors are reportedly in hiding, and the school is now under heavy surveillance.

But the assault on UAM and the revelation of Marco's identity—whether authentic or not—is unlikely to undermine sympathy for the Zapatista cause. In fact, even before the unmasking of Marcos it was already well known that many Zapatista leaders, including Marcos, were "foreigners," white urban intellectuals attached to Nicaragua's Sandinistas and to left-wing groups within the country. Despite their presence, however, few have ever doubted that the Chiapas rebellion is deeply rooted in the centuries-old grievances of Mexico's indigenous people. And their unhappiness is shared by millions of other poor Mexicans whose poverty will only grow worse in the wake of the peso's devaluation.

The plight of the Zapatistas is symbolic: in their struggle lies Mexico's future. Although I left Mexico in 1985, I often reflect on how crucial my UAM experience was in shaping my political and artistic views. Since then, I've become a writer and a scholar, and adopted a new language. In the process, I've acquired a new mask of my own. Evidently, the ski-masked Subcomandante Marcos is also a bookish academic, although a less reticent, more militant one. Apparently, in leading the Zapatistas' guerrilla movement, he has easily bridged the gap between words and action. Being a UAM alum, I confess that as a student I often saw armed rebellion as the only solution to the problems that plagued Mexico. After all, reasoned debate has rarely carried the day in my native land.

Today I live far from Mexico, and I've become a peaceful advocate for democracy. But I can't really blame some of my college friends and acquaintances for choosing a more confrontational approach. No matter what the Mexican government may claim, they certainly aren't terrorists.

13 / THE ADVENTURES OF MAQROLL

Portentous dreamer, irredeemable traveler, subtle monarchist and conversationalist *extraordinaire,* Alvaro Mutis is the inhabitant of an unique, self-sufficient cosmos—endless, without timetables and borders, a universe of excitement and horror alien to most of us. His creatures are bizarre and wondrous: arms dealers, buccaneers, and corsairs, students of Saint Francis, guerrilla fighters, mutineers, clairvoyant prostitutes with little attachment to society. They go about doing their habitual errands without much fanfare, common men and women either living a nomadic life or settled in remote, enchanting regions of the globe. But only after getting acquainted with their inner world do we realize that their solitude and moral ambiguity are incommensurable, just like ours. Joseph Conrad is an obvious reference point: in some way, Mutis's creations also seem to cry repeatedly, in a whisper, as if addressing a strange image, a strange vision: "The horror! The horror!"

But his is not a literature about the repercussions of colonialism. He doesn't display any real interest in nationalism and racial interaction. Instead, he is solely obsessed with the act of wandering, the art of belonging nowhere and becoming one's own hero. Mutis is a master utterly unconcerned with our present ideas of equality and justice, a perpetual sojourner whose real home is the airport and the hotel room. For years he has kept such a peripatetic schedule that, as his friends put it, he often runs the risk of turning into an apparition. Bogotá is his birthplace, Brussels gave him an early education, and Mexico is where he has spent his adult years—but more often that not Mutis can be found en route to Majorca, the Balkan states, and Levant, spending an afternoon drinking cognac at an old friend's house or talking the night away in a cozy bar. More than anything, his select group of devotees, which grows steadily as time goes by, is eternally grateful for his creating Maqroll the Gaviero, also an obsessive voyager (the word *gaviero* in Spanish means mast-man, lookout), a misanthrope and a contemporary Golem of sorts whose stature in the realm of fantasy seems to have acquired a life of its own.

About Maqroll's origin and past almost nothing is known. He is described as "a born anarchist who pretends not to know that about himself, or to ignore it." He can be spotted pronouncing statements like "The disappearance of our species would be a distinct relief for the universe. Soon after extinction, its ominous history would be totally forgotten. There are insects better able to leave more permanent and less fatal traces of their passage than those left behind by the human race." Depending on when one comes across his labyrinthine path, Maqroll's face can be well shaved or covered by a thick graying beard. He speaks little but smiles frequently. He often walks with a makeshift bamboo crutch, and is portrayed as an elusive entrepreneur who, like Don Quixote, makes trotting a philosophy. He thinks of himself as always traveling "at the edge of chasms compared to which death is a puppet show," but he's not a visionary: windmills are windmills and his Dulcinea is not one but many women, all painfully real. Not unreasonably, Octavio Paz has described Maqroll as "a personage of romantic ancestry," and what his eyes "discover—quicksand, the dense, dwaried vegetation of malaria, immense salt marshes, obelisks and squared towers, a geometry of prisons, offices and slaughterhouses—is not so much a physical world as a moral landscape. . . ." He is the perfect Byronic hero: melancholic, defiant, brooding on some mysterious, unforgivable sin of the past.

Mutis has spent his whole creative career chronicling, mapping, sorting out Maqroll's jumbled misadventures, first through poetry, then through a series of carefully crafted novellas. (A book of his poetry in English was translated by Alastair Reid and Alexander Coleman.) Maqroll's debut dates back to when Mutis wrote *Memoria de los hospitales de Ultramar,* in his late twenties, and his complete poetic incarnation was compiled in its Spanish original in the early seventies, under the title *Summa de Maqroll El Gaviero: 1948–1970.* Then, more than a decade later, the first four narrative episodes of his saga, brief novellas of about ninety pages, including the most famous, "The Snow of the Admiral," began to show up individually. Three more have been added to the canon since 1990, but readers in the Hispanic world often have difficulty collecting them because they appeared in various countries under the aegis of different publishers. Expertly translated by Edith Grossman, all are now available in English in a couple of compact, elegant volumes, the first of which appeared in 1992 and the second was just issued.

The added effect is nothing short of thrilling. Mutis's style is clear, dry, plain, and caustic. Maqroll emerges as a lucid, enchanting figure—a metaphor for dislocation and incessant search. He dies many deaths and then revives without much explanation. We see him living an austere life, with hardly a penny in his pocket. All we know about him is somewhat unreliable, as it comes from his companions and acquaintances and through personal diaries, lost manuscripts, delayed correspondence, second-hand chronicles, and accidental meetings. He's never comfortable, always in a transient state, a man for all seasons: We see him become a rug smuggler, participate in guerrilla activities in South America, be active in a gold rush, transport Muslims from Yugoslavia to Mecca, and be in charge of a brothel in Panama. I must once again make reference to his lucid remarks: "What you don't control always turns against you," he argues at one point. "What happens is that people don't understand this. Well, people, you know, people aren't worth very much. Nothing bothers me more than people. A poet from my country, who would have been a good friend of yours and an ideal companion in breaking open bottles of the densest alcohol in the most unbelievable taverns, used to say: 'Ah, all those ignorant people always expressing their opinions!'" Although Maqroll's is clearly the abstract landscape of our human imagination, he often gets involved with real-life people, most memorably Mutis's own life-long friends—say the poet Gonzalo Rojas and the painter Alejandro Obregón. But for as much as people tell us who he is and where he is found, no one is actually capable of deciphering his underhanded identity. Not even Mutis. And thus, Maqroll remains a paradox—the everlasting fugitive.

What he isn't, and what some would expect him to be, is a modernist symbol, an emblem to decipher the handicaps of our present way of perceiving reality. That's because Mutis has never had the slightest interest in politics. He's a Catholic who considers himself "a Ghibbeline, a monarchist, and a legitimist." He acknowledges never to have voted in an election. By his own account, the last political event that truly attracts his attention is the fall of Constantinople into the hands of the infidels on May 29, 1453. "I was born in Bogotá on the feast of the Sainted king, Louis IX of France," he once wrote. "I do not discount the influence of my patron saint in my devotion to monarchy." But politics have always found a way to permeate his life, accidentally and otherwise. He belongs to a generation of Colombian writers—Manuel Mejía Vallejo, Pedro Gómez Valderrama, and Plinio Apuleyo Mendoza—born in the twenties (in his case 1923), who took five decades to make a commitment to the novel as literary genre. In spite of its alien disposition to the social and ideological upheaval of the time, *La balanza,* his first book, co-authored with Carlos Patiño Roselli, was unexpectedly burned in 1948, amid the arson and looting that took place after the assassination of the liberal leader Jorge Eliécer Gaitán. And in 1956, while working in the Colombian branch of the Esso oil company, Mutis was involved in a financial scandal. Apparently he had used discretionary funds to buy his friends useful presents, including one of the first typewriters García Márquez ever had. When things got heated he had to run to exile in Mexico. Although he was never found guilty, he was incarcerated for a couple of years while a legal battle to extradite him was under way. (His experiences in prison are the subject of his first novel, *Diario de Lecumberri.*)

Whenever one talks about Mutis one must talk about Colombian letters today, and inevitably once must come to the blinding, splendid figure of García Márquez: the compass, the lighthouse that signals the way to understand every precursor, contemporary and successor. But unlike what nearsighted critics want us to believe, the author of *Love in the Time of Cholera* isn't an influence on Mutis; ironically, it's perhaps the other way around: Mutis was already very much in control of his chimeras and distinctive style in the late forties, whereas García Márquez, five years younger, took command of his fictional universe only after *No One Writes to the Colonel,* in 1958. At any rate, the liaison between the two is solid and intricate. García Márquez ranks Mutis as "one of the greatest writers of our time" in a blurb reproduced a thousand times. For a while Mutis contemplated the idea of writing a novel about Simón Bolívar's last days, but only managed to publish a fragment: "El último rostro." Realizing the project had incredible potential but would probably not be finished, among other things because Mutis has committed himself to the Maqroll saga and because his entire oeuvre has a tendency to be fragmentary, García Márquez asked to borrow it to produce *The General in His Labyrinth*. Also, they keep on paying tribute to each other in their respective work: García Márquez, for instance, appears in passing in "A True History of the Encounters and Complicities of Maqroll the Gaviero and the Painter Alejandro Obregón," part of "Triptych on Sea and Land," the last novella included in the book under review. Likewise, the French translation of *One Hundred Years of Solitude,* which appeared before Gregory Rabassa's, was half dedicated to Mutis and his wife Carmen.

The thread linking the four novellas in *The Adventures of Maqroll,* among themselves as well as with those included in the previous volume translated in English, is the protagonist himself. Sometimes he's at center stage but other times his role is small. He comes across people like Abdul Bashur, a Lebanese shipowner whose only dream is to find a perfect ship. In "The Tramp Steamer's Last Port of Call," at least the first half, Mutis himself commands our attention as he coincidentally finds himself on several occasions followed by the *Halcyon,* a ship whose captain, Jon Iturri, has a love affair with Bashur's sister. Each of the adventures is autonomous and self-contained, even if certain motifs and characters keep on reappearing. As we finish one novella after another, we occasionally find ourselves perplexed, even annoyed by the fragmentary nature of Mutis's oeuvre. But sooner rather than later it becomes clear that Maqroll's perils are to be enjoyed in small doses, allowing their language to hypnotize us, their baroque attention to detail carries us away to a higher intellectual dimension. Mutis's talents are directed toward fragmenting the world, not uniting it.

His aristocratic attitude toward society (he descends from José Celestino Mutis, an eighteenth-century Spanish priest who arrived in South America to found the so-called Botanical Expedition) makes him a writer's writer—or if not, a writer for the initiated and highly sophisticated. He shies away from the spotlight. While he puts his whole self into Maqroll's pilgrimage, he knows, even while often ridiculing his own effort within the text, that it will only make him a celebrity among an educated elite. "I . . . attempt to leave some mark in the memory of my friends by narrating the trials and tribulations of the Gaviero," he writes. "I don't believe I will achieve very much along this road, but no other seems open to me." His literature is obviously influenced by Jules Verne, Emilio Salgari, the *Poema del Mío Cid* and the chivalry novel, and the fabulous first chronicles of the New World. Adventure is his main motif and the whole globe is his stage. And if when compared to Conrad (about whom he has written an enlightening, evocative essay), Patrick O'Brien, Melville, and Cervantes, Mutis's creatures can feel light, unsupported by a philosophical system pushing us to question our ethical values and our sanity, after one finishes reading his amazing novellas it's clear that he's an expert at understating his views. Maqroll questions reality by simply living as a ghost in the margins of history. In his mouth, the expression "The horror! The horror!" is not an indictment of our reckless morality but of human nature as a whole. As Montaigne would observe, he personifies the type of person that abandons his life for a dream to know it's true worth, only to discover that it is worthless.

[1995]

14 / FELIPE ALFAU

> Whom do we write a novel for? Whom do we write a poem
> for? For people who have read a number of other novels, a
> number of other poems. A book is written so that it can be
> put beside other books and take its place on a hypothetical
> bookshelf. Once it is there, in some way or another it alters
> the shelf, expelling certain other volumes from their places
> or forcing them back into the second row, while demanding
> that certain others should be brought up to the front.
>
> —Italo Calvino,
> *The Uses of Literature*

In a pseudo-essay ironically titled "Kafka and His Precursors,"
Jorge Luis Borges argues that every writer not only creates his successors
but also, and primarily, his precursors. That is, after reading Franz Kafka
or Lewis Carroll, we look back for earlier works that show a slight influence, a gentle touch typical of their style. Felipe Alfau (b. 1902,
Barcelona), who after a brief critical success in the late 1930s vanished
into oblivion, to be resurrected in the late 1980s, turns Borges's dictum
upside down. Although it's easy to locate Alfau's precursors—say,
Laurence Sterne or Diderot—looking for his successors is where one is
likely to get into trouble. Since very few read him between the end of the
Second World War and the late eighties, how could we recognize his
style in, say, John Barth, Robert Coover, or Thomas Pynchon? And yet,
how could we not?

To put it another way, here is a tempting parable. Imagine, for a moment, that the history of world literature made a mistake and forgot to
include Miguel de Cervantes and the *Quixote* in its festive narrative parade. Or better, that the Spaniard wrote his masterpiece in 1605 and
1615, as he actually did, but only a selected club of initiated friends had
the pleasure of reading it, and then the book disappeared from human

150

memory without a trace. Suddenly, several hundred years later, a publisher in Madrid by pure chance rediscovers it, and people recognize
traces of its craft in subsequent writers from Europe, the United States,
and even Hispanic America. Yet none knew of him. What then? One
sole interpretation: Cervantes was a prophet who foresaw the artistic
mood and metabolism of the future.

Precisely that, I believe, is the case of Alfau. *Locos: A Comedy of Gestures,* a novel—or a "nivola" if Miguel de Unamuno had been its major
influence—was published in 1936 in a limited edition by Farrar &
Reinhart. It was enthusiastically reviewed by Mary McCarthy and others, yet it disappeared from the literary scene without a trace. The writer,
the son of a lawyer who frequently traveled to the West Indies and the
Philippines, had been raised in Guernica and Madrid, and had emi-
grated to New York with his family in 1916, at age fourteen. Although he
took some courses at Columbia University, he was self-educated, with a
deep love for music and mathematics, and a disdain for conventional
literature. During his youth, Alfau was for a while a music critic for *La
Prensa,* an up-and-coming Spanish-language newspaper in Manhattan.
In his heart he nourished the dream of one day becoming an orchestra
conductor but couldn't. So after a few years, picking up English in the
streets, he wrote a novel in his adopted language. He had a very hard
time selling it, perhaps because of its avant-garde techniques and its
Iberian English. It clearly was a book ahead of its time. Meanwhile, in
1929 Doubleday published his children's book, *Old Tales from Spain,* a
compendium of invented stories about bullfighting and the Spanish way
of life and imagination. As he tells it, Alfau did both books not because
he wanted to become a professional writer but in order to earn money.
By then he had already married his first wife and had a daughter. But
any intelligent reader of the novel knows that Alfau is far from tradi-
tional. If he was looking for commercial success, he was on the wrong
track. Yet in various other ways, he wasn't.

The price of *Locos: A Comedy of Gestures* was $2.50. The publisher
paid him $250 for the manuscript and included it as the first title of a
series of signed editions intended for a select club of subscribers. It has
no conventional plot. The author himself meets the characters—
Lunarito, Gastón Bejarano, Don Benito, Juan Chinelato, Doña Micaela,

García, Don Graciano Báez, Sister Carmela, and Father Inocenicio—in a bizarre gathering place in Toledo called Café de los Locos. They discuss many topics: panhandling and theft, love and violence, metaphysics and music, all intertwined in anecdotes, recollections, and philosophical dissertations. Reviewing the new edition fifty years later, a *New Yorker* critic said that although "Alfau wrote with a confidence astonishing in a twenty-six-year-old [the novel was completed in 1928], beneath the comedy and the surrealistic effects and the glare and shadows," the pages were inhabited by a "whispered secret," a mysterious light—as if the author was "gestur[ing] to his public from his side of the peculiar one-way mirror that is reflexive art."

Read before World War II, while John Dos Passos, F. Scott Fitzgerald, Dashiell Hammett, Ernest Hemingway, and Raymond Chandler had their fingerprints on everything literary, the book is a compelling curiosity. Today, it's a revelation. One can trace Alfau's "influence" on Italo Calvino, Vladimir Nabokov, Barth, Pynchon, Spain's Luis Martín-Santos, and even on Borges himself (b. 1899). Yet none of them knew about him. Or at least, not until 1988. His precursors, on the other hand, are the Maupassant of "Le Horla," Luigi Pirandello, and of course the lucid narrative tradition of *Tristram Shandy*. What strikes us as astonishing is the fact that for over fifty years, Alfau was an influential writer without readers.

When the Dalkey Archive Press reissued the novel, it was a sensation. Mary McCarthy wrote an epilogue about how, when she first read *Locos* and reviewed it for the *Nation*, it changed her way of perceiving literature. "It was my fatal type," she wrote. "What I fell in love with, all unknowingly, was the modernist novel as detective story." Alfau includes Sherlock Holmes in his cast, and surrounds the story with the suspense derived from such questions as: Will the characters disobey their creator? Can they fight for freedom? In Italy, France, and Holland, translations soon followed, and in Spain it was published by the prestigious imprint Seix Barral.

In 1990, *Chromos,* the only other novel by the author and one which not a single publisher wanted back in the forties, saw the light, and was nominated for the National Book Award. Paul West, one of the judges, wrote: "Finished in 1948, [the novel] sets an imaginary Alfau dreaming in front of old calendar pictures by the light of a match. Before the flame gutters, a real novel has come to him: a tart and eloquent, sly and feisty kaleidoscope of New York Spaniards, wrought in fire amid the *cante hondo* of the heart by a hunger artist almost lost, unpublished, to oblivion." Full of fiction-within-fiction devices, it contains almost the same cast of characters. The theme now moves around a group of actors, fantasists, mathematicians, singers, guitarists, all of Iberian origin, who endlessly discuss life, physics, and relativity in a Manhattan that hardly notices them. And indeed, as in *The Brothers Karamazov, Don Quixote,* and *The Arabian Nights,* within the novel there's another novel, as if art suddenly decided to stop describing life and began to imitate itself.

Besides the two novels and the children's tales, he also wrote another book: a collection of poems, *La poesía cursi.* It was handed by the author to Steven Moore, senior editor at the Dalkey Archive Press, after recognizing the dedication the publishing house had given to his work. There are a few remarkable features that need to be discussed regarding the text: first and foremost, the fact that it is poetry and not fiction. Alfau is a prose writer who happens to write poetry, not vice versa. Second, the book was written in Spanish and not in English. It consists of twenty-two poems, some clearly better, more inspired than others, all with a careful metrical system and following a format in vogue in the late nineteenth century with many South American *modernistas* like Rubén Darío, Julián del Casal, José Martí, and Manuel Gutiérrez Nájera.* The dates of composition range from 1923 to 1987; that is, from a time even before *Locos* was written to a year prior to its reissue. The themes are often autobiographical and have an immediacy that apparently results from personal experiences, like the death of a companion or the daily contact with Afro-Americans in New York City. Why was it written in Spanish and not in English if Alfau made the transition in his novels? *La poesía cursi* is a rebuttal of Romanticism, but it emerges from the very ranks of the Romantic movement and its sense of life. Thus, parody is the book's

---

* I use *modernista* in the Hispanic-American sense: the literary movement that started in 1885 and finished approximately in 1915, that included, besides these authors, Leopoldo Lugones and Delmira Agustini. See the illuminating essay by Octavio Paz, "Tradition and Metaphor," part of his Charles Eliot Norton Lectures, published under the title *Children of the Mire* (Cambridge: Harvard University Press, 1974), 115–41.

signature.* Alfau tries to caricature the sweep and atmosphere of Romanticism, with its drive for spontaneity, creative freedom, an inflated emotional engagement with the universe, and with its opposition to Rationalism.

In the Iberian peninsula, the nineteenth-century Romantic movement, to which Alfau indirectly refers, had as its founding fathers the Duque de Rivas and José de Esponceda. Yet its major promoter was Gustavo Adolfo Bécquer, a poet born in 1836 who met his death at age thirty-four, who aimed at simplicity and economy in his verses. Some of his themes—despair, memories, deep emotional insights, and the inevitability of love—appear in *La poesía cursi.* As it stands, the cadence of the prosaic humorist Ramón de Campoamor and that of the idealist Gaspar Núñez de Arce can be felt in several stanzas, which could be read as a tribute to the late masters. And although the book suggests that Alfau is promoting himself as a Romantic, it is evident he is keeping his distance from the lyricism, and even symbolism, of his precursors. The very first sonnet, titled "Romanticism," is a sardonic description of the "suicidal" spirit emulated by Wordsworth, Coleridge, Goethe, and Bécquer. It includes two typically Romantic terms: the anxiety of life, and human egotism. Yet the author clearly criticizes the attitude by arguing, in the last stanza, that this literary movement of eros and pathos is incapable of accepting and inhabiting our contradictory reality.

In general, the characters and scenes that permeate the volume are easily recognizable: the unmerciful scientist and collector of butterflies (called by Alfau "The Naturalist"); youth as a vanishing state of happiness; a train as a metaphor of the passing of time; the wish of the individual to be integrated into the whole; and death as an irrevocable event. Alfau juxtaposes, and at times masks, these elements with Spanish and New York leitmotifs: for instance the ethnic mix of blacks and whites, or a folkloric song of Castille, "La pájara pinta." Here and there, one gets a Borgesian sentence ("It's an ideal picture / painted in the mirror's moon")

---

*"A Parody" was the author's subtitle for *Chromos* (shortened from "A Parody of Truth," his earlier choice), but it was eliminated by the editor at the time of publication. If one agrees that the term denotes an exaggerated imitation of a work of art, it's clear that the narrative tone in the novel, as well as in *Locos,* is nothing but parodic—that is, possessed by the instinct to burlesque pompous human behavior.

or a Darío twist ("expressing the horror of dying without the assurance of being able to remember he was once alive"). One or two poems have explosive themes, like the one titled "Afro-Ideal Evocation," a call for blacks to return to Africa. But altogether, Alfau's poetic voice is very much his own: sarcastic, baroque, and theatrical.

No doubt his literary persona is quite puzzling. By the time the earliest poems of *La poesía cursi* had been written, an irrevocable, widely publicized literary transformation had taken place in Spain and Hispanic America at least a decade earlier. He writes as if Romanticism was still a movement to be ridiculed and overturned, yet the *modernistas* in Nicaragua, Cuba, Mexico, or Argentina had already undertaken this task. Octavio Paz argues that the revolution of Rubén Darío and José Martí, which gave us immortal pieces such as "Walt Whitman" and "Dos patrias," was nothing but a sort of south-of-the-border Romanticism. The argument is debatable; be that as it may, by 1920 almost every single South American *modernista*, from Darío to Julio Herrera y Reissig and Agustini, was already dead.* And in Spain, where Juan Ramón Jiménez had enthusiastically embraced their revolution, another deep transformation had taken place, one in search of national roots and a distinctive collective power.

One ought not to forget that Alfau is a contemporary of Pedro Salinas, Jorge Guillén, Rafael Alberti, Dámaso Alonso, Vicente Aleixandre, and even Federico García Lorca. They renewed Spanish poetry, at times injecting it with folkloric tendencies or with a Rimbaud-like attitude toward the wonders of life and nature. Yet the author of *Chromos* does not seem to know anything about them. His conscious decision to leave his homeland, so it would seem, ultimately resulted in a total lack of interest in the literary trends of the Hispanic world. And even more surprising is the fact that, as in his novels, his poems totally ignore the Spanish Civil War. Nowhere can one find an allusion or an indirect reference to it. All this makes Alfau not only an anachronistic writer but

---

* This particular text, "Cuento de niños/A Children's Tale," is similar in tone and structure to a work by the Colombian poet José Asunción Silva (1865–96), "Los maderos de San Juan," included in his collection *El libro de versos*. Both intertwine a folkloric song with a more tragic, ultimately fatalistic comment on life and hope. Federico García Lorca, by the way, cultivated the same poetic contrasts, drawing his images from popular rhymes and legends.

also, and more astonishingly, an artist unaffected by his intellectual and aesthetic surroundings, living in a universe of his own creation.

I personally discovered Alfau in 1988, when Mary McCarthy's afterword to the new Dalkey Archive edition of *Locos* was published in the *New York Review of Books*. A mystical experience immediately took place. All of a sudden, deep at heart I felt I could have been Felipe Alfau if only I had been born not in 1961 but sixty years earlier. This might sound eccentric, even presumptuous. I had had a similar sensation once before—with Pinhas "Der Nister" Kahanovitch, a Soviet-Jewish writer who died as a result of Stalin's purges. I remember running to Butler Library at Columbia University to get hold of anything written by this obscure Spaniard, and, to my surprise, found the 1936 edition of his only known novel, the very same one McCarthy was discussing. The volume had never been borrowed before by a reader. In three hours or so I devoured its two hundred-some pages, and began nurturing the hope of someday meeting Alfau. I wrote a letter to Steven Moore, senior editor at Dalkey Archive, and as an answer, I was told the Spaniard refused to receive any visitors, although I should try. The address—436 West 27th Street, apt. 9H—and phone number followed.

That same night I called. Somebody with a peculiar, matured voice responded. Alfau was out of the country, he claimed, perhaps in Europe. He had sublet his apartment and was not expected back for several months. The man said *su apellido*, his own last name, was García, by profession a taxidermist. The joke was clear. A protagonist, along with Dr. José de los Ríos, in his fictionalized universe, he had become a real entity to protect the writer's privacy. Indeed, Alfau had intelligently foreseen this Scheherazade-like metamorphosis: characters have a way of growing independent, of rebelling against their creator's will and command, of mocking their author, of toying with him. . . . Wonderful, I thought—an invitation to a beheading where life and fiction intertwine.

Who is Felipe Alfau? I asked the question time and again over the next few months. The typical answer I got, paraphrasing Edmund Wilson's comment on Agatha Christie's *The Murder of Roger Ackroyd*, was, who cares? Nobody knew him, nobody gave a damn. Notwithstanding, a link, a communion between him and me, had been established. I knocked at his door several times, but García always refused to allow me in, until I finally decided to play the game—to unveil Alfau's identity, to live on a Pirandellian stage, to decapitate him and unveil myself. One August afternoon, after I rang the bell and he inquired who the visitor was, I answered, Felipe Alfau. He opened the door and a few days later we were chatting about his literature and past. A friendship began.

To think of Alfau's response to his literary rediscovery is to invoke J. D. Salinger and even Pynchon. The three have done everything to evade publicity and escape the plight of fame. Since they live in virtual seclusion, biographical information about them is scarce, and it seems that they actively perpetuate their own mystery. The author of *Locos* and *Chromos,* now living in a nursing home in Rego Park, Queens, has as his only interest now to leave this world as soon as possible. "It's very boring," he argues, "and can only get worse."

His relevance today comes from his disturbing, remarkable voice. The language question is fundamental in understanding him. Why did he switch to English after having written journalistic pieces in Spanish? The reason, I think, is rather simple: back in the twenties, he knew he was an avant-garde writer, and that to be appreciated, it would have to appear in what was then New York City's major vehicle of communication. At the time, his motherland was engaged in a cruel and ultimately meaningless civil war, and any artistic product read in Manhattan or Paris, written by a Spaniard, had to be concerned with ideology and the battle against fascism. Although a supporter of Francisco Franco, he was not interested in politics. His decision to change languages links him with Nabokov, Jerzy Kosinski, Joseph Conrad, the U.S. poet laureate Joseph Brodsky, and the Cuban novelist Guillermo Cabrera Infante. Thus, he belongs to that new branch of Hispanic literature, written in the United States, that must be translated into Spanish in order to be read in Buenos Aires, Mexico City, or Barcelona. But not only did Alfau jump from one code to another, he actually makes the linguistic dilemma one of his central themes. Here is the potent opening paragraph of *Chromos:*

> The moment one learns English, complications set in. Try as one may, one cannot elude this conclusion, one must inevitably come back to it. This applies to all persons, including those born to the language, and, at times, even more so to Latins, including Spaniards. It manifests itself in an awareness of implications and

intricacies to which one had never given a thought; it
afflicts one with that officiousness of philosophy
which, having no business of its own, gets in everybody's way and, in the case of Latins, they lose that
racial characteristic of taking things for granted and
leaving them to their own devices without inquiring
into causes, motives or ends, to meddle indiscreetly
into reasons which are none of one's affair and to
become not only self-conscious, but conscious of
other things which never gave a damn for one's existence.

Alfau's odyssey exemplifies the fate of Hispanic writers in the United
States. When compared to other ethnic minorities—Jewish, African,
Asian, Italian—it seems that the writers of Puerto Rican, Cuban, or
Chicano background find it difficult to enter the literary mainstream.
Although Hispanic authors have been part of the U.S. literary scene since
the last century, today most people know more about the Hispanic rela-
tives of William Carlos Williams, George Santayana, or John Dos Passos
than about the art of an Hispanic–North American author. This country's
Eurocentrism (understood as the heritage of mainly Italy, France, Great
Britain, Eastern Europe, and even Russia) discourages paying much attention to anything south of the Río Grande.

Also, there is the fact that since 1492, when Christopher Columbus
first set foot in what would be called the Americas, there have been two
different stories cohabiting in the vast continent: the success of the north
and the defeat of the south. That mere fact makes it even harder for
Anglo-Saxon culture in New York to recognize as equal that of the inheritors of Luis de Góngora and Lope de Vega. But Alfau's value tran-
scends egalitarian feelings and ethnic qualities. It stands on its own as
the contribution of someone living in the abyss existing between two
realities, in the margin, on the edge. His work belongs to two distinct
traditions, and thus has a dual referential code. It is the result of a personal, linguistic, and cultural identity that is difficult to grasp. Felipe
Alfau is a product of that no-man's-land—somewhat like Kafka's characters, a frontier dweller.

[1991]

15 / THE BRICK NOVEL

Our fin-de-siècle has solidified the intercourse between encyclopedias and the novel. In his last memo for the next millennium, Italo
Calvino suggested the term *hypernovel* to describe the by-product of
their relationship, an all-knowing, all-encompassing fictional narrative
whose virtues defy time and space. The term brings to mind images of
immoderation and excess, and portrays its creators as gluttonous, Epicurean artists given to dissipation, which indeed they are. Enthralled by
its richness, possessed by its "challenge to eternity," Calvino described
the standard hypernovel as a formidable text of modulating structures
and accumulative shape mirroring our vast epistemological ambition
and our licentious linguistic drive. He then went on to list Flaubert's
Bouvard et Pécuchet, George Perec's *La Vie mode d'emploi,* and Carlo
Emilio Gadda's *Quer pastissiaccio brutto de Via Merulana,* as precursors.
But many more titles ought to be added to the list, including the ubiquitous ones by Cervantes, Rabelais, Laurence Sterne, Diderot, and Machado
de Assis, which are at the very inception of this most promiscuous of
literary subgenera.

Other practitioners have also come forth with alternative terms: *nivola*
(Miguel de Unamuno), *anti-novel* (Raymond Queneau, William H.
Gass), *novel-almanac* (Severo Sarduy), *carnival-novel* (Guillermo Cabrera
Infante), *total novel* (Perec), *androgynous novel* (Milorad Pavic), *jigsaw
puzzle–novel* (George Simon, Julián Ríos), and *Nirvana-novel* (Julio
Cortázar). Since James Joyce remains the most outstanding, the most
talked-about, the most enigmatic of contemporary promoters, some
critics have suggested distinguishing writers as Prejoycean and
Postjoycean (or, what's worse, as coming "Before the *Wake*" and "After

the *Wake*"). But the discrimination seems to me neither useful nor convincing: it recognizes encyclopedic novelists as inhabiting a galaxy that rotates around a single, solitary center, when in fact other cores, equal in stature, if not more magnanimous, act as centripetal forces.

What characterizes the encyclopedic novel, first and foremost, is its mammoth proportion—its "brick-like nature," to use John Barth's word. Oscillating between a length of 500 and 1,250 pages, it is unmistakably chubby, overblown, and corpulent. (More, according to Carlos Fuentes, is "an exaggeration.") Then there's the issue of plot, which is often made to appear secondary and inconsequential. The confusion of perception is what matters, not the progression of a storyline. Its main purpose isn't to entertain but to challenge, to perplex and obfuscate. It doesn't approach life progressively but— Perec's word—"horizontally." That is, instead of narrating one life or more chronologically and realistically from point A to point C, it devotes its energy and space to describing a bulk of atemporal experiences, which are often presented arbitrarily. What's more, in spite of the common perception, this type of giant fiction is not disenchanted with the universe and with literature but, on the contrary, fully enchanted with its own possibilities. And as far as its linguistic dimension goes, it is fair to say that language is used less as a conduit and more as a primary protagonist and as an inexhaustible pyrotechnics machine, a powerful volcano erupting all sorts of ingenious pirouettes, riddles, rhymes, and puns. In short, its utopian objective is to embrace reality as a whole, to leave absolutely nothing out, which results in an awesome array of information organized capriciously, shifting viewpoints, and a multiple and often confusing cast of characters.

Light reading, obviously, the encyclopedic novel is not. On the other hand, its uttermost desire might well be to infuriate its audience. And yet, it would be a big mistake to think that its scope is only scholarly. Regardless of its cerebral approach to the world, its design reaches way beyond academic circles. (In most cases, its practitioners are not even college professors.) Thus this type of book thrives on the idea that general readers today have reached an amazing degree of sophistication and that parody and self-reflection, *sine qua non* in a time like ours where tastes are broad and eclecticism is the norm, are needed to put some degree of separation between life itself and the act of thinking about it.

Expansiveness, excess, and endless regeneration are of course also qualities of baroque art, a style so conscious of its own potentials, as Borges has argued, that it almost borders on the cartoonish. This brings me to a major point I want to make: this type of novel's novel, so meretricious, so tawdry and ornate, is quintessentially baroque and its abundance of accessories, its gaudy spirit helps explain why it flourishes with a vengeance south of the Río Grande. After all, the baroque signals a density of culture, a *mare magnum* of identities typical of the Hispanic psyche. With very few exceptions, Havana, Buenos Aires, and Mexico City, the three major cultural metropolises in Latin America, have been its sole crib and have seen this tricky narrative prosper. The first city is akin to jubilees where masks, mulatto music, and politics intertwine; the second to volumes about exile and melancholy; and the third to disquisitions on the inescapable weight of history. And precisely that baroqueness of style, a signature of Spain's Golden Age, is a synonym of *ingenio,* the capacity for various kinds of wit through ornamentation. (Since being rediscovered in 1927, the poet Luis de Góngora, it's a common fact, has become a Nietzschean superman for the Latin America's intelligentsia.) And that, of course, is Fernando del Paso's trademark. Indeed, he perceives the novel as a broad, heterogeneous enterprise, hugging many subjects and epochs, an endless mirror, an anything-goes receptacle, generous, formless, and thus easily malleable, with a vast and splendid history traceable anywhere and pointing everywhere.

Del Paso was for many years a publicity agent and is known today not only as an accomplished novelist but as a highly revered painter (he is influenced by Salvador Dalí, Magritte, and Escher). He began his literary career early on dreaming to become a doctor. "In the beginning I wanted to be a doctor . . . ," he once said to an interviewer, "but actually, I had a very romantic, very literary idea of medicine. I could not have been a doctor because I can't stand blood, foul odors, and things like that: they all terrify me. Well, I wound up studying chemistry and economics. But I did not study medicine for a stronger reason: I met my wife-to-be and wanted to get married. And you can't study medicine and be married." Medicine, nevertheless, never abandoned him: *Palinuro of Mexico* is plagued with scientific references, which easily trespass the knowledge of specialists. "My literary formations began when I was eighteen or nineteen," del Paso told an interviewer. "At the time I read a great deal, mainly translations, because then I could read neither English nor French (*Ulysses,* for example, I read for the first time in the old translation by J. Salas Subirat). The first author who awakened me to language, so to speak, was Miguel Hernández. In *El rayo que no cesa* I discovered a world I had not suspected existed and that I also had inside myself, and I wrote a series of sonnets in 1958 published under the title *Sonetos de lo diario.* I then began to read a great many novels and plays. The number of authors whom I got to know at that time was enormous: William Faulkner, Thomas Wolfe, John Dos Passos, Ferdinand Ramuz, and other great masters of the novel, mainly North Americans. In addition, of course, *Ulysses* and the Mexicans Juan Rulfo, Fuentes, etc. . . . Then, in England, I reread a great deal, from Sartre to Lewis Carroll."

Del Paso is a bookish writer, then, although not a scholarly one. His baroqueness, his derivative *joie de vivre,* full of innuendoes, of unexpected masks, of subdued forces pushing to explode, of labyrinthine paths, is precisely what makes him tick. It explains, I guess, why he finds his native cultural home so perfectly homey: he is a consummate impersonator, a mummer, a writer's writer, but one still fighting to keep a sense of originality. As he himself has claimed, Tristram Shandy is his Jesus Christ, Joyce his Virgin María, and the Spanish language his canvas. Notice the following quote:

> I consider that *Ulysses* is a sort of sun installed at the center of the Gutenberg Galaxy, which illuminates not only all the works which followed it but all of universal literature that preceded it. Its influence is definite and unique in modern Western literature. . . . *Finnegans Wake* is a comet of great magnitude moving away from us at the speed of light, in danger of becoming lost for ever. But there is also the possibility that it will return one day and be better understood. Joyce's most important aspect for me is what has been called his "total" or "totalizing" practice of fiction, because I am interested in books not only as macrocosms but also as microcosms. This attitude implies two further aspects: the mythical background and linguistic revolution. But it also implies an anticolonial posture, because it presupposed a very highly

personal analysis by the writer of history, that of his
country, the West as a whole, and the world—quoting from memory, "History, that nightmare from
which I am trying to awake." But it also implies
sexuality, of course, which only acquires human
dignity when it is liberated.

Del Paso's remarkable literary status was established early on, when his
first novel, *José Trigo*, about a railway strike and the migration of workers from rural areas to urban centers, for which he won the Xavier
Villaurrutia Prize, appeared in 1967. Three years later he was part of
Iowa's Writing Program, where he first drafted *Palinuro of Mexico*. Since
then his personal library has expanded very little. It includes a rich historical novel, *Noticias del Imperio*, about the French intervention in
Mexico, and particularly about Maximilian of Hapsburg, his wife Carlota
of Belgium, and their ill-fated reign in Mexico (1862–67), known as
"the Second Mexican Empire," as well as a biography of Juan José Arreola,
a crucial figure in south-of-the-border letters instrumental in shaping
the art of a number of writers, among them the poet and essayist José
Emilio Pacheco. But it's his second novel which I'm personally most
fond of, one that more than fifteen years after its original appearance
remains a puzzle, an enchanting homage to confusion, and is, in my
judgment, a perfect embodiment of Calvino's hypernovel.

To reinvent the world anew from the perspective of an omnipresent,
Rashomon-like child is its primary intent. Critics have described it as
"Gargantuan," confirming, "for those who doubt it, that Latin America
really is a part of the Western civilization," that Hispanic literature is
indecorously self-referential, allowing for "a replication of the Joycean
trajectory and the optimum conditions for its assimilation." Although,
according to my estimates, relatively few have made the effort of reading
647 pages (the natural augmentation of the Spanish language makes the
original some 90 pages longer that Elizabeth Plaister's stellar British translation), the adventurous ones, in the words of the American critic John
S. Brushwood, have indeed undergone "a highly imaginative experience."

Published in 1977 and awarded the prestigious Rómulo Gallegos
Award, *Palinuro of Mexico* belongs to a time in Latin American letters,

between the early sixties and the late eighties, when readers couldn't satisfy their hunger for encyclopedic novels. Not surprisingly, it has been compared to Cortázar's *Hopscotch*, Augusto Roa Bastos's *I, the Supreme*, José Lezama Lima's *Paradiso*, and Cabrera Infantes's *Three Trapped Tiggers*, although, as the British critic Gerald Martin once rightly argued, its linguistic texture is "insufficiently demanding to stretch the reader's consciousness to the dimensions required by del Paso's Ulyssean perspective." And I agree: unlike its counterparts in the Hispanic world, the novel is more accessible but also less rewarding in linguistic terms— more conventional and less nightmarish.

And yet, true to its subgenre, it defies easy summary. The plot, if any, circles around a certain Palinuro, whose main obsession is the act of creation in its multiple varieties: artistic invention, sexual intercourse and procreation, health and sickness, recreation, acculturation, as well as transmigration. The scenario allows del Paso the opportunity for long disquisitions on history, time, and the meaning of things. In short, the book is about everything and nothing—medicine, eschatology, resistance and affirmation, linguistic and psychological emigration, atemporal love, Mexican history from pre-Colombian times to the 1968 student massacre in Tlatelolco Square, in which Palinuro dies (*"Acta est Fabula:* The Comedy is Over"). Its characters are ambiguous and evasive: Palinuro and Estefania, its protagonists, are by turns siblings, cousins, lovers, and mere companions. Their ancestors, Uncle Esteban, Grandmother Altagracia, Aunt Clementina, Uncle Federico, are globetrotting figures whose stage fluctuates between London, Prague, the Crimea, Paris, and Mexico's capital. Innumerable references (names, places, entire scenes) pay tribute to *Alice in Wonderland* and Laurence Sterne. Chapter 25, entitled "Palinuro on the Stairs: or, The Art of Comedy," is an autonomous play using characters from *La Commedia dell'Arte:* Harlequin, Scaramouch, Pierrot, Colombine, Pantalone, and others, and indeed, del Paso has published the segment separately, as an independent volume. The point of view constantly shifts. At times Palinuro tells the story; other times he talks of himself and those around in second and third person. In a vampiresque twist, he becomes an anonymous entity and his cousin Walter assumes the narrating. A colorful parade of historical and literary figures keeps on resurfacing: Ché Guevara,

Ambrose Bierce, Swift, Ho Chi Minh, and countless Latin American luminaries: José Asunción Silva, Rubén Darío, Pancho Villa, and others.
Nothing is certain—except, perhaps, the novel's concrete existence.

Del Paso's Mexico is at once mythical and mythological. Time is cyclical, history is a spiral leading to nothingness. In fact, *Palinuro of Mexico*
might be read as a parodic reading of a Diego Rivera mural: color, lots of
color surrounding omnipresent luminaries, and the message an amorphous, indecipherable, vacuous collective identity made of various races,
religions, and political backgrounds. But the novel is not an inconsequential quagmire. It reflects the rapid national modernization and deep
collective introspection that took place south of the Rio Grande from
the end of World War II to 1968. As the nation's capital became an all-
encompassing octopus, with tentacles everywhere, the Partido
Revolucionario Institucional, the corrupt ruling party in power since
1929, solidified its bureaucratic power. The result was a sense of suffocation, the perception that, on the road to being, in Octavio Paz's words,
a "contemporary of the rest of humankind," Mexico was selling its soul
to the devil. It was losing whatever authenticity it once had. Fuentes,
known as an *enfant terrible* (he is del Paso's elder by seven years), brought
out *Where the Air Is Clear,* an ambitious examination à la Balzac of the
social and political tensions ubiquitous in Mexico City. Shortly after, a
new antiestablishment generation sprang up, known as *La Onda,* whose
work was modeled after the Beatniks in the United States and the French
nouveau roman. It included writers like José Agustín and Gustavo Sainz
and promoted a less conventional, more anarchic, free-thinking Beat-
nik novel, spontaneously written, loosely structured, with innumerable
links to foreign cultural influences, contaminated by history, autobiography, and nonfiction. Del Paso analyzes the destruction and renewal in
the country's culture and ponders where it's going and at what cost. He
reflects on the increasing openness of Mexico to the outside world, its
cosmopolitanism, the democratic spirit felt among the populace, which
ultimately results in conflagration and tragedy.

His contribution walks hand-in-hand with Fuentes's, whose work
champions encyclopedism in Mexico. A couple of years before del Paso's
novel, Fuentes published *Terra Nostra,* a narrative pilgrimage from 1492
to the twenty-first century with the Spanish language as its leading star;

and in 1987, *Christopher Unborn,* an apocalyptic vision of anti-utopia set in an overpopulated Mexico City on October 12, 1992. Clearly Fuentes's goal, which he easily achieved, was to insert Mexico in the torrent of international fiction, to bring his native country to the international literary banquet. Not suprisingly, his books pay homage to infinite novelistic playfulness. But Fuentes's charismatic personality and the seriousness with which he undertakes his itinerant role of "cultural ambassador of Hispanic America," have somehow eclipsed *Palinuro of Mexico.* As my reader will soon find out, del Paso, thank God, isn't Fuentes: his vision is more intimate and legible, less rambunctious and pedantic. While he also establishes a dialogue with his Mexican contemporaries (including Salvador Elizondo, *La Onda* writers, and Fuentes himself), he doesn't reprimand. Nor does he lecture or look down at his reader. Instead, he creates a game of mirrors through which his troubled native country is perceived as a reflection, an addition, an appendix to a global European and American consciousness.

So, is *Palinuro of Mexico* a bona-fide "postmodernist" novel? I guess so, although I have deliberately avoided using this most academic term, which emerges within strictly scholarly boundaries and has little significance to the world at large. Yes, when one applies John Barth's famous qualifiers, del Paso's book does appear to be "self-conscious" and "self-reflective." It's anti-rationalist, anti-realist, anti-bourgeois, but "without a material adversary." It's eclectic, loose; it "performs" under "a spirit of anarchy," and it doesn't seem to be written *against* somebody, the way, for instance, Ezra Pound attacked the Edwardians and Proust wrote "against" Sainte-Beuve. But postmodernism is an empty word. Modernism, according to Webster, is "the philosophy and practice of modern art; *esp.:* a self-conscious break with the past and a search for new forms of expression." Unlike Fuentes, whose mature work becomes more and more "Bakhtinian" as times goes by, del Paso isn't an academic writer: he's a "modern" writer, from the Latin *modo,* "just now." His work is about Mexico's difficult history and arduous present, about the ambitions of an all-encompassing knowledge, about freedom of body and mind, and about the demons of possibility.

[1996]

16 / THE LATIN PHALLUS: A SURVEY

Somos el duelo a muerte que se acerca fatal.
—Julia de Burgos

I envision a brief volume, a history of Latin sexuality through the figure of the phallus, not unlike Michel Foucault and René Magritte's *Ceci n'est pas une pipe:* a compendium of its capricious ups and downs, ins and outs, from the Argentine Pampa to the Rio Grande and the Caribbean. An essay in representation, it would begin with the intimidating genitalia of the sovereigns of courage, Hernán Cortés, Francisco Pizarro, and Spanish explorers like Hernando de Soto and Cabeza de Vaca. It would make abundant display of the often graphic art of the gay awakening of the early seventies, shameless in its depiction of the male organ. And it would conclude, perhaps, with the ribbing of feminists. Here, for instance, is a poem by Cherríe Moraga, for one of its last pages:

> there is a man in my life
> pale-man born infant
> pliable flesh his body remains
> a remote possibility
> in secret it may know many things
> glossy newsprint female thighs
> spread eagle wings
> in his flying imagination
>
> soft shoe
> he did the soft shoe
> in the arch that separated the living
> from dining room
> miller trombone still turns his heel
> and daughter barefoot and never pregnant
> around and around and around

soft-tip
penis head he had
a soft-tipped penis that peeked out
accidentally one kitchen cold morning
between zipper stuck and boxer shorts
fresh pressed heat lining those tender white-meat loins

wife at the ironing board:
"what are you doing, jim, what are you doing?"
he nervously stuffed the little bird back
it looked like Peloncito
the bald-headed little name
of my abuelita's pajarito

Peloncito
a word of endearment
never told to the child
father
yellow bird-man
boy

Let me map the ambitions of my little book by starting at the beginning. The Iberian knights that crossed the Atlantic, unlike their Puritan counterparts in the British Colonies, were fortune-driven bachelors. They did not come to settle down. As Cortés wrote to Charles V in his *Cartas de Relación,* the first conquistadors were trash: rough, uneducated people from lowly origins. Their mission was to expand the territorial and symbolic powers of the Spanish crown; their ambition in the new continent was to find gold and pleasure. And pleasure they took in the bare-breasted Indian women, whom they raped at will and then abandoned. A violent eroticism was a fundamental element in the colonization of the Hispanic world, from Macchu Picchu to Chichén Itzá and Uxmal. The primal scene of the clash with the Spaniards is a still-unhealed rape: the phallus, as well as gunpowder, was a crucial weapon used to subdue. Machismo as a cultural style endlessly rehearses this humiliating episode in the history of the Americas, imitating the violent swagger of the Spanish conquerors. (This, despite the Indian legends that Cortés was the owner of a tiny, ridiculous penis.)

The hypocrisy of the Church played a role as well. Although the priesthood bore witness to the rapacious sexuality of the Spanish soldiery, *fingieron demencia:* they pretended to be elsewhere. Simultaneously, they reproduced the medieval hierarchy of the sexes that prevailed in Europe: man as lord and master, woman as servant and reproductive machine. In his insightful book *Demons in the Convent,* the journalist and anthropologist Fernando Benítez eloquently described how the Church in the seventeenth century established an atmosphere of repressed eroticism. The archbishop of Mexico City, Aguiar y Seijas, a demonic man who walked with crutches and nourished a thousand phobias, *detested* women: they were not allowed in his presence. If, in a convent or monastery, a nun walked in front of him, he would *ipso facto* cover his eyes. Only men were worthy of his sight—men and Christ. In the religious paraphernalia of the Caribbean, Mexico, and South America, Jesus and the many saints appear almost totally unclothed, covering only their private parts with what in Spanish is known as *taparrabo;* whereas the Vírgen de Guadalupe, the Vírgen de la Caridad, the Vírgen del Cobre, and a thousand other incarnations of the Virgin Mary are fully dressed.

In a milieu where eroticism reigns, my volume on the Latin phallus is obviously far from original. In Oscar Hijuelos's Pulitzer prize-winning novel *The Mambo Kings Play Songs of Love* (1989), the male organ plays a crucial, obsessive role. The narrative is a sideboard of sexual roles in the Hispanic world. Nestor and Cesar Castillo, Cuban expatriates and musicians in New York City, personify Don Quixote and Sancho Panza: one is an outgoing idealist, the other an introverted materialist. Throughout Nestor's erotic adventures, Hijuelos refers to the penis as *la cosa:* the thing. Its power is hypnotic, totemic even: when men call on women to undo their trousers, women reach down without looking to unfasten their lover's buttons. The novel's libidinal voyeurism even extends to incestual scenes, like the one in which Delores, Hijuelos's female protagonist, finds herself in touch with her father's sexuality.

> In imitation of her mother in Havana, Delores would cook for her father, making do with what she could find at the market in those days of war rationing. One night she wanted to surprise him. After he had taken to his bed, she made some caramel-glazed *flan,* cooked up a pot of good coffee, and happily made her way down the narrow hallway with a tray of the quivering *flan.* Pushing open the door, she found her father asleep, naked, and in a state of extreme sexual arousal. Terrified and unable to move, she pretended that he was a statue, though his chest heaved and his lips

stirred, as if conversing in a dream. . . . He with his suffering
face, it, his penis, enormous. . . . The funny thing was that,
despite her fear, Delores wanted to pick up his thing and
pull it like a lever; she wanted to lie down beside him and
put her hand down there, releasing him from pain. She
wanted him to wake up; she didn't want him to wake up. In
that moment, which she would always remember, she felt
her soul blacken as if she had just committed a terrible sin
and condemned herself to the darkest room in hell. She
expected to turn around and find the devil himself standing
beside her, a smile on his sooty face, saying, "Welcome to
America."

For a culture as steeped in sexuality as our own, it is strange that the
substance of our masculine identity remains a forbidden topic. We are terri-
fied of exposing the labyrinthine paths of our unexplained desire, of engaging in what the Mexican essayist and poet Octavio Paz once called "the
shameful art of *abrirse*"—opening up and losing control, admitting our
insecurities, allowing ourselves to be exposed, unprotected, unsafe. We are
not Puritans; our bodies are not the problem. It is the complicated, ambiguous pathways of our desire that are too painful to bear. We have adopted the
armature of our Spanish conquerors: Hispanic men are machos, dominat-
ing figures, rulers, conquistadors—and also, closeted homosexuals. In *The
Labyrinth of Solitude,* Paz has been one of the lonely few to criticize male
sexuality:

The macho commits . . . unforeseen acts that produce
confusion, horror and destruction. He opens the world;
in doing so, he rips and tears it, and this violence pro-
vokes a great, sinister laugh. And in its own way, it is
just: it reestablished the equilibrium and puts things in
their place, by reducing them to dust, to misery, to
nothingness.

Unlike men, Hispanic women are indeed forced to open up. And they are
made to pay for their openness: they are often accused of impurity and
adulteration, sinfulness and infidelity. We inhabitants of the Americas live
in a nest of complementing stereotypes: on one side, flamboyant women,
provocative, well-built, sensual, lascivious, with indomitable, even bestial

nerve and intensity; on the other, macho men. Both seemingly revolve around the phallus, an object of intense adoration, the symbol of absolute power and satisfaction. It is the source of the macho's self-assurance and control, sexual and psychological, and the envy of the Hispanic woman. Our names for the penis are legion; besides the *parajito* of Cherríe Moraga's boxer-short reverie, it goes by *cornamusa, embutido, flauta, fusta, garrote, lanza, másta, miembro viril, pelón, peloncito, pene, pinga, plátano, príapo, pudendo, tesoro, tolete, tranca, verga,* and *zurriago,* among many others.

Where to begin describing the multiple ramifications of the adoration of the phallus among Hispanics? In the Caribbean, mothers rub a male baby's penis to relax him, to force him out of a tantrum. In Mexico the *charros* (*guasos* in Chile, *gauchos* in Argentina) are legendary rural outlaws, independent and lonely men. Their masculine adventures, clashes with corrupt landowners and politicos, live on through border ballads, known in the U.S.-Mexican border as *corridos,* and *payadores,* a type of South American minstrel who accompanies himself with a guitar. (The celebrated no-budget film by Robert Rodriguez, *El Mariachi,* is a revision of this cultural myth.) The Latin man and his penis are at the center of the Hispanic universe. Ironically, more than one rebellious Hispanic artist, including Andres Serrano, has equated the Latin penis to the crucifix. Which helps understand what is perhaps the greatest contradiction in Hispanic male sexuality: our machismo, according to the dictionary an exaggerated sense of masculinity stressing such attributes as courage, virility, and domination. Take bullfighting, an erotic event like no other, supremely parodied in Pedro Almodóvar's film *Matador.* Where else can the male strike such provocative sexual poses? Carlos Fuentes described the sport in his book *The Buried Mirror:* "The effrontery of the suit of lights, its tight-hugging breeches, the flaunting of the male sexual organ, the importance given to the buttocks, the obviously seductive and self-appraising stride, the lust for blood and sensation—the bullfight authorizes this incredible arrogance and sexual exhibitionism." Essentially bestial, the *corrida de toros* is a quasi-religious ceremony unifying beauty, sex, and death. The young bullfighter, an idol, is asked to face with grace and stamina the dark forces of nature symbolized in the bull. His sword is a phallic instrument. A renaissance knight modeled after Amadís de Gaula or Tirant Lo Blanc and parodied by Don Quixote, he will first subdue and then kill. *Viva el macho!* Blood will be spilled and ecstasies will arrive when the animal lies dead, at which point the bullfighter will take his hat off before a beautiful lady and smile. Man will prevail, the phallus remains all-powerful, and the conqueror will be showered with red flowers.

The Hispanic family encourages a familiar double-standard. Few societies prize female virginity with the conviction that we do. But while virginity is a prerequisite for a woman's safe arrival at the wedding canopy, men are encouraged to fool around, to test the waters, to partake of the pleasures of the flesh. Virgins are *mujeres buenas:* pure, ready to sacrifice their body for the sacred love of a man. Prostitutes, on the other hand, are hedonistic goddesses, *mujeres malas,* safeguards of the male psyche. Like most of my friends, I lost my virginity to a prostitute at the age of thirteen. An older acquaintance was responsible for arranging the "date," when a small group of us would meet an experienced harlot at a whorehouse. It goes without saying that none of the girls in my class were similarly "tutored": they would most likely become women in the arms of someone they loved, or thought they loved. But love, or even the slightest degree of attraction, were not involved in our venture. Losing our virginity was actually a dual mission: to ejaulate inside the hooker, and then, more important, to tell of the entire adventure afterwards. The telling, the story of the *matador* defeating his bull, the conqueror's display of power, was more crucial than the carnal sensation itself. I still remember the dusty art deco furniture and the blank expression of the woman. She was there to make me a man, to help me become an accepted member of society. Did we talk? She asked me to undress staightaway and proceeded to caress me. I was extremely nervous. What if I were unable to prove myself? The whole ceremony lasted twenty minutes, perhaps less. Afterward I concocted a predictable cover, announcing to my friends that the prostitute had been amazed at my prowess, that I had made her *very* happy, that she had been shocked at my chastity.

We told tall tales to compensate for the paucity of our accomplishments. After all, a prostitute is an easy triumph. Even consensual sex is an unworthy challenge for the aspiring macho. Courting women with serenades and flowers, seducing them, undressing and then fucking them, *chingar,* only to turn them out: that's the Hispanic male's hidden dream. *Chingar* signifies the ambiguous excess of macho sexuality. Octavio Paz's exploration of the sense of term concludes that the idea denotes a kind of failure: the active form means to rape, subdue, control, dominate. *Chingar* is what a macho does to women, what the Iberian soldiers did to the native Indian population, what corrupt politicos do to their electorate. And the irreplaceable weapon in the art of *chingar,* the key to the Hispanic worldview, is *el pito,* the phallus.

Not long ago, while writing on the Chicano Movement of the late sixties, I came across the extraordinary figure of Oscar "Zeta" Acosta, defender of the dispossessed. Born in 1935 in El Paso, Texas, Acosta became a lawyer and activist, well acquainted with César Chávez, Rodolfo "Corky" González, and other political leaders of the era. An admirer of Henry Miller and Jack Kerouac, and a close friend of Hunter S. Thompson, whom he accompanied in his travel to Las Vegas (Acosta is the 300-pound Samoan of *Fear and Looting in Las Vegas*), Acosta wrote a couple of intriguing novels about the civil rights upheaval in the Southwest: *The Autobiography of a Brown Buffalo,* published in 1972, and *The Revolt of the Cockroach People,* which appeared a year later. Both volumes detail a man's night of passage from adolescence to boastful machismo. A cover photograph by Annie Leibovitz showed Acosta as a Tennessee Williams–type, a perfectly insecure macho with flexed muscles and spiritual desperation in his eyes: he is in an undershirt and stylish suit pants, fat, the lines in his forehead quite pronounced. He is thirty-nine years old and looks a bit worn out. Besides this picture, nothing is certain about him, except, perhaps, the fact that in the early seventies he went to Mazatlán, a resort area and port on Mexico's Pacific coast, and disappeared without a trace.

The moral of Acosta can be used to understand what lies behind the ostentation and bravado of the macho: a deep-seated inferiority complex. The size and strength of the penis is the index of masculine value, as well as the passport to glorious erotic adventure. Inevitably, then, it is also a boundless source of anxiety.

Acosta is all emblem of the insecure Hispanic male. His machismo could not hide his confusion and lack of self-esteem. He spent his life thinking his penis was too small, which, in his words, automatically turned him into a fag. "Frugality and competition were my parents' lot," he writes, describing his and his brother's sexual education. "The truth of it was [they] conspired to make men out of two innocent Mexican boys. It seems that the sole purpose of childhood was to train boys how to be men. Not men of the future, but *now.* We had to get up early, run home from school, work on weekends, holidays and during vacations, all for the purpose of being men. We were supposed to talk like *un hombre*, walk like a man, act like a man, and think like a man." But Acosta's apprenticeship in masculinity was undermined by the embarrssment of his tiny phallus. He perceived himself as a freak, a virile metastasis.

> If it hadn't been for my fatness, I'd probably have been able to do those fancy assed jackknifes and swandives as well as the rest of you. But my mother had me convinced I was obese, ugly as a pig and without any redeeming qualities whatsoever. How then could I run around with just my jockey shorts? V-8's don't hide fat, you know. That's why I finally started wearing boxers. But by then it was too late. Everyone knew I had the smallest prick in the world. With the girls watching and giggling, the guys used to sing my private song to the tune of "Little Bo Peep"
> ... "Oh, where, oh where can my little boy be? Oh, where, oh where can he be? He's so chubby, *pansón,* that he can't move along. Oh, where, oh where can he be?"

Acosta is a unique figure among male Chicano novelists, in that his bitter, honest reflections do nothing to enhance his machismo.

> I lost most of my religion the same night I learned about sex from old Vernon. When I saw the white, foamy suds come from under his foreskin, I thought he had wounded himself from yanking on it too hard with those huge farmer hands of his. And when I saw his green eyes fall back into his head, I thought he was having some sort of seizure like I'd seen Toto the village idiot have out in his father's fig orchard after he fucked a chicken.
> I didn't much like the sounds of romance the first time I saw jizz. I knew that Vernon was as tough as they came. Nothing frightened or threatened him. He'd cuss right in front of John Hazard, our fag Boy Scout leader as well as Miss Anderson [our teacher]. But when I heard him OOOh and AAAh as the soap suds spit at his chest while we lay on our backs inside the pup tent, I wondered for a second if sex wasn't actually for sissies. I tried to follow his example,

but nothing would come out. With him cheering me on, saying, "Harder, man. Pull on that son of a bitch. Faster, faster!" it just made matters worse. The thing went limp before the soap suds came out.

He advised me to try it more often. "Don't worry, man. It'll grow if you work on it."*

Taboos die hard, if they ever do. After emigrating to the United States in 1985, my identity changed in drastic ways. I ceased to be Mexican and became Hispanic, and my attitude toward homosexuals underwent a metamorphosis. Still, that transformation took time. Even as homosexuals entered my peer group, and became my friends, I was uneasy. At times I wondered whether having homosexual friends would make others doubt my sexual identity. Though I've never had an intimate encounter with another man, I have often wondered what I would feel, how I would respond to a kiss. As José Ortega y Gasset said: *Yo soy yo y mi circunstancia,* I am the embodiment of my culture.

My father had taught me to show affection in public. When departing, he would kiss me without inhibition. But as I became an adolescent, I heard my friends whisper. Was I secretly a deviant? To be an Hispanic man was to hide one's emotions, to keep silent when it came to expressing your heart. We are supposed to swallow our pain and never cry *como una niña,* like girls. Keep a straight face, suck it up—*sé muy macho.* Many Hispanic adolescents still find role models in the confident and aggressively reserved stars of the Golden Age of Mexican film, black-and-white celebrities like Pedro Armendáriz, Jorge Negrete, and Pedro Infante, Hispanic analogues of James Dean and John Wayne. These figures were classic macho: ultra-masculine Emiliano Zapata mustaches, closely cropped dark hair, a mysterious Mona Lisa smile, thin, well-built bodies, and an unconquerable pride symbolized by the ubiquitous pistol. Vulnerability means cowardice. Deformity was not only evidence of weakness but a sign of unreadiness to face the tough world. In spite of his verbal bravura, Cantinflas, the Charlie Chaplin of Spanish-language films like *Ahí está el detalle,* was antimacho: poorly dressed, bad-

---

* I developed these reflections on Acosta's identity in my book *Bandido* (HarperCollins, 1995).

mouthed, short, unhandsome, without a gun and hence probably possessed of a tiny phallus.

Among Hispanics, homosexuals are the target of nearly insurmountable animosity. If the Latin phallus is adored in heterosexual relations, it is perceived as wild, diabolic, and uncontrollable for homosexuals. Reinaldo Arenas, the raw Cuban novelist who died of AIDS in New York City in 1990, argued that Latin society comprises five classes of homosexual: the *dog-collar gay*, boisterous and out, constantly being arrested at baths and beaches; the *common gay*, who is sure of his sexual identity but who never takes risks, save to attend a film festival or write an occasional poem; the *closeted gay*, a man with a wife and children and a public profile, who is reduced to sneaking off to the baths without his wedding ring; the *royal*, a man whose closeness to politicians and people of power allows him to be open about his sexual identity, to lead a "scandalous" life, while still holding public office; and finally the *macho*, whose cocksure bravado is intended to fend off questions about his sexual identity. It goes without saying that most gay men are forced to assume the less public personas.

In his second book, *Days of Obligation*, Richard Rodriguez includes an essay, "Late Victorians," about his own homosexuality and AIDS. He ponders the impact of the epidemic. "We have become accustomed to figures disappearing from our landscape. Does this not lead us to interrogate the landscape?" Very few in the Hispanic world have dared to address the subject: Hispanic gays remain a target of mockery and derision, forced to live on the fringes of society. To be gay is to be a freak, mentally ill, the sort of abnormality José Guadalupe Posada, the celebrated turn-of-the-century Mexican lampooner, often portrayed in his sarcastic cartoons: a creature with legs instead of arms, a dog with four eyes. And yet, homosexuality, a topic few are willing to address in public, is the counterpoint that defines our collective identity. Despite the stigma, homosexuals have been an ubiquitous presence in the Hispanic world, a constant from the Cuban sugar mill to the colonial *misión*, from Fidel Castro's cabinet to the literary intelligentsia. And, like St. Augustine's attitude toward the Jews, the established approach toward them follows the maxim: Don't destroy them, let them bear witness of the lawless paths of male eroticism. They are the other side of Hispanic sexuality: a shadow one refuses to acknowledge—a "they" that is really an "us." Again, the language betrays us: the panoptic array of terms for homosexual includes *adamado, adelito, afeminado, ahembrado, amaricado, amujerado, barbalindo, carininfo, cazolero, cocinilla, enerve, gay, homosexual, invertido, lindo, maría, marica, mariposa, ninfo, pisaverde, puto, repipí, sodomita, volteado, zape,* to name only a few.

I recall an occasion in which one of my Mexican publishers, the Colombian director of the extraordinarily powerful house Editorial Planeta, sat with me and a gay friend of mine from Venezuela. In a disgusting display of macho pyrotechnics, the man talked for the better part of an hour about the size of his penis. His shtick was full of degrading references to homosexuals, whom he described variously as kinky, depraved, and perverted. The presence of a self-identified "queer writer" at the table only stimulated his attack. He suggested that the United States was the greatest nation on earth, but that sexual abnormality would ultimately force its decline. Days later my Venezuelan colleague told me that the publisher had made a successful pass at him that very night. They shared a hotel room. This sort of attitude isn't uncommon. The Hispanic macho goes out of his way to keep appearances, to exalt his virility, but he often fails. Sooner or later, his glorious masculinity will be shared in bed with another man.

In the Mexico of the seventies in which I grew up, common sense had it that machos were the unchaste victims of an unsurpassed inferiority complex. Unchaste victims—impure, yes, but sympathetic characters, and commanding figures. Homosexuals, on the other hand, were considered oversensitive, vulnerable, mentally imbalanced, unproven in the art of daily survival. At school, the boys were constantly made to test their muscular strength. Girls were allowed to cry, to express their emotions, while we *men* were told to remain silent. If to open up was a sign of feminine weakness, to penetrate, *meter,* meant superiority. Sex—fucking—is how we prove our active, male self, subduing our passive, female half. Physical appearance was fundamental to this regime: obesity and limping were deviations from the norm, and hence effeminate characteristics.

Who is gay among us? It's a secret. We simply don't want to talk about it. Although a few essays have been written about Jorge Luis Borges's repressed homosexuality, the topic is evaded in Emir Rodríguez Monegal's 1978 biography. Borges lived most of his life with his mother and married twice: once, briefly, in his forties, and then to María Kodama a few months before his death in 1986, in order to turn her into the sole head of his estate. His writing is remarkable for its lack of sexuality. When his stories do verge on the intimate, they portray only rape or molestation. Still, the matter is hushed up, the details of a life subordinated to the dense lyricism of an oeuvre. Undoubtedly, concern for the master's reputation can explain some large part of the silence.

Take the case of John Rechy, whose 1963 novel *City of Night,* a book about hustlers, whores, drugs, and urban criminality, garnered him accolades and a reputation as one of the most promising Chicano writers of his generation. Shortly thereafter Rechy's book was categorized as a "gay novel," a stigma that tarred the book for Hispanic readers in the United States. It is only recently, since the onset of the North American gay rights movement, that Rechy's achievement has been reevaluated. And then there's Julio Cortázar, the celebrated Argentinean novelist and short-story writer responsible for *Hopscotch.* In 1983, at the peak of his fame and just a year before his tragic death, he made a trip to Cuba and then New York, there to address the United Nations about the *desaparecidos* in South America. Cortázar was alone, and lonely, as a strange sickness began taking over his body. He lost his appetite, became thinner, became susceptible to colds. After his divorce from Aurora Bernárdez some fifteen years previous, he had been involved with a number of women and men, although he tried desperately to keep his homosexual encounters secret. In the depths of his solitude, he told Luis Harss, he began to lose confidence in his own writing. A symbol of liberation for many Hispanics, Cortázar, so the rumor goes, probably contracted AIDS. He died in Paris, on 12 February 1984, when the epidemic was still largely unrecognized, its details elusive to scientists and never openly discussed. A number of Cortázar tales deal with homosexuality and lesbianism, including "Blow-Up," "The Ferry, or Another Trip to Venice," and "At Your Service." The last, the story of an elderly servant woman working as a dog-sitter in a wealthy Parisian home, moved a Cortázar specialist to ask him about his own homosexuality. He answered quite impersonally, with a lengthy dissertation on the general subject, a history of homosexuality from the open love of the Greeks to the present-day climate of ostracism and homophobia. "The attitude toward [it]," he suggested, "needs to be a very broad and open one, because the day in which homosexuals don't feel like . . . persecuted animals . . . they'll assume a much more normal way of life and fulfill themselves erotically and sexually without harming anyone and by being happy as much as possible as homosexual males and females." He concluded by applauding the more tolerant atmosphere of select North American and European societies. One might assume that the profound questions of sexuality and repression broached in this discussion would have had severe, productive, repercussions in the critical work on one of the giants of Latin American literature. But Cortázar's gay life, like Borges's, remains a forbidden issue.

Since the sixties, gay artists in Latin America have worked to put Latin homosexuality on the map. They have devised strategies to name the unnameable and map a symbolic picture of our collective erotic fears. The Argentine Manuel Mujica Láinez's 1962 novel *Bomarzo,* for instance, equates the male organ, and homosexuality in general, with the monstrous. Thanks to him and to many others (José Ceballos Maldonado, José Donoso, Carlos Arcidiácono, Reinaldo Arenas, José Lezama Lima, Richard Rodriguez, Manuel Puig, Virgilio Piñera, Severo Sarduy, Xavier Villaurrutia, Luis Zapata, and Fernando Vallejo), a small window of vulnerability has been created, a space for the interrogation of suffocating, monolithic sex roles. The most significant of these, to my mind, are Puig, Arenas, and José Lezama Lima. *Kiss of the Spider Woman,* Puig's most celebrated work, directed for the screen by Héctor Babenco, portrayed a forced male relationship in a unspecified prison in Latin America. The film made waves from Ciudad Juárez to the Argentine Pampa with its startling conclusion, a kiss between a macho Marxist revolutionary and a gay man, and the suggestion that the characters complemented each other.

Puig is one of the principal characters in the long history of homophobia and gay bashing in the Hispanic world. In the early seventies the committee for the prestigious Seix Barral award in Spain selected his first novel, which the filmmaker Néstor Almendros and novelist Juan Goytisolo openly endorsed. But the publisher rejected the recommendation of the selection committee because of Puig's sexual orientation. He was similarly stigmatized in his native country, where the Peronists banned his work, calling it "pornographic propaganda."

Puig died in his mid-fifties in 1990, in Cuernavaca, Mexico, during a bizarre (and suspicious) gall bladder operation. Was it AIDS? Puig chose to keep silent about his impending demise. At the time I was preparing a special issue of *The Review of Contemporary Fiction* about his *oeuvre* and had been in contact with him. I last saw him at a public reading at the 92nd Street Y a few months before his death; he looked thin but energetic. There was no mention of an illness. Of course, having been burned so many times before, it was unlikely that he would open up now. Two years after Puig's death, Jaime Manrique, the Colombian author of *Latin Moon in Manhattan* and a close friend of Puig, reconstructed the gay subtext of Puig's life in a moving reminiscence, "Manuel Puig: The Writer as Diva," for *Christopher Street*. After considering the possibility of Puig opening up, *abrirse,* in public, Manrique concluded that whatever honors Puig could still hope for were infinitely more secure with his personal secrets kept hidden. In the end, he had moved back to Cuernavaca with his beloved mother, spending the last months of his life "busy building his first and last home in this world," a fortress closed to strangers, filled with Hollywood memorabilia. Puig's death is emblematic of the fate of the Hispanic gay.

Puig's work was remarkably tame, at least with regard to the representation of the Latin penis; he feared the persecution of the Argentine military, and only ever depicted its image in a short section in the novel *Blood of Required Love.* Like most gays in the Hispanic world, Puig was trapped between his sexual preference and the prejudices of the larger society. And yet, what is distinctive about him and the literary generation that came of age in the wake of the sixties is the desublimation of the phallus. Puig and other gay writers began a process of *apertura:* they have named names, celebrated and mocked Latin masculinity and the omnipresent phallus.

Reinaldo Arenas is probably the best-known openly gay writer from Latin America. His writings explore Latin sexuality and the phallus with eloquence. His final years, prior to his suicide—years marked by extreme fits of depression, a chronic and abrasive pneumonia, paranoia, and increasing misanthropy—saw him complete a surrealist novel, an autobiography, the last two installments of the *Pentagonía,* a five-volume novelization of the "secret history of Cuba." *Before Night Falls,* the autobiography, is destined to become a classic. It traces Arenas's birth in Holguín in 1943 as well as his rural childhood; his difficult transition to Havana, his friendships with Virgilio Piñera, José Lezama Lima, Lydia Cabrera, and other important Cuban artists and intellectuals; his "youthful loyalty" to Castro's socialist regime and his subsequent disenchantment with the revolution; his betrayal by a family member; the persecution, "re-education," and imprisonment he suffered in Havana's infamous El Morro prison because of his homosexuality; his participation in the 1980 Mariel boatlift; and his bondage experiences in Florida and Manhattan.

Dictated to a tape-recorder and then transcribed by friends, *Before Night Falls* is one of the most incendiary, sexually liberating texts ever to come from Latin America. Published posthumously in 1990, shortly after the long-suffering author committed suicide in his New York City apartment, it appeared in English in 1993. Its confessional style and courageous depiction of homosexual life make it a remarkable and haunting book. Its impact on the Spanish-speaking world, including Spain (where it appeared under the prestigious Tusquets imprint), has been enormous. "I think I always had a huge sexual appetite," writes Arenas. "Not only mares, sows, hens, or turkeys, but almost all animals were objects of my sexual passion, including dogs. There was one particular dog who gave me great pleasure. I would hide with him behind the garden tended by my aunts, and would make him suck my cock. The dog got used to it and in time would do it freely."

Guillermo Cabrera Infante, a fellow Cuban, summed up Arenas's career in an obituary published in *El País:* "Three passions ruled the life and death of Reinaldo Arenas: literature (not as game, but as a consuming fire), passive sex, and active politics. Of the three, the dominant passion was, evidently, sex. Not only in his life, but in his work. He was a chronicler of a country ruled not by the already impotent Fidel Castro, but by sex. . . . Blessed with a raw talent that almost reaches genius in his posthumous book, he lived a life whose beginning and end were indeed the same: from the start, one long, sustained sexual act. . . ." And indeed, Arenas repeatedly describes his sexual intercourse with animals, family members, children, old people, friends, lovers, and strangers. The volume ends with a personal letter, written shortly before Arenas's death, in which he bids farewell to friends and enemies. "Due to my delicate state of health and to the horrible emotional depression it causes me not to be able to continue writing and struggling for the freedom of Cuba, I am ending my life," Arenas writes. "Persons near to me are not in any way responsible for my decision. There is only one person to hold accountable: Fidel Castro."

The autobiography details his multifarious sexual encounters. He recalls the fashion in which he was abused by his grandfather, his close attachment to his mother, a woman who left Cuba early on in the child's life to make money for the family by working in Florida. What's remarkable is the fact that the book comes out of the Spanish-speaking world, where erotic confessions are few, and seldom related to politics.

> In [Cuba], I think, it is a rare man who has not had
> sexual relations with another man. Physical desire over-

powers whatever feelings of machismo our fathers take upon themselves to instill in us. An example of this is my uncle Rigoberto, the oldest of my uncles, a married, serious man. Sometimes I would go to town with him. I was just about eight years old and we would ride on the same saddle. As soon as we were both on the saddle, he would begin to have an erection. Perhaps in some way my uncle did not want this to happen, but he could not help it. He would put me in place, lift me up and set my butt on his penis, and during that ride, which would take an hour or so, I was bounding on that large penis, riding, as it were, on two animals at the same time. I think eventually Rigoberto would ejaculate. The same thing happened on the way back from town. Both of us, of course, acted as if we were not aware of what was happening. He would whistle or breathe hard while the horse trotted on. When he got back, Carolina, his wife, would welcome him with open arms and a kiss. At the moment we were all very happy.

Arenas's other major work, the *Pentagonía* quintet, is similarly obsessive about sex and politics. Though the text has fascinated critics for some time, it continues to scare lay readers. All exercise in literary experimentation modeled after the French *nouveau roman,* the first three volumes, *Singing from the Well, The Palace of the White Skunks,* and *Farewell to the Sea,* display a fractured narrative and convoluted plot that often make them appear impenetrable. *The Assault,* the fifth installment, is the most accessible. A compelling exercise in science fiction, it is structured as a tribute to Orwell's *1984* and Kafka's *The Castle.* It is narrated by a government torturer, a leader of the so-called Anti-Perversion Brigade, who spends his days visiting concentration camps and prisons looking for the sexual criminals to annihilate. The book's nightmarish landscape is a futuristic Caribbean island deliberately similar to Cuba under Castro's dictatorship. At the heart of the book is the torturer's search for his mother, whom he glimpses from afar but seems unable to approach. He is passionate and inscrutable in his hatred for her, ready to undertake any action that might lead to her destruction. The book opens: "The last time I saw my mother, she was out behind the National People's Lumber Cooperative gathering sticks." Approaching her, the narrator thinks to himself: "This is my chance; I knew I could not waste a second.

I ran straight for her, and I would have killed her, too, but the old bitch must have an eye where her asshole ought to be, because before I could get to her and knock her down and kill her, that old woman whirled around to meet me." With macabre echoes of Luis Buñuel, the allegory is not difficult to decipher: pages into the book, the reader comes to understand that the torturer's mother is Castro himself. As the search for her continues in various "Servo-Perimeters" of the land, Arenas prepares us for a colossal encounter, savage and profane. In the final scene, Arenas's protagonist fearlessly employs his penis one last time: he fucks and then kills his lover, whose identity is dual: his own mother, whom he describes as a cow, and the Resident, as Fidel Castro himself.

> With my member throbbingly erect, and my hands on my hips, I stand before her, looking at her. My hatred and my revulsion and my arousal are now beyond words to describe. And then the great cow, naked and horrible, white and stinking, plays her last card; the sly bitch, crossing her ragged claws over her monstrous breasts, looks at me with tears in her eyes and she says *Son.* That is all I can bear to hear. All the derision, all the harassment, all the fear and frustration and blackmail and mockery and contempt that the word contains—it slaps me in the face, and I am stung. My erection swells to enormous proportions, and I begin to step toward her, my phallus aimed dead for its mark, the fetid, stinking hole. And I thrust. As she is penetrated, she gives a long, horrible shriek, and then she collapses. I sense my triumph—I come, and I feel the furious pleasure of discharging myself in her. Howling, she explodes in a blast of bolts, washers, screws, pieces of shrapnel-like tin, gasoline, smoke, semen, shit, and streams of motor oil. Then, at the very instant of my climax, and of her final howl, a sound never heard before washes across the square below us . . . While the crowd goes on moving through the city, hunting down and destroying to the accompaniment of the music of its own enraged whispering, I tuck the limp mass of my phallus (now at last spent and flaccid) into my overalls. Weary, I make my

way unnoticed through the noise and the riot (the crowd
in a frenzy of destruction, like children, crying *The
Resident is dead, the beast at last is dead!*), and I come to
the wall of the city. I walk down to the shore. And I lie
down in the sand.

It is the singular achievement of the gay Cuban writer Lezama Lima to
have provided an accounting of the Latin phallus equal to its inflated importance in the Hispanic world. Lezama Lima (1912–76) was the author of
Paradiso, published in 1966, a book hailed by Julio Cortázar and others as a
masterpiece. It was a remarkable text: in the words of the critic Gerald Martin, the text rendered "both classical and Catholic imagery, lovingly but also
scandalously, achieving the remarkable double coup of offending both the
Catholic Church and the Cuban Revolution through its approach to eroticism in general and homosexuality in particular." Chapter VIII details the
promiscuous sexual adventures of young cassanovas Farraluque and Leregas.
Leregas's penis, which would swiftly grow from the length of a thimble to
"the length of the forearm of a manual laborer," becomes legendary among
his classmates:

> Unlike Farraluque's, Leregas's sexual organ did not
> reproduce his face, but his whole body. In his sexual
> adventures his phallus did not seem to penetrate but to
> embrace the other body. Eroticism by compression, like
> a bear cub squeezing a chestnut, that was how his first
> moans began. The teacher was monotonously reciting
> the text, and most of his pupils, fifty or sixty in all, were
> seated facing him, but on the left, to take advantage of a
> niche-like space, there were two benches lined up at
> right angles to the rest of the class. Leregas was sitting at
> the end of the first bench. Since the teacher's platform
> was about a foot high, only the face of his phallic colos-
> sus was visible to him. With calm indifference, Leregas
> would bring out his penis and testicles, and like a wind
> eddy that turns into a sand column, at a touch it became
> a challenge of exceptional size. His row and the rest of
> the students peered past the teacher's desk to view that
> tenacious candle, ready to burst out of its highly pol-

ished, blood-filled helmet. The class did not blink and its silence deepened, making the lecturer think that the pupils were morosely following the thread of his discursive expression, a spiritless exercise during which the whole class was attracted by the dry phallic splendor of the bumpkin bear cub. When Leregas's member began to deflate, the coughs began, the nervous laughter, the touching of elbows to free themselves from the stupefaction they had experienced. "If you don't keep still, I'm going to send some students out of the room," the little teacher said, vexed at the sudden change from rapt attention to a progressive swirling uproar.

The chapter becomes increasingly daunting as the florid prose continues.

An adolescent with such a thunderous generative attribute was bound to suffer a frightful fate according to the dictates of the Pythian. The spectators in the classroom noted that in referring to the Gulf's currents the teacher would extend his arm in a curve to caress the algaed coasts, the corals, and anemones of the Caribbean. That morning, Leregas's phallic dolmen had gathered those motionless pilgrims around the god terminus as it revealed its priapic extremes, but there was no mockery or rotting smirk. To enhance his sexual tension, he put two octavo books on his member, and they moved like tortoises shot up by the expansive force of a fumarole. It was the reproduction of the Hindu myth about the origin of the world.

The phallus remains an all-consuming image for Hispanic society, whether as the absent, animating presence in the *repressive* culture of machismo or the furtive purpose of the *repressed* culture of homosexuality. It is the representation of masculine desire, a fantastic projection of guilt, shame, and power. Hyperactive bravura and suppressed longing are its twin modalities.

Like its subject, my little text on the Latin phallus has swelled to gargantuan proportions. I now envision an open book, steeped in the infinite richness of reality, a Borgesian volume of volumes incorporating every detail of every life of every man and woman in the Hispanic world, alive and dead—the record of every innocent or incestuous look, every masturbatory fantasy, every kiss, every coitus since 1492 and perhaps even before. The book is already in us and outside us, simultaneously real and imaginary, fatal and prophetic, *abierto* and *cerrado*. As a civilization, we *are* such a history—a living compendium of our baroque sexual behaviors. From Bernal Díaz del Castillo's chronicle of the subjugation of Tenochtitlán to Mario Vargas Llosa's novella *In Praise of the Stepmother*, from Carlos Fuentes's climax in *Christopher Unborn* to José Donoso's *The Obscene Bird of Night* and his untranslated erotic novel *La misteriosa desaparición de la Marquesita de Loria*, from Lope de Vega's Golden Age *comedies* to Sor Juana Inés de La Cruz's superb baroque poetry and Cherríe Moraga's *peloncito*, the tortuous history of our sexuality is the story of the Latin phallus. In a continent where tyranny remains an eternal ghost and democracy (the open society, *la sociedad abierta*) an elusive dream, the phallus is an unmerciful dictator, the totemic figure of our longing.

[1995]

17 / TRANSLATION AND IDENTITY

The original is unfaithful to the translation.
> —Jorge Luis Borges, "On
> *Vatek,* by William Beckford"

I

Translation, its delicious traps, its labyrinthine losses, was at the birth of the Americas, and I am often struck by the fact that to this day, the role language played during their conquest is often minimized, if not simply overlooked. There's little doubt that without the "interpreters," as Hernán Cortés referred to them, an enterprise of such magnitude would have been utterly impossible. Although *la conquista* was a military endeavor encompassing social, political, and historical consequences, it was also, and primarily, a verbal occupation, an unbalanced polyglot encounter. More than a hundred different dialects spoken from the Yucatán peninsula to modern-day California were reduced to silence, and Spanish became the ubiquitous vehicle of communication, the language of business, government, and credo. Through persistence and persuasion, Cortés and Pizarro, to name only the most representative warriors, took control of the powerful Aztec and Inca empires. Cortés, for one, was astute enough to convince their unprepared, naive monarchs, Moctezuma II and Cuauthémoc, that he indeed was Quetzalcóatl, the Plumed Serpent, a bearded god the Aztec calendar had been prophesying as a triumphant sign for the coming of a new age. But to make themselves understood, he and his Spanish knights were constantly on the lookout for a very special type of soldier: the translator, capable of using words as weapons, reading not only the enemy's messages but its mind as well; someone who, in modern terms, would be not only perfectly multilingual but, more important, a cultural analyst able to explain one culture, one *weltanschauung* to another. Only by enlisting a "word wizard" were they able to achieve their goals; translators needed to be true loyalists, part of the invader's army, at once supporters and promoters who would eventually have a share of the gain and make victory their own.

These reflections recently came to mind during a pleasant afternoon reading sacred Nahuatl poetry. Indeed, although I don't purport to be a specialist in pre-Columbian literature, my interest in the ancient cultures of the Americas has produced ongoing readings and book collecting, and I was happily wandering through the work of Daniel G. Brinton, the first American ever to translate from the Nahuatl into English, when I was struck by the obvious: the difficulty of making the pre-Columbian people accessible to modern readers. Their poetry, an expression of their vision of time, their dreams and frustrations, has changed countless times in front of our very eyes; they are what we want them to be; and what one commentator believed they were is light-years away from the views of others. In spite of many generous scientific discoveries, dating back to the early nineteenth century, about Macchu Picchu, Tenochtitlán, and other ruined population centers, the pre-Columbians are nothing but our own image reflected in a distorted mirror: the observer observing himself in others. From the moment it clashed with European culture to our fin-de-siècle, Nahuatl civilization was betrayed and misrepresented, then renewed and reinvented, by innumerable interpreters. More than five hundred years after their tragic subjugation, their world-view remains a puzzle—alien, exotic, unclear to us—the product of adventurous scholars (mostly Mexicans) unmasking a certain facet, contradicting a predecessor, searching for lost sources. And although since World War II the new discoveries have been nothing but outstanding, the added collective efforts are still incomplete; they certainly don't present a fair, comprehensive view simply because the Nahuatl civilization was almost erased by the European invaders. Finding clues to its identity is a challenge worthy of a superhuman detective.

All this signals the impotence of translation, the act of bridging out by means of language. Obviously, finding such useful "bridges," such vital entities, has proven to be an incredibly difficult task. For purposes of argumentation, let me focus on Cortés's conquest of Mexico. Bernal Díaz del Castillo, in his chronicle of the conquest of Tenochtitlán, recounts how, around 1517, two Mayans, Melchorejo and Julianillo, were captured in the Yucatán peninsula by Capt. Francisco Hernández de

Córdoba. In spite of their shyness and introversion, which we would probably interpret today as a lack of desire to cooperate, they were forced to become interpreters. In keeping with their new role, they were treated better than other prisoners of war. After traveling to Cuba to answer the questions of a governor anxious to know if their land had any gold mines, and thus passing the crucial test of a tête-à-tête with the highest authority, Melchorejo and Julianillo were asked to dress up and behave like Europeans. They were given their own hamlet in Santiago; they were required to attend mass and were indoctrinated in the ways of the Church, and they were taught as much oral Spanish as they could digest. But in spite of the intense training, their patrons remained suspicious of the Indians' ultimate motives and service, mainly because, as Díaz del Castillo puts it, Melchorejo and Julianillo were incapable of looking one in the eyes. They had an obnoxious way of looking down to the floor, not as a sign of respect, but to evade contact. And, just as expected, when the interpreters traveled to Cozumel with the expedition of Juan de Grijalba, it was clear to many that the Spanish message was only being partially conveyed to the natives, if only because, after a friendly exchange, the enemy didn't show up for the next agreed-upon meeting. The Spaniards, needless to say, were very worried.

We know very little about Melchorejo and Julianillo. Unlike the military heroes of the time, these translators are but a footnote in history, their words overshadowed by the weaponry of those interested in action, in wealth, in fame, not in communication and understanding. Even if their skills were indeed questionable, they deserve some sort of acknowledgment; instead, their fate, I'm afraid, is the one commonly granted to translators: oblivion. While their death is actually recorded by Díaz del Castillo, it is done only in passing, without much fanfare; they have no monuments and their memory is never celebrated. Julianillo apparently died either of sadness or as a victim of one of the many epidemics decimating the native population at the time. Melchorejo, on the other hand, had a more heroic, if also more tragic, death. He changed sides around 1519, when he understood that Cortés's real intentions were disastrous. Rather than delivering his translation in a cold, straightforward, objective manner, after the crucial battle in Tabasco, he took off his European costume, regained his Indian identity, and ran to his people to explain what he knew. But his was not a happy welcome: after listening to what he had to say, the Tabascans killed him in revenge for his many lies, his betrayal, and his hypocrisy.

No doubt the most distinguished bridge between languages and cultures during the conquest of Mexico, at least the one mythologized since early on, was a woman whose name is as evasive as her biography, but one who, we know for sure, acted as an interpreter wholeheartedly and with very few reservations. Known as Marina, Malina, Malinalli, Malintzin, and Malinche, she was at once a translator, Cortés's concubine, and an endeared presence among the Spanish army—Latin America's counterpart to Pocahontas. Some historians believe she was born in a small town some forty kilometers from Coatzacoalcos, was sold as merchandise after her father's death, and became Cortés's mistress (she mothered one of his sons, Martín Cortés) after he stole her from a high-ranking official. Cortés himself mentions her often in his *Cartas de Relación,* and so does Díaz del Castillo in his chronicle. Whereas Melchorejo and Julianillo remain in shadow, Malinche is famous: her stature inspires and infuriates, so much so that Mexicans apply the term *malinchista* to a person who sells his country to foreign forces for his own sake. Malinche knew the value of sleeping with the powerful commander of the Spanish army. She was fluent in many native dialects and quickly picked up the rules of Spanish; above all, she understood the role of translator as loyalist and charlatan. Aside from interpreting, her function was to advance her lover's military purposes. Her words were intimately linked to her body: one couldn't function without the other; the message and her personal beliefs were deeply intertwined. In short, Malinche personifies the translator as concubine. Scorned for years, Mexicans today perceive her as the true mother of the nation, the woman who used her body to betray her people, who incorporated European manners into her repertoire while incubating the mestizo race.

Malinche, of course, was never an impartial, objective interpreter; far from our modern view of what literary translators are called to do, she wasn't looking for aesthetic beauty, for honest communication across cultures. Her role was purely strategic: she misled and deceived her peers and ultimately helped dismantle the Aztec empire. She used words as artillery to unveil the secrets of the Aztec mind and thus helped Cortés and his men appreciate the real strength of their enemy. But it would be a mistake to assume that her role as word wizard was something new and alien to the Nahuatl and other autochthonous people. Interpreters such as she must have prevailed in Mexico between the late fourteenth and early sixteenth centuries. In order to interact, to do business, the many pre-Columbian cultures that populated Mesoamerica before 1492 were surely in need of interpreters. While a true *lingua franca* did not exist, dialects were considered more or less important depending on the force their speakers exerted. Thus the Nahuatls, the Mayans, the Otomis, and other groups were somehow acquainted with the business of adapting their words for those lacking knowledge of their tongue. Yet all this can be an understatement if one fails to realize that, once aligned with the Spaniards, translators such as Malinche were involved in a sophisticated form of deception. They could see the military advantage the invaders had over the natives; they were witnesses to a catastrophe of immense proportions; and yet, more often than not their personal interests had more weight than the suffering of their people. It's the classical portrait of the Latin American scoundrel: once in power, the Spaniards granted them high esteem and celebrated them as heroes. And while these translators (mostly aborigines) are obviously not to be blamed for the dynamite the Europeans fired against the native population, they certainly played a crucial role in their tragic disappearance. Since the Nahuatl conceived the idea of preserving one's past only through oral tradition (an advance alphabet was still in the making when the Spaniards arrived), European chroniclers—liberal friars and priests devoted to saving what was being demolished—could not do enough to rescue aboriginal culture from being eclipsed. Their own capacity to understand native culture was limited, linguistically and psychologically. Consequently, what we have left today is but a minuscule slice of ancient native Mexican civilization. Add to this the fact that since 1523 other so-called interpreters have obscured the lens through which we could have begun to appreciate Nahuatl culture. Proselytes found Christian imagery in ancient manuscripts, for example, destroying and revamping old texts. To understand the implications of the conquest in Mexico, imagine who we would be today if only a twelfth of *The Divine Comedy* was all that was available from ancient and medieval Europe—and not in Italian but in a language totally forbidden to us.

II

As a result, the corpus of pre-Columbian literature available today is quite small. For argument's sake, take Nahuatl poetry again as an example: what we have are no more than twenty sacred hymns, collected by Fray Bernardino de Sahagún; songs scattered in several annals and testimonies; the manuscript of *Cantares mexicanos y otros opúsculos*, collected by an anonymous priest and kept at Universidad Nacional Autónoma de México; and the manuscript of *Romances de los señores de la Nueva España*, housed at the University of Texas at Austin. Most of what we know about the Nahuatl people is a result of the intense scholarly studies of Angel María Garibay and Miguel León Portilla. The lack of familiarity with the original culture makes the translation process unfair and problematic: translations are first done into Spanish, and then into other European languages. A few exceptions occur: Eduard Seler, for example, has worked directly in German. Daniel G. Brinton was the first ever to bring Nahuatl poetry out from obscurity in his books *Rig Ved Americanus* and *Ancient Nahuatl Poetry*, both published in Philadelphia at the end of the nineteenth century and translated directly into English. Brinton's work was based on the manuscript of *Cantares de los mexicanos*, which, as he stated from the outset, was an incomplete transcription by one Abbé de Bourbourg, signaling, once again, the innumerable abuses to which this type of material has been exposed. How much or how little of the final work was a product of Brinton's own making has been a subject of speculation. León Portilla, Seler, and Garibay have found his translations loyal, if extravagant. Brinton's anthropological obsession to compare the Nahuatl civilization to ancient India also puts him in trouble. But more than anything else, his erratic English makes for a questionable, if interesting, version. Still, Brinton's work is amazing in that it needed no intermediary language. León Portilla himself has recently published a collection of his own, *Fifteen Poets of the Aztec World*, where he translates into English material he anthologized in 1967 and subsequently expanded on at least five occasions. This collection is immensely more reliable than Brinton's; his technique, yet again, employed Spanish as the bridge language.

Correlating Brinton's work with León Portilla's can be a frustrating act. More than a hundred years of research and analysis run from the pages of one into the other. Brinton only had a segment of the Nahuatl legacy in front of him; he had no predecessors to map his route; and more important, he was unable to individualize poets because other historical sources were still unknown. And yet, in spite of his many short-comings, his Victorian English translations ought to be acknowledged because he happily inaugurated a tradition that is slowly expanding. His task as interpreter, perhaps unconsciously, was an attempt to undo what Julianillo, Melchorejo, and Malinche had helped to achieve: the closing of the Nahuatl mind. But one should approach the texts cautiously once one is past the initial sense of joy felt in coming for the first time face-to-face with a universe long gone. I cannot but encourage the reader to consult *Fifteen Poets of the Aztec World,* which identifies individual poets and comments historically and literally on themes and motifs: flowers, life as a dream, the cravings of the heart, the death of a monarch, the passing of time, and so on. The effort to establish a link between the two translations will not be meaningless and will somehow help reduce the endless chain of misinterpretations that has victimized Nahuatl literature. The work of Garibay and León Portilla has done much to disclose what translators and interpreters during the colonial period and afterwards had actively misinterpreted.

Nowadays we thankfully have volumes such as J. Richard Andrews's *Introduction to Classical Nahuatl,* which begin to unveil the Nahuatl language and world-view for us. We are beginning to learn, for example, to what extent the Nahuatl people were devoted to contemplation and the role poetry played in society. We have also been able to penetrate the oeuvre of a handful of Nahuatl poets, most important King Netzahual-cóyotl (1401–72) and Aquiauhtzin de Ayapanco (circa 1430–90). Diego Durán, in his *Historia de las Indias,* describes the Nahuatl poet as playing a crucial role among the elite: rulers were constantly surrounded by singers and dancers, and rhymes were taught to children in school. Concerts, sometimes from early morning to nightfall, were performed in front of a large audience, and beloved poets, accompanied by melodious instruments, were asked to perform in public. If the importance of music, lyrics, and dance in modern Mexican villages is any sign, Durán's words must be true: people rejoice in fiestas and use poetry to recount individual or collective anecdotes and happenings. Sahagún,

Clavigero, and Torquemada explained that Nahuatl poetry was divided into historical and fictitious plots. But Garibay and León Portilla have taken us much farther: they explored the fiesta as ritual, analyzed the sacred hymns known as *Teocuícatl,* and made available what León Portilla calls *la visión de los vencidos,* the Indian accounts and eyewitness testimony of the conquest. After Brinton opened the door, they expanded our horizon.

But Brinton and his successors are as much interpreters as they are translators, bridges in the tradition of Melchorejo, Julianillo, and Malinche. Brinton's language of reception, English, allowed him to open up, in his own terms, the pre-Columbian mind to Western civilization. Similarly, Cortés's and Pizarro's translators, albeit reluctantly, had made accessible to Europeans their own personal interpretation of the Americas by means of explaining in a rudimentary Spanish their non-Western linguistic codes. The overall result is nothing but a global misapprehension; one could even say delusion. A sense of this verbal maze can be captured in full the moment one realizes that Hispanics and Brazilians today communicate in a language that is theirs only by imposition. The fact that they talk, the fact that they read and write in Spanish and Portuguese, already carries a degree of falsification. In order to insert themselves into Western culture, they have appropriated, or have been appropriated by, a communication vehicle that wasn't theirs in the first place. In short, as a result of its colonial history, Latin America, to paraphrase Robert Frost, is what is lost in translation. It is also what is lost in interpretation.

Literature, more specifically the art of fiction, is the magnifying glass which more clearly exposes the abyss between reality and language, world and word. Why have the region's artists and writers been so imaginative and its politicians so unimaginative? The answer, perhaps, is that in the eyes of foreigners, the colorful, exotic, or, to use the fashionable term *magical,* reality south of the Rio Grande has always been a field of dreams. We might not know much about the pre-Columbian civilizations, but what is clear from the historical artifacts we have inherited (hieroglyphics, codices, vessels, and architectural wonders) is that they had a florid fantasy life. André Breton once described Latin America as "a Surrealist Continent," a land where chaos and the unknown, the instinctual and the unconscious, prevail—a land, clearly, essentially un-Western. Others have added layers to his concept, describing it as "marvelous." But the Cuban musicologist and homme de lettres Alejo Carpentier, in his famous 1949 prologue to *The Kingdom of This World,* tried to reverse Breton's concept. After a trip to Haiti, he argued that Latin America was the perfect stage of *lo real maravilloso,* where the triteness of Europe was left behind, where the search for an imaginary utopia is mixed with astonishing surprises, where the world is always in a stage of unfinishedness. He realized during his journey

> that the presence and authority of the real marvelous was not a privilege to Haiti but the patrimony of all the Americas, where, for example, a census of cosmogonies is still to be established. The real marvelous is found at each step in the lives of the men who inscribed dates on the history of the Continent and who left behind names still borne by the living: from the seekers after the Fountain of Youth or the golden city of Manoa to certain rebels of the early times or certain modern heroes of our wars of independence, those of such mythological stature as Colonel Juana Azurduy.

And yet, to make "the real marvelous" accessible to internal and external observers requires its translation to bring it to a "standard" code of communication. When the Mexican thinker José Joaquín Fernández de Lizardi plots *The Itching Parrot,* when the Chilean poet Pablo Neruda shapes his masterpiece *Canto general,* when the Guatemalan Miguel Angel Asturias delivers *El Señor Presidente,* when the Brazilian mulatto Joaquim Maria Machado de Assis writes his *Epitaph for a Small Winner,* and when Isabel Allende gives the final touches to *The House of the Spirits,* the appropiation of a nonnative language has been completed to deliver a view of this side of the Atlantic to international readers, the very same readers educated by Ovid, Dante, Cervantes, and Shakespeare. The images might be original, but not so the verbal code. In fact, we can even talk about a form of linguistic cannibalism: in order to be members of Western civilization, Latin Americans need to be initiated into, and then are forced to perfect, the language of the invader. Cannibalism, as a metaphor of the struggle to at once define and translate oneself to the rest of the world, is certainly not a new idea. In runs throughout the chronology of the whole hemisphere, acquiring different masks, being called by different names, depending on the context. In Brazil, for instance, Oswald de Andrade, while stationed in Paris in the 1920s with his wife, painter Tarsila do Amaral, awoke to the possibilities of the so-called primitive art of his own country as a source of inspiration. And some years after returning home in 1923, he published the *Manifesto Antropófago*. Its central message, in the words of critic Edward Lucie-Smith, was that "Brazilian artists must devour outside influences, digest them thoroughly and turn them into something new"; in other words, to use the verbs and punctuation, the manners and excesses of Europeans ad nauseam until a refreshing view, a distinctive Brazilian approach to the universe, can be recognized. Translation as anthropophagy.

All this makes any translation from Spanish into English, or for that matter any other European language, an attempt at removing what was already once removed. If what Malinche conveyed to Cortés is already a falsification, a deformation, an interpretation, her words, or what she purportedly said, once they are translated from Spanish into another tongue, take the listener even farther away from the original source. By this I'm not suggesting, at least not in concrete terms, that whenever he writes, García Márquez, or any of the other Latin American literati before or after him, is, in essence, translating himself. His native vocabulary is his by subject of inheritance: he was born into, and raised in, Quevedo's language; and for that simple reason it's his as much as it's Quevedo's. One cannot forget, obviously, that, as a product of endless transformations, Spanish itself is a hybrid, a sum of parts, an addition. Its roots can be found in vulgar Latin, in Arabic, in Castilian and other Romance tongues of the Middle Ages and Renaissance. Besides, like all other languages, Spanish is the property and product of its speakers, no matter who they have been and where they have lived. This means that García Márquez, by virtue of history, is as much its owner as any Spaniard today. And yet, Aracataca, where the Colombian was born in 1928, was a landscape where pre-Columbian languages and dialects were used. That is, its usage necessarily implies the eclipse of other grammatical structures, subdued by external forces.

Furthermore, when the Spanish knights and Catholic proselytes arrived, they didn't only bring their physical presence but, also, and more important, a whole set of values and traditions, which include, among a vast array of offerings, the novel and verse poem as we know them. In order for *One Hundred Years of Solitude* to be written in the mid-sixties, its author needed to be immersed, in one form or another, in the European novelistic tradition: he had to know what the novel as cultural artifact is about, its purposes and limitations. He obviously had to be acquainted with at least a small number of early practitioners. For García Márquez to revolutionize the genre, he first was required to be familiar with it. He was first required to impregnate himself in its European style and language. When writing it, he unconsciously, one could even say inadvertently, cannibalized a foreign artistic vessel and, even if it was his from his very birth on, he also appropriated an outside tongue.

What kind of collective identity emerges from this act of losing and regaining oneself in translation? A complex question. Since Cortés and Pizarro, the continent has been inhabited by a conflicted view of itself. Where does it belong: to the Iberian peninsula or to the native Aztec, Inca, Quechua, Olmec, Mayan, and other pre-Columbian world-views? Spanish, no doubt, is spoken without the discomfort of knowing it is a borrowed language. And yet, the whole region lives in a permanent state of nostalgia, of longing for a past that is long gone but could perhaps be rescued, relived, renourished. Identity, then, is a schism, a division, a wound—a sense that, in the translation process, the original and the copy will never match.

III

I should say at this advanced point that, while the two previous sections were devoted to the amazement and paradoxes of translation, my original intention in this essay was to talk about something altogether different: the discovery of Latin American letters by United States readers. But as I began to write, I realized that the topic was really of marginal importance when compared to a number of subdivisions: first and foremost, translation as a concept in the Southern Hemisphere; and second, the idea of discovering another culture by means of language. I was therefore forced to take a step back to reflect on the role played by translators during the early stages of the conquest, and then to link their product—what they do—to collective identity. My argument can be summarized as follows: the birth of Latin America is also the overshadowing of many aboriginal tongues; in order to enter Western history, the continent has been forced to appropriate a foreign, nonnative vehicle of communication; consequently, its collective identity is shaped as a hybrid. (Cortázar used the image of the *axólotl* and Octavio Paz the salamander—a fish in permanent mutation.) Obviously, this hybrid is not only cultural but linguistic, a sum of alien words, of apparently unrelated masks, used to define something emerging in a different verbal dimension. That's why it is vastly ironic that Hispanics and Anglo-Saxons share a common border: their intermingled histories are a succession of misunderstandings and abuse, a chronology of miscommunications and, like the 1523 conquest of Tenochtitlán, a loss in translation.

It has been repeated to exhaustion that the United States and the rest of the Americas are divided by a bleeding injury: the Rio Grande, a nonnavigable 1,880-mile-long river. This isn't only a physical border but a mental and verbal one: to the north, a methodical, Puritan culture, perfectly suited to its mathematical English; to the south, a culture of confusion using Spanish and Portuguese, ill-conceived Romance languages designed for romance, remorse, and melancholy.* Identity was a maze for Hispanics and as progressive line for Anglo-Saxons. When the British Puritans settled in the thirteen colonies, they didn't face a challenging power like the Aztec or Inca empires. Their encounter with the natives was largely a matter of reaching out to distant frontiers. Their enemy wasn't as well-equipped militarily, as philosophically sophisticated, as the populations found by the Spanish and Portuguese knights. Also, miscegenation, both genetic and verbal, was never a real issue, not on a scale comparable to Hispanic culture. The results are two worldviews drastically opposed, two incompatible visions. The two have shared a *diálogo de sordos*, a conversation made of laws and treaties designed to ease the tension, to make more manageable the illegal immigration waves, the unfair economic pacts that constantly threaten to push these neighbors to a flagrant confrontation. Let's not forget that the United States, while calling itself, presumptuously no doubt, America, is also part of

---

* See my book *The Hispanic Condition: Reflections of Culture and Identity in America* (HarperCollins, 1995).

the Americas, but a very different one at that—forcing others to see her as different, superior, in a class of her own.

And where are the Melchjorejos and Julianillos of the border, writers and translators attempting a concurrence? Shrieking on both sides. The literature produced in *el norte* has always been popular across the border, thanks to innumerable, often anonymous translators. Shortly after Washington Irving's 1828 biography of Christopher Columbus was issued in Great Britain, it was already available in Spanish, first in Madrid and Barcelona, and immediately after across the Atlantic, in large urban capitals of the Southern Hemisphere. In the same vein, Domingo Faustino Sarmiento's masterful *Life of Facundo: Civilization and Barbarism* evidences the impact of James Fenimore Cooper's fictional frontier dwellers in Argentina and Chile. José Martí and Rubén Darío, to name only two of the most distinguished *modernistas*, were not only well acquainted with, but strongly influenced by, Walt Whitman, Ralph Waldo Emerson, and the New England Transcendentalists. Edgar Allan Poe was a decisive force behind the naturalist stories of Uruguayan Horacio Quiroga. All this proves that, by means of translation, Latin America has been well equipped to follow the intellectual and artistic trends of its neighbor up north.

But by the early sixties, when John Dos Passos, Ernest Hemingway, and William Faulkner were names ubiquitous among readers in Bogotá, Mexico City, and Montevideo, few if any in the United States knew anything about the literature of their southern neighbors. While a couple of bibliographies were available, there was no reflective census of what had been done in terms of Latin American literature in translation, a much-needed enterprise that would help us understand the awakening of Anglo-Saxons to Hispanic and Brazilian cultures. Among the early enthusiasts was Daniel G. Brinton, whose translations of the Nahuatl into English, as I stated earlier, helped introduce, anthropologically and poetically, a forgotten civilization. Until the late twenties, Darío was probably the region's most distinguished man of letters, but he was far better known in Spain (thanks to his friend, Juan Ramón Jiménez) and only rarely was he mentioned north of the Rio Grande. Quiroga's *Stories of the Jungle* appeared in London in 1923, translated by Arthur Livingstone and published by Methuen, but they failed to be reprinted in the United States. Few translators were active, and those who were had tremendous difficulty convincing editors to embark on south-of-the-border projects. An exception was Harriet de Onís, born in 1899 and wife of the Columbia University professor Federico de Onís. A folklorist fluent in both Spanish and Portuguese, de Onís was a crucial innovator in bringing attention, through her 1935 English translation of Ricardo Güiraldes's *Don Segunda Sombra*. She was also responsible for disseminating the works of Cuban ethnographer Fernando Ortíz, Colombian essayist Germán Arciniegas, Bolivian feminist Argentina Díaz Lozano, and the early novels of Brazilian Jorge Amado. Hers was a slow revolution: a colleague of hers, Earle K. James, brought out a translation of José Eustasio Rivera's *The Vortex* in 1935, but it wasn't until the forties that her translations and those of other enthusiasts would begin to reach a less minuscule audience, often thanks to anthologies, which have served to offer an assortment of styles. (Very few and scattered anthologies were published from the twenties to the forties, including Isaac Goldberg's *Brazilian Tales,* Waldo Frank's *Tales from Argentina,* and Angel Flores's *Fiesta in November*).

Mexico's proximity to the United States, the interest of such writers as Graham Greene, Mike Gold, and Katherine Anne Porter in the 1910 revolution of Pancho Villa and Emiliano Zapata and its aftermath, as well as the late 1930s expropriation of the oil industry, brought particular attention to its native writers. The inventory, while not vast, is intriguing: Enrique Munguía's now dated translation of Mariano Azuela's classic *The Underdogs* appeared in 1929, followed by de Onís's 1930 translation of Martín Luis Guzmán's *The Eagle and the Serpent.* Then Katherine Anne Porter, whose own stories in *Flowering Judas* were set in Mexico, published in 1942 a translation, with preface, of Fernández de Lizardi's *The Itching Parrot.** But not only Mexicans were in vogue: de Onís translated the Peruvian Ciro Alegría, a now-forgotten novelist very popular before and during World War II. Chilean María Luisa Bombal created her own outstanding translations of *The House of Mist* and *The Shrouded*

---

* Actually, Porter cheated: it wasn't her translation but Eugene Pressly's, begun in Mixcoac and finished in Paris; she originally wanted to promote Pressly's work, but when, after polishing it a bit, she showed it to some agents and was rejected, she decided to give her name to it.

Woman in the late forties, a decade that also saw Mexican José Ruvueltas's talents appreciated north of the border. Bombal, perceived today as a forerunner of "magical realism," is the first renowned Latin American writer to "refurnish" herself, to perform an act of self-translation. The practice would gain recognition several decades later, in part as a strategy by authors to escape being misunderstood and as an attempt to establish direct contact with editors. Among those who wrote originally in English, or "adapted" their own oeuvre, were Borges, with his "Autobiographical Essay," first published in *The New Yorker*; Manuel Puig, with his novel *Eternal Curse to the Reader of These Pages*; Guillermo Cabrera Infante, with *Holy Smoke*; João Ubaldo Ribeiro, with *Sargeant Getulio* and *An Invisible Memory*; and Carlos Fuentes with his essays in *Myself with Others* and *The Buried Mirror*.

It wasn't until coinciding events of the sixties—Borges being awarded the Formentor Prize (he shared it with Samuel Beckett), Asturias receiving the Nobel Prize for Literature in 1967, and the explosive literary boom that brought international attention to García Márquez, Cortázar, Mario Vargas Llosa, Cabrera Infante, Donoso, and Fuentes—that things began to change, thanks in large part to translators like Gregory Rabassa and Helen Lane, many of whom have been my teachers, mentors, and friends.

In order to succeed in their task, translators often have needed to strike relationships with the writers they translate. Rabassa, for one, believes that "it often depends on a writer's knowledge of English and on political circumstances." Cortázar, he claims, was very helpful.

> Most of the changes he made in *Hopscotch* were his own doing. García Márquez also gives you a free reign. He has an open mind, a sort of Joycean attitude. He accepts any kind of interpretation of his works, sometimes one way out in left field. When I would show him my work, he would say: That's right! That's right! Which means that he is a real writer in the sense that he is unconscious about the moves he makes in his work and can see something he didn't know existed before. I had a beautifully dangerous triangular situation with José Lezama Lima in Ha-

vana. Because of the Communist regime, direct communication wasn't good. Also, he was difficult about
his work. He was put in touch with me through
Cortázar, a great admirer of his. I would send pages
to Cortázar in Paris, and he would give them to a
courier he knew in the Cuban embassy in Paris, who
would go to Havana, give them to Lezama Lima, and
then back to Paris and New York. We got going pretty
well until about halfway through, Cortázar become
persona non grata. Communication stopped. By then I
was enough into it, so I finished the job trying to stay
as close to the author's intentions as possible. All this
to say that I do like to send manuscripts to the author. I would send to Vargas Llosa, for instance, and
it would come back with a little note: 'No, I meant
this instead of that.' He would give me a synonym,
but it wouldn't work.

But other translators prefer dealing with what Baudelaire once described as "dead literary corpses." That is the case with Toby Talbot, responsible for bringing to English Jacobo Timerman's *Prisoner Without a
Name, Cell Without a Number.* Although, as she once argued, working
with living writers like Humberto Constantini and Luisa Valenzuela has
helped Talbot resolve issues that fall in the gray area between English
and Spanish, the relationship can also become a bilingual tug-of-war.
"Constantini fought over every epical *y* and we negotiated fiercely for
inclusion or deletion," she recalls. Dead authors, on the other hand, "seem
to be the ones looking most fixedly over my shoulder."

If, as Ezra Pound once stated in *ABC of Reading,* literature is news
that stays news, translators have the capacity of renewing the news, refreshing it time and again. Original works of art, once they enter the
canon, cannot be touched; but translations often prove obsolete by virtue of their antiquated language. Fresh new translations are required to
satisfy new reading appetites. Thus it is foreseeable that in the near future Rabassa's translation of *One Hundred Years of Solitude* or Donald
Yates's faithful rendition of Borges's short stories, will be replaced by
others, more akin to their time. The future Angel María Garibays and
the Miguel León Portillas, with their useful academic tools, will unravel

misunderstandings we are probably unaware of today. They will take us much farther, exploring rituals, analyzing attitudes, and making available a sort of *visión de los vencidos* for the next millennium. The energy and passion of this extraordinary group of contemporary translators will be seen as inaugural yet replaceable. But it won't matter. Guilty as they might be of distortion, the original opening up of a secluded universe, the championing of the Americas in the eyes of foreigners, exotic or otherwise, has already been achieved, thanks no doubt to their effort. They are the modern Melchorejo and Julianillo, direct descendants of Daniel G. Brinton. Reluctance has been left behind. They don't have to escape their patrons; on the contrary, they are wise, active participants in the translation encounter. There's little doubt that the region lives today in far less isolation, in far more dialogue, than a century ago. Silence has been replaced by words, and words in one language have traveled to another. In that sense, Harriet de Onís and her successors are yet another crew of courageous explorers in the tradition of Sir Walter Raleigh and, why not?, Alvar Nuñez Cabeza de Vaca: they reach out to the geography of the imagination. They penetrate latitudes forbidden to most people, they interpret, they make accessible the inaccessible—they improve us by expanding our horizons. The old saying *traduttore, traditore* applies in that their effort entails a degree of treason. (In order to make an imaginary reality available, they have to falsify, to personalize, to adapt its message to their own language and culture; and adaptation necessarily carries along a degree of distortion). In spite of this, their vision has also been crucial to breach an abysmal gap: they reinvent; they enter an already furnished house and redecorate it, and their craft has particular significance precisely because it applies to a region whose birth has been perceived as a colossal misunderstanding, a chaotic *mélange* of words, facts, and acts. Ironically, what was once lost in translation during the *conquista* of the Americas can now be reconquered by the exact same means.

[1996]

18 / TONGUE SNATCHER

Tongue snatching, the art of switching from one language to another, has always been popular among writers, but it has acquired particular urgency as a result of massive migration. Baruch Spinoza, among the legendary examples, while native in Dutch and Spanish, wrote the *Ethics* in Latin; Sh. Y. Abramovitch (*aka* Mendele Mohker Sforim), the nineteenth-century, Eastern European Jewish writer responsible for establishing the Yiddish literary tradition, managed to go back and forth between Yiddish and Hebrew, often with the same essential story, only to discover how differently it is articulated in each medium; Joseph Conrad abandoned Polish to opt for English, his third language (French was his second), and though he did not begin learning English until he was in his twenties, he soon became one of the most revered masters of Shakespeare's language; Vladimir Nabokov was perfectly fluent in Russian and English, transforming both through his intricate, elegant novels; Manuel Puig wrote books in Spanish, English, and Portuguese; and Fernando Pessoa's Portuguese self was, in his own words, "dormant" when he wrote English poetry, which helped him recreate himself as Alexander Search when he alternated between Portuguese and English.

The list is endless and malleable enough to includes names such as Samuel Beckett, Arthur Koestler, Ngugi wa Thiong'o, Isak Dinesen, Eugène Ionesco, Wole Soyinka, Jorge Luis Borges, Kamala Das, George Santayana, Alberto Gerchunoff, Franz Kafka, and Anita Desai, to name only a few. It also ought to include Hector Bianciotti, whose "original" language is the Piedmontese dialect; Spanish is his mother tongue, French his adopted one. His current literary medium is French, in which his memoir, *What the Night Tells the Day,* originally published in Paris in 1992, is written, and from which it has come to the United States, courtesy of Linda Coverdale's lucid translation.

The great imperial languages (English, Latin, Spanish, French, Arabic) have been a magnet to the largest number of tongue snatchers, who often embrace another tongue in order to find a larger audience, to escape political persecution, or simply to reinvent themselves. In Bianciotti's case the three options apply. Born in 1930 in Argentina, of his dozen books to date, including *Sans la Miséricorde du Christ,* the first four were written in Spanish and the remaining in French. Apparently, what moved him to travel to Europe at age twenty-five was the unquestionable desire to escape the bucolic, homophobic atmosphere of his childhood. But when, half a decade later, he settled in Paris once and for all, he realized he was undergoing a profound metamorphosis: not only was Cervantes slowly becoming his past and Paul Valéry his present, but Bianciotti was in the process of acquiring a totally different personal identity and a brand new self. A quintessential tongue snatching phenomenon: the mother tongue replaced by the wife tongue.

Underscored by gender, these terms—mother and father tongues—seem to me ineffective. Whereas the nation is perceived as a patrimony (*Das Vaterland*), language is approached as an expression of the matriarchal realm: the womb, the umbilical cord. One's liaison to the original language is instinctive, even primitive; in the adopted tongue, on the other hand, the eternal feeling is that of extraneousness, as if one was condemned to live forever in somebody else's house. Maternal words seem original, authentic, but adopted words never loose the quality of being borrowed. The distance between both tongues might seem small to some but in fact is abysmal. In a way, tongue snatchers become their own translators, their own interpreters; but in spite of their amazing linguistic knowledge, they never feel quite on their own in either case. Frequently, as in the case of Bianciotti, they appear to be ostracized in a room of their own.

Open any biographical dictionary of Latin American literature: he is nowhere to be found; data about his upbringing and literary beginnings are still scarce, in spite of the fact that his books, in their original or in translation, are available in Spain, and that he is only a bit younger than

Gabriel García Márquez and Guillermo Cabrera Infante, and not much older than Manuel Puig. He is equally absent from most Francophile encyclopedias, notwithstanding Bianciotti's current status in contemporary French letters: he has worked as critic for *Le Nouvel Observateur,* is a member of Gallimard's *comité de lecture,* helping select the titles that will be published annually in France, and is currently literary correspondent of *Le Monde.* But even if his work frequently receives high praise from native French speakers, not always known for their welcoming manners, he, as most tongue snatchers, is and will always be an outsider.

Divided into sixty relatively small chapters, *What the Night Tells the Day,* as any standard memoir, begins at the beginning, in Bianciotti's cradle. He evokes the haunted pampa of his infancy, a landscape in the northern province of Córdoba rooted in its Catholicism and largely composed of Italian immigrants. His was a farmers' milieu: poor, uncosmopolitan, irredeemably pastoral, where machismo reigned. The scenario is a symbol of Latin America as a whole—unsuitable, unfinished, *in medias res,* in constant state of decay. Our house, he claims, "— a rather imposing building designed for a different kind of life, and for people other than farm workers—showed signs of ambitious plans that had come to grief. The bathroom, for example, where no one over took a bath because there was no running water; or the gallery with the checkerboard floor in black and red, completed on one side by assorted lozenges of different sizes and colors, with cement patches here and there filling the inevitable gaps."

The first half of his book is devoted to family life, particularly to siblings, his oppressive father, an Italian immigrant fluent in the Piedmontese dialect who would always keep records of money young Bianciotti borrowed from him, and his enigmatic mother, whom he never quite learned to love. "Driven by life," he writes, "we strive relentless to escape our parents, so that the heart—and this we realize only at their deaths—always lags behind." His environment forbade him to touch himself and others, and so it was natural that when masturbation took over, he was badly reprimanded. His body, he was told, was sinful, bestial, uncontrolled, in desperate need of domestication. Soon, as Bianciotti discovered gay pleasures, first in the image of Tomasito Carrara, a young visitor, and later personified in Florencio, another farmer boy, reprimand turn into condemnation.

Escape and evasion were the only solutions, and he found them, at least temporarily, in the priesthood. Attracted by Franciscan friars, at age eleven he entered a seminary; his decision to embrace a religious career makes me think of Sor Juana Inés de La Cruz, the genial nun responsible for immortal sonnets and *redondillas* written in Mexico at the end of the seventeenth century. Rather than a crystalline love for Jesus Christ, what probably possessed the two was the desire to run away from their immediate environment and to find time to read and reflect. The monastery as refuge.

However, not Sor Juana but Puig, whose childhood was also spent (or, as he would say, wasted) in the Argentine pampa, is the true voice, the flavor, the ethos to be invoked, time and again, between Bianciotti's lines—especially his early novels, such as *Betrayed by Rita Hayworth,* also about repressed male sexuality. Puig's attempt was to capture the morose atmosphere of middle class banality and boredom, the collective obsession with Hollywood movies and soap operas. Bianciotti's memoir, on the other hand, is a study of solipsistic indulgence and restraint. The leitmotif in his autobiography is memory: its ephemerality, its fugitiveness. He appears less concerned with social attitudes than with an individual exploration. The two writers also complement each other in their approach to homosexuality: as effeminate as he was, Puig always seemed to me to oscillate between caution and explosion. Bianciotti, in turn, is more introspective, nondenouncing, an enlightened French intellectual possessed by his inner demons. Still, both ought to be placed, on equal terms, alongside Calvert Cassey, Reinaldo Arenas, José Lezama Lima, Luis Zapata, and Silviano Santiago, all gay writers who live and die under the weight of machismo, even if Bianciotti stands alone in his view of Latin America as a prison he managed to escape, a hell left behind, repelled and fully buried.

When Bianciotti moved to Buenos Aires in his early twenties, he was part of a generation confronted with the rise of Peronism. He worked for a while for a notary, moved in literary circles, and got involved with a woman who had a pregnancy and an abortion. Soon he was miraculously, almost mysteriously, handed in a ticket to travel to Naples—a ticket to his future. His Argentine period concluded in 1925, as does the book under review.

I have described it as autobiography, but this is only half true. The publisher bills it as a novel, perhaps because names have been changed to protect the identity of those alive and facts manipulated to fit the passing of time. The strategy highlights the volume's artificial dimension, its *literariness*. So as to force chronology out of its progressive, lineal shape, the narrative oscillates, inconsistently at times, between the past and present tense. The effect is daunting: people and scenes that might otherwise be believed at face-value acquire a ghost-like presence. Everything seems at once real and unreal, authentic and fabricated. I guess that's why, in essays and interviews, Bianciotti has coined the term *autofiction,* to imply the intertwining of real facts and invented material. "I think that autobiography is impossible," he once claimed. "Memory offers flat images, like photographs. Something very important that lasted for years can end up reduced to a few moments." He adds: "When one has developed a taste for words, for cadences, for the phrase, there's nothing to be done, one lies. One lies."

Not lies but a banquet for words is indeed what Bianciotti's book is about. A particularly sweeping aspect compares the writer's awakening to the act of reading. In spite of his limited education, his father, apparently, truly loved books. Somehow he managed to have around copies of *Don Quixote,* "which nobody ever read," as well as Jorge Isaac's *María, Amalia* by José Mármol, and *Quatrevingt-Treize* by Victor Hugo. A personal turning point came on a Sunday in August 1945, when, disappointed in the priesthood, Bianciotti fell in love with Paul Valéry's poetry. Catholicism was no longer the answer when Valéry suddenly died and an issue of a literary supplement of *La Nación,* in Buenos Aires, was devoted to him. Bianciotti read it, was swept away by *La Soirée avec Monsieur Teste,* first in Spanish translation, then in French with a companion dictionary to help him out. He made his way through the text, deciphering it with much difficulty, and was never the same. He writes: "'Stupidity is not my forte.' Valéry, who did not care for fiction, had taken it up so that he might write that first sentence without any appearance of vanity. I would have been so pleased to be worthy of the phrase; as I was not, I admired it. On the other hand, I took my secret motto from these four words found on the second page: 'I have pre-ferred myself.' And with time, without noticing it, I added a fifth, the adverb *always,* between the verb and its auxiliary."

Verb and auxiliary: In light of the metalinguistic reveries from which it flourishes, what's surprising, to me at least, is the almost total reluc-tance by Bianciotti to reflect on language and translingualism. At one point he does state that his parents used Piedmontese among them-selves, "doubtless to safeguard their secrets, so that for me the mother—or father—tongue, around which the soul takes shape, will always be the forbidden language." But nothing more. And yet, to paraphrase Marshall McLuhan, in this book, perhaps more than in many other, the medium is the message. Bianciotti's soul has been shaped and reshaped. The fact that his personal memory comes to us though a linguistic look-ing-glass makes it incredibly vibrant, a life performed in the abyss where words have no owner, lost and found in translation. Tongue snatching at its best.

[1995]

19 / HELLO COLUMBUS

A symbolic man is a man's name without a self.
—Zdenek Saul Wohryzek,
An Improbable Life

I

I have been fascinated by Christopher Columbus since I was a little boy. The legend of his Sephardic blood, the vision of him as either the traitor or the savior of the oppressed, the coincidence of his arrival in the Bahamas in 1492, Spain's annus mirabilis—the year of the final unification of Castile and Granada by the Catholic kings and of the official edict proclaiming the expulsion of the Jews from the Iberian peninsula—these historical facts and ancestral rumors were enthusiastically promoted by my part-Russian, part-Mexican grandmother, a descendant of a globe-trotting family with previous incarnations in Eastern Europe, Palestine, and South America. Our delightful afternoon conversations, which took place regularly during a period of almost a decade in her old-fashioned living room, transformed her opinions into stimulating fantasies that haunted me for a long time and left stamped indelibly on my mind a sense of the heroic and the futile.

She was intentionally ambiguous. Often she would portray the admiral as disoriented, uneducated, and dumb; on other occasions, however, she would bestow upon him a kind of celestial power, turning him into a sort of messiah ready to embark on an enterprise that seemed beyond the scope of most of his contemporaries but that for him appeared an easy task. Two facets then, two dimensions—two masks. If I was never sure how to understand his legacy and behavior, it was clear without a margin of doubt that in my grandmother's eyes the Genoese had possessed the talents of a superior individual, that he was a man like no other. This aura of excellence, this unique, magnanimous, poetic quality, was one reason for my fascination. I soon understood that the admiral she fantasized about was nothing but an invention she would joyfully

210

create to make Columbus concrete, to feel close to him, to make him part of herself. Always waiting for the apocalypse and the redemption of God's world, she would distort the facts to accommodate the biographical data (she had learned a lot about him in newspapers, magazines, and pseudoscientific books) to her own set frame of mind. He was a savior because she wanted him to be one, because she needed a figure who could have rescued thousands of Jews from the terrible fate that awaited them in the torture chambers of Tomás de Torquemada's Inquisition. Or she perceived him as a traitor because, having had some influential power over Queen Isabella (she was sure they had been passionate lovers), he never did enough to save his doomed fellow Jews and other foreigners in Spain. By the time I grew up to become a bookish adolescent, I looked for the truth and found it, but only partially. I read everything that fell into my hands. Wondering why my grandmother could never make up her mind about Columbus, I was ultimately forced to understand the profound subjectivity and contingency with which history has approached this gigantic figure. And I embraced a kind of antihistoric stance because I came to understand that Columbus is, for the most part, whatever people want him to be.

The mariner's adventure, I also concluded, had been from the very beginning a literary event. Fully conscious of his role, Columbus, a terrible speller and perhaps speaker, kept a journal that was later lost and then found, rewritten, and edited by the Spanish priest and historian Fray Bartolomé de Las Casas. The text is full of suggestive descriptions of his Iberian environment and of what he saw on this side of the Atlantic. Having a good sense of the power of the written word, he would occasionally send ravishing if inaccurate letters to friends and patrons in Spain, and when hard times darkened his future he even dropped a line or two to the Vatican. As a reader, one Roland Barthes would have liked, he wrote down his own thoughts and impulsive comments in the margins of book pages, as he did with Marco Polo's account of his voyages to the Orient.

Besides his own writing, pamphlets big and small began to be published in Europe, from Venice to Lisbon, from Marseilles to Seville, immediately after his first and second voyages. They conveyed rumors about his Jewish origin, conflicting reports about his mysterious friendship with an unknown Icelandic pilot, unconnected ideas about the unexplained death of his wife and his affair with Beatriz Enríquez de Arana, and other infamous stories. By the time he died in 1506, at the age of fifty-five, penniless and not knowing the true scope of his success, the lands across the Atlantic Ocean were attracting other travelers and serving as a source of inspiration for the collective imagination—and his life was being recounted already as an epic adventure.

Since then innumerable creative and historical writings, both fictional and nonfictional, have been produced. Every author, it is clear, has his own agenda: Columbus has proved to be as malleable a historic figure as one could find, a shapeless stone waiting for the sculptor. But time has shown that objectivity about him is also attainable. Empirical evidence, in the Maimonidean (and Popperian) sense, tells us that even if we cannot positively prove many details of the admiral's life, we can at least dispel falsifiable claims, as indeed some researchers have done. The verifiable facts are on file, and although full knowledge of Columbus's life is impossible, much of the history of his life is perfectly distinguishable from fiction. The mysterious fate of a handful of essential manuscripts— for instance, his journals (most of the narrative material we have about Columbus was transcribed by Las Casas)—the loss of a crown, the loss of a decisive map, these possibilities have encouraged detective novelists to compose thrillers in the tradition of Umberto Eco's *The Name of the Rose*. In these scholastic plots the discovery of a missing link would change forever our fragile perception of reality. Nevertheless, in addition to the overcrowded flow of fiction, numerous scholarly articles and books on aspects of the admiral's life have appeared at an incredible rate every year, as if repeating his biography, searching his past, is a form of therapy in our quest to find the origin of modernity. The stuff of literature is everywhere to be found in his complex legend—his obscure childhood, his struggle to raise enough money to accomplish his project, the poverty he suffered with his son Diego after becoming a widower, the mutinies by both his Spanish crew and the Taino natives before that crucial 12 October and after. Fiction writers have played with Columbus's biographical data ad infinitum to invent plausible endings to unfinished stories or to revamp those that already end conclusively.

There are at least twenty valuable, if controversial, biographies of Columbus available in English, including those by Washington Irving, Salvador de Madariaga, Simon Wiesenthal, John Noble Wilford, and Samuel

Eliot Morison. More than a hundred novels, plays, oratorios, and poems were written between the nineteenth and twentieth centuries alone, most of them by Iberians and North and South Americans, but a good many of them also by Greeks, French, Italians, and other Europeans. The tone and content are constantly changing: the Genoese is canonized or crucified and is depicted as an illuminated mystic, a prophet, a businessman, a courageous freedom fighter, a devoted Christian, and a messiah. For the most part, writers south of the Rio Grande have attempted to show his villainous face, while those in the North and in Europe prefer to perceive him as the inaugurator of an illustrious historical destiny.

Take, for instance, Washington Irving's biography, which heavily borrows from the scholarship of the Spanish scholar Martín Fernández de Navarrete. Irving, who became fluent in Spanish, was invited by Alexander Everett, then the U.S. ambassador in Madrid, to do a quick translating job of the Navarrete research on Columbus. Depressed, anxious, in a middle-age crisis about his struggle to become a well-known writer, and ready to leave England, the creator of "Rip Van Winkle" happily accepted the offer. But when he saw the dryness of the material he decided it needed embellishing. The result was a four-volume narrative account of the life and times of the Genoese, published in London in 1828, that mixed truth and fiction. Since Irving felt the division in his own identity between his European ancestry and his childhood and education in the United States, his mariner is a bridge between the old and new civilizations, a link between the two continents. In a way, that was precisely how Washington Irving wanted to be perceived by his contemporaries. Hence, Columbus's face reflected Irving's—a mirror.

A completely different view is offered by Alejo Carpentier, the baroque Cuban novelist and music critic who wrote the 1979 novel *The Harp and the Shadow*. His conception of Columbus is that of a gold-thirsty explorer, a liar and charlatan who, after getting Queen Isabella's attention and love, described the Americas in a magical, surrealistic fashion, distorting reality, corrupting it. In fact, what Carpentier wants to prove is that the so-called magical realism movement (*lo real maravilloso*) subscribed to by South American writers such as Gabriel García Márquez and himself embodies nothing new: it reaches back to the sixteenth century, when the admiral talked about rivers of gold and exotic, chimerical animal beings. His mariner is very much the usurper of a whole native tradition, a victimizer, the metaphorical source of all the suffering for five hundred long years by Hispanic America. Carpentier, it should be said, was a participant, albeit not a fully committed one, in Fidel Castro's 1959 socialist revolution. He was also a devoted scholar of Cuban music and folklore who spent part of his lifetime in exile for opposing repressive regimes. Thus, his view of the mariner is furiously negative: he attacks Columbus as a wrongdoer and debunks his glorified stature. Columbus, his face symbolizing evil, acquires the metaphysical appearance of Carpentier's own enemy.

Others who have drawn portraits of the Genoese include Joel Barlow, Walt Whitman, William Carlos Williams, Rubén Darío, Paul Claudel, Friedrich Nietzsche, and James Fenimore Cooper. Each inserted his own message in his portrait; each advertised the qualities he liked the most and hid or deformed those he detested. As the admiral was lying on his deathbed in Seville, a myth was being born: Christopher Columbus the literary character, a narrative entity with a thousand different countenances, a man of resemblances, a chimera.

Most of the first literary texts describing his voyage were poems, including those by the seventeenth-century Mexican nun Sor Juana Inés de la Cruz and the Revolutionary-era American poet Philip Freneau. But that generic predilection soon changed. After 1792, and especially after the publication of Washington Irving's life account, there was an explosive production of novels, for two simple reasons, one historical and the other literary. First, the Genoese's life and legacy had come to be used for nationalistic purposes as the past was slowly made fully conscious in the Americas. The emergence of Columbus as a full-scale historic figure reached an apex only with the consolidation of the United States as an international power and with the economically and politically unstable rise of the South American republics. As Kirkpatrick Sale claims in his 1990 volume, *The Conquest of Paradise*, during the years immediately after his death the mariner was in a complete shadow. Nobody cared for him, and his contribution was largely ignored. But soon the population of the Americas increased considerably, and literature acquired a crucial role in the soul-searching process of exploring the collective past. Intellectuals and artists defined themselves by finding historic figures who legitimated their shared ancestry. If in 1692 the centennial of his so-called discovery was not celebrated in the new territories, by the time of the tricentennial in 1892 Columbus had become a legendary figure. Academic institutions, such as Columbia University, formerly King's College, were named after him, as were towns, squares, public monuments, and artistic events everywhere north and south of the Rio Grande. Through this transformation, Columbus acquired larger-than-life features.

The second reason for the nineteenth-century plethora of novels about the Genoese has to do with aesthetic and generic artistic trends in Europe and the Americas. The rise of the novel as a literary genre is fairly recent compared with poetry and drama. Only after Cervantes, Daniel Defoe, and Jonathan Swift left a mark on the seventeenth and eighteenth centuries with their lucid, imaginative prose did Europe witness a marked increase in novelistic adventures. Immediately after 1492 other literary genres prevailed, but by the eighteenth century this new literary form had captivated the contemporary mind more than any other and had acquired an unparalleled popular status. The rapid development of sophisticated printing and book manufacturing techniques during the first part of the twentieth century has pushed the genre even further. More historical and fantasy novels have been published since World War I than in any other period of literary history. And Columbus has been a favorite novelistic character.

II

Bertrand Russell once forcefully argued that if some one hundred men had been removed from European history, we would still be groping through the labyrinths of the Middle Ages. It's a persuasive idea. Perhaps for some the absence of Christopher Columbus from the history of North and South America, and for that matter from world history, would not mean much. After all, if he had not opened up a new geographical dimension across the Atlantic, somebody else would have, as indeed, Amerigo Vespucci and other sailors and voyagers succeeded in doing during and after the fifteenth century.

In fact, there is little doubt that the Vikings, among them Leif Eriksson and Thorfinn Karlsefni, all great shipbuilders and courageous warriors, did it before that crucial, memorable year of 1492. By the eleventh century, more or less while the Normans were conquering England and the Crusaders were embarking on the bloody recovery of the Holy Land from the Muslims, these Scandinavians had already settled in Germany, France, and Spain. And around the year 1000 they founded a colony in the region of New England. The reasons for their territorial outreach included overpopulation, quest for trade, internal dissension, and a passion for adventure. Yet the Vikings, we know, ultimately vanished and their legacy evaporated when Christianity was introduced into Scandinavia, thus giving rise to the emergence of strong, self-protecting kingdoms in Norway, Denmark, and Sweden. And since history is nothing but the version of past human events as perceived and recorded by the winners, not the losers, today Eric the Red and his itinerant followers are not considered the "official" discoverers of the so-called New World. Columbus has that honor.

But what if Russell's playful supposition were actually true? What if the admiral never existed? What if he is only an invention of the human imagination which likes to play tricks, is fond of dreams, magic, and unreality, and gets lost in physical and intellectual labyrinths? If so, in almost no other case have our imaginings been so vivid, so exuberant, so prolific. With the probable exceptions of Jesus Christ, the prophet Muhammad, and William Shakespeare, no other individual has ever awakened as much passion and controversy, generated as many rumors surrounding his life and achievements, and inspired as prolific an imaginative effort to darken or enlighten his endeavors. If Christopher Columbus is indeed an invention, humankind certainly has to be congratulated for its fertile, everlasting creativity.

At any rate, the end of a millennium always brings nightmare prophecies of doom and apocalypse, as well as ambitious reconsiderations. Already, as our restless, violent twentieth century is coming to its conclusion, the ominous scriptural visions of disaster, of ecological collapse and socioeconomic Armageddon, are cropping up everywhere. Even as the irrevocable collapse of Marxism has inspired the rebirth of messianic, democratic hopes for a new global ideology that could save the whole of humankind, witch-hunting and secret ritualistic organizations are working to alter people's views and influence religious beliefs. The year 1984, the date George Orwell suggested would be representative of the totalitarian Stalinist state, has been replaced with the year 2000.

What will the new century bring us? Will our overpopulated, intoxicated planet be able to survive? Can we ever escape fraternal blood spills and ancestral ethnic rivalries? Are humans meant to become robots? Will art as we know it today be part of our collective future? In Spain exactly five hundred years ago, in 1492, similar speculations were in vogue. The battles to reconquer Andalusia from the Moors had been successful. Just as Antonio de Nebrija was compiling his grammar of the Castilian language in Salamanca, Isabella and Ferdinand, the Catholic monarchs, decided to reinvigorate the kingdom by getting married and joining forces, uniting Granada and Aragon. It was also during that year that the Jews were expelled from the Iberian peninsula, thus eliminating, or at least dismantling, all foreign power inside the proud new nation. Catholicism was unanimously revealed as the one and only religion, and the Church conducted the Inquisition—the dreadful search for chastity and *la pureza de sangre.*

Not all was vanity and glory. The empire's finances were actually stumbling: citizens were refusing to pay the taxes randomly collected, and institutions like the army were devouring mammoth amounts of money. Overexpenditure was also the result of lavish government parties and the lack of administrative planning. All these factors contributed to a xenophobic atmosphere and an unhappy population. To balance the budget, the state had to find new capital through viable financial alternatives that would decrease social unrest without threatening the grandiose life-style of the court and aristocracy. To make things worse, commercial routes to Africa and the Indies in Asia were under a blockade by the Turks, endangering the economic stability of Spain as well as Portugal. A new trade line had to be found—that, at least, appeared to be the best solution. On this volatile, potentially explosive stage, Columbus made his entrance.

An unknown Italian mariner, he had been seeking support from Portuguese and Spanish government officials, as well as from private entrepreneurs, to try out his idea that the only way to find a new trade route was to sail westward from the Canary Islands. He had been trying to raise funds for several years and was disheartened by the poor results.

But suddenly his luck changed. With the support of Queen Isabella, the money finally came through, mainly from the pockets of rich *marranos,* or crypto-Jews. And a courageous adventure was set in motion, one that eventually proved to be a liberating, ecstatic experience.

The mariner's true motives are in dispute. If indeed he was looking for a viable commercial route to the Indies to reinvigorate the Spanish kingdom, he seems to have been a disoriented oceanographer with little knowledge of sailing techniques, a fortunate fellow at the right time and place. His marine calculations were often mistaken, and his data frequently incomplete and wrong. Artists, historians, and intellectuals, among them the Argentine novelist Abel Posse, argue that Columbus's admiration for Marco Polo, the Venetian who had set foot in Cathay (China) in 1266 and reached the court of Kublai Khan, transformed his passion for sailing from an adolescent infatuation into a lifelong career. In the Genoese's eyes, this enterprising, spirited Italian was the true role model: he had been looking for Cipangu (Japan), a legendarily wealthy island, half-paradise, half-reality, full of gold, located on the map some 30° to the east of Cathay. Columbus wanted to duplicate Marco Polo's success by attempting a similar voyage by another path.

But a handful of academics and independent scholars have argued that during his first voyage from Palos to the Bahamas Columbus had a hidden agenda: sailing westward across the Atlantic, with money raised from wealthy Jewish businessmen, was secretly a plan to look for a new land where the *conversos*—Jews who because of the torture and merciless persecutions of the Inquisition had openly converted to the Christian faith but in truth remained loyal to their ancient Hebrew heritage—could freely practice their original belief. Whatever the actual facts, the Spanish empire, in financial trouble and facing social unrest, needed a gold mine to balance its budget and was lucky enough to find it in the Americas. Thus Columbus became a sort of messiah, an economic wizard.

Perhaps there is at least partial truth in each of these views: it was a search for a new trade route, a quest for money and richness, fueled by fear of an apocalypse and anxiety about things to come in the imminent new century. All of these ingredients helped Columbus to shape his loyalties, to justify his navigations, and to get people around him to make his dreams become a reality. When the admiral first reached Guanahaní

(Watlings Island) and later on Juana (Cuba), Hispaniola (Haiti and the Dominican Republic), and San Juan Bautista (Puerto Rico), a new era had begun.

It was not a very happy era, however, and it was one that could tolerate both success and disaster. After Columbus reached the New World—according to some, not before stealing important maps and information from an Icelandic pilot—the fruits of his success were savored by almost everybody except him. Others who were perhaps as uncompassionate and ambitious but no doubt more bloodthirsty immediately took advantage of his precarious position and left him poor and forgotten. Having been named sole governor of all new territories beforehand, his titles and properties were revoked or taken away by old friends and loyalists. After Queen Isabella's death, even King Ferdinand, instead of fulfilling his official promises, hurried to repossess the mariner's legacy. There was nothing new, I should add, in this opportunism; after all, intrigue and disloyalty have always crowned grandiose human enterprises. The mariner's successors, among them conquistadores such as Francisco Pizarro and Hernán Cortés, with their respective armies in Mexico and Peru, were cruelly barbaric toward the native population, although some missionaries tried to stop their atrocities by acting as the voice of morality. Hispanic America eventually became a wasteland. In contrast, the United States ended up a triumph of progress and civility. Why? One of the many reasons is that the vast territory of the North was not settled by sophisticated native empires like the Aztec and Inca that had to be ousted. The British colonists, although abusive and entrenched, didn't need to dismantle a powerful civilization, but scattered tribes without a solid and well-equipped army.

Could Columbus foresee the outcome of his 1492 trip and the three that followed? Some say he could, and that he should be held accountable for his crimes against humanity and those of his successors. Others perceive him on the other hand, as an unwitting product of an imperialist, violent epoch.

Shortly after that decisive year of 1492, two very distinct, almost antagonistic realities emerged north and south of the Rio Grande. The passengers on the *Mayflower* were inheritors of the Puritan tradition. Their dream was to begin anew far away from England, to create an improved version of their motherland based on the manners, laws, and reason of their forefathers. Not only were these Calvinists fortunate enough not to find a huge Indian empire ready to oppose them, but their contact with another race did not extend to miscegenation; their ethnic ancestry remained pure and their Protestant religion was left intact. They were motivated to work hard and to make progress, giving birth to the myth of a new Israel, the chosen people of the New World. Their dream became a success. But Cortés, Pizarro, and the other conquistadores came with a different attitude: they arrived to destroy, to proselytize, to exploit, to rape, to kill. Moctezuma II and Cuauhtémoc, the last two Aztec emperors, confused them with Quetzalcóatl and other divine entities; instead of battling them, the Aztecs sent jewelry, gold, and exotic gifts to greet them. Immediately afterwards, the Church began baptizing "infidels," treating the Indians in an ambiguous, two-faced fashion: priests like Fray Bartolomé de Las Casas, a champion of Indian rights in colonial times and one of Columbus's biographers, had a benevolent, philanthropic attitude toward the native environment, both human and natural; but others—the majority, unfortunately—supported the cruel laws enacted by the Spanish crown and perpetuated in the Americas by the viceroyships. The conquerors, whether sexually abusing or simply "buying" native females, fathered bastard mestizo children of mixed ethnic background—half-Spanish, half-native. In the words of José Vasconcelos, an early twentieth-century Mexican philosopher who became minister of education, *la raza de bronce* (the bronze race) was born. Yet pitiless plagues and other natural disasters quickly took a toll, killing a high percentage of that new race. As a result, Hispanic American civilization has been marked by violence, chaos, and repression. Octavio Paz claims in his 1950 psychological and intellectual study *The Labyrinth of Solitude* that the collective identity of Hispanic America is obtuse, introspective, and full of fears and tremors. While the nations of North America became successful new societies, Mexico, Peru, Argentina, the Caribbean nations, and other parts of the region were unable to find political, military, and financial stability. Theirs is the legacy of what Las Casas called the "black legend," his account of the disasters and massacres perpetrated by the Spaniards in the newly explored lands. Probably nowhere in the world do two civilizations as dissonant and contrasting live side by side, divided only by the muddy flow of the Rio Grande. Distant neighbors, indeed.

A book that attempts to explain why the Europeans were cruel, merciless, and deceiving in Hispanic America is *The Conquest of America,* published in French in 1982 and written by the renowned French literary critic of Russian descent, Tzvetan Todorov. His thesis, phenomenological in nature, is that when making a discovery, an immature self most often finds what it is looking for, not the true reality surrounding it. "We can discover the other in ourselves," he argues, "realize we are not a homogeneous substance, radically alien to whatever is not us: as Rimbaud said, *Je est un autre.* But *others* are also "I"s: subjects just as I am, whom only my point of view—according to which all of them are *out there* and I alone am *in here*—separates and authentically distinguishes from myself." As a product of his time, Columbus, who was not a particularly avant-garde individual but was full of energy and had a talent for overcoming obstacles, was incapable of understanding the environmental and aboriginal treasures he found in the Americas. With a set frame of mind, he interpreted what he saw according to his own dogmatic *weltanschauung.* More than an itinerant voyager, he was a tourist interested only in a segment, not the whole complexity, of reality. He failed both in communicating with the Indians and in realizing the vastness of his enterprise because, according to Todorov, he was always the dupe of his illusions. But not only Columbus is to blame: the European travelers, especially the Iberian ones, arriving in the New World were representatives of an unripe civilization incapable of accepting or living in peace with other cultures. The "civilized man" was self-righteous and individualistic, an egomaniac. Recognizing the Aztecs and Incas as humans, as equals, would have entailed dialogue. But the Genoese and his successors traveled across the Atlantic to find wealth and, perhaps, to discover another facet of themselves, though not a self different from their own. They massacred, destroyed, and burned because power could not be shared. Had they acknowledged the inherent difference between Europe and the Americas, their attitude, claims the French critic, would have been totally different. But it could not have been: in 1492 feudalism still prevailed in Aragón and Castile; the principles of *liberté, egalité, et fraternité* and the growth of the bourgeoisie, already apparent in England, France, and Germany, were still in embryonic form in the Iberian peninsula and would take centuries to fully germinate.

III

Thus, we have two viewpoints on Columbus's achievement. According to one, the 1492 discovery of the Americas was a benign event, a true beginning, that enlarged the material and spiritual resources of humankind. The opposing view, that Columbus opened the door to tragedy, is more pessimistic. Disastrous yet foreseeable consequences unfolded that far surpassed any other tragedy in history up until then and perhaps ever since. More people died in plagues—according to some estimates, close to seven million—, wars, and religious conversions because of the confrontation between these two civilizations—the European and the native—than in World Wars I and II, the Vietnam War, the Crusades, the U.S. Civil War, the French Revolution, and all other battles that have ever occurred.

Amplifications of these two views are always at hand. Proponents of the first view refer to Columbus's reaching the Americas as a *discovery*. In the second view, it was only an *encounter*, since you can only discover that which you don't know but already exists. The "discovery" group argues that it was a glorious moment in history that should be celebrated with an annual holiday and centennials; the "encounter" group believes that it should be remembered only by a moment of mournful silence. Two opposing portraits of the Genoese emerge: hero and villain, saint and scoundrel.

In 1992 the governments and cultural institutions of the Southern Hemisphere—where the catastrophe has been felt far more than in the United States—supported the encounter thesis when it came to celebrating the quincentennial. In Madrid, Rome, Hollywood, London, and Washington, D.C., however, there was a readiness to celebrate and money to spend. The supporters of the discovery thesis planned innumerable fiestas full of color and fireworks, museum exhibits, operas, films, public television programs, outer-space projects, diplomatic gatherings, and the publication of some thirty-five commemorative books. With as much energy, the opponents—among the most important was the Alliance

for Cultural Democracy in Minneapolis—sabotaged the occasion; they claimed their campaign reached back to Fray Bartolomé de Las Casas and his accusation of European atrocities.

The year 1892, it should be noted, saw a big Columbus party as well, although not quite as generous and polemical as the 1992 fete. Rubén Darío, the archfamous Hispanic American poet of the time, traveled to Spain under the sponsorship of several South American governments, but instead of delivering a congratulatory sonnet, he read a confrontational poem accusing Columbus of rape and holocaust. His voice, nevertheless, was not loud. The admiral was honored north and south, east and west. A memorial to the mariner was unveiled at the southwest corner of Central Park in Manhattan, and in Chicago, a city consumed by fire in 1871 but rebuilt with magnificent skyscrapers, there were colorful festivities. The Czech composer Antonín Dvořák wrote his 1893 symphony *From the New World* for one of the celebrations. That same year, the World's Fair held near Chicago was known as the World's Columbian Exposition. By then, of course, France and North America had well-established, democratic, constitutional governments, and some Hispanic American nations, among them Mexico and Argentina, were tentatively independent.

In 1992 the polemic turned sour and the celebration revealed the hypocrisy in Columbus's position. The novels and poems produced before and during the year-long happening, including *The Dogs of Paradise* by Abel Posse and *Christopher Unborn* by Carlos Fuentes, were full of candor and criticism, reflecting a new multicultural global order and the reshaping of the collective identity. With the end of World War II, countries in Africa, Oceania, Asia, and Hispanic America sought their independence. The end of colonialism gave rise to the idea of internationally recognized human rights. With time, that worldview has matured. "Multiculturalism is not a plot of some left-wing professors in the U.S.," claims Garry Wills. "It is the most obvious of global facts, in a world where the 'natives' are telling Columbus how to behave, rather than the reverse. That, oddly, is a cause for celebration. The next century will not be [North] America's to call its own—or any other single nation's. We are all in a boat together, and Columbus must travel with us now as a fellow passenger, no longer the skipper." At the end of the twentieth

century the world believes that history can no longer be written by Europeans alone. New artistic and intellectual centers have emerged in what was once the periphery of culture—Buenos Aires, Johannesburg, Tel Aviv, Mexico City, Cairo, and Tokyo—as has the sense of an integrated planet, what the Canadian mass-media analyst Marshall McLuhan calls "the global village." Since the late 1950s and 1960s, writers such as Gabriel García Márquez, Milan Kundera, Nadine Gordimer, Chinua Achebe, and Mario Vargas Llosa have been promoting a different, multilingual, multiethnic order.

The attempt to make a villain out of the mariner has particularly angered a handful of intellectuals and more than a few conservatives in the Anglo-Saxon world. If we remember the victims of the Holocaust perpetrated by Adolf Hitler, claim some, why gather in joyful parties on an occasion that also marks the massive killings of millions of Indians in the Southern Hemisphere? To respond, Karl Meyer, an editor of the *New York Times,* wrote a brief essay in 1991 entitled "Columbus Was Not Eichmann." He argues, not without logic, that living as we do in a self-righteous age, the arguments against the sailor tell more about us than about him. The conquistadores were not war criminals, he claims, at least not like the deranged, machinelike commanders and soldiers who served Hitler and his merciless army. Although the violence perpetrated by the Spaniards was far beyond any reasonable limit, "what needs to be added is that cruelty was the common currency of power among Europeans, and indeed among less-than-noble high Indian civilizations." Meyer offers a passage from Sir Walter Raleigh in which the British courtier and man of letters depicts life in the *evil* Spanish empire; Meyer then writes: "The colonizers had much to answer for. But to ignore their achievements travesties history. Europeans passed judgment on themselves, thus nurturing the very universal norms that enable people today to throw mudballs at their ancestors." Indeed, Meyer has a point. After the 1863 abolition by Abraham Lincoln of slavery, with its endless repercussions, after World War II, after the civil rights movement of the 1960s, we now live in an aggressive age that professes little tolerance for cruelty. To identify with the victim has become a fashionable ideological stand. A revised view of 1492 forcefully argues that blood was the ink with which the conquerors wrote their signature. Yet history is nothing

but the need of the present to comprehend and find meaning in the past. And each epoch colors the past with tones that legitimize its own moral and spiritual values.

Looking at Columbus as a treacherous saboteur may be nothing but a mirage in which we are trying to find the victim we always wanted to be. Thomas Aquinas is said to have argued that God has power over everything but the past. Although history is unchangeable and we are forced to live with both its happy and horrendous consequences, our interpretation of past events can vary. Perhaps the best way to approach a controversy of this magnitude is with some degree of humor. Finding the humorous side has always been the job of Russell Baker, a newspaper columnist and the celebrated author of *Growing Up*. "Listening to these charges," Baker argues in a hilarious article, "you get the impression if it hadn't been for Columbus there'd be no air pollution, no grim Interstate highways or ugly housing developments marring the continent's beauty, no mountains of burning tires or reeking gasoline refineries blighting the landscape." He goes on to say that the perfect paradise that the Americas could have been if the admiral had not arrived also has its *serious* disadvantages. If the Genoese had not discovered the new territories, some other traveler, perhaps in the nineteenth or early twentieth century, would have, and money would have begun to flow in, eventually turning the newfound lands into an amusement tourist park, a Disneyland of sorts. "The trouble is, though, that once the tourist dollars start flowing, residents of the new-found continents are going to be under heavy pressure to make a mess of Paradise. I don't know about you, for instance, but I'm not going to be in a hurry to go until they build some decent highways and motels and a few places where you can get a cheeseburger at 3 o'clock in the morning." Baker finishes by admitting that, indeed, Columbus opened the door to a long list of maladies: "slavery, capitalist exploitation, cultural arrogance, racism, sexism, ethnic jokes and steroids. . . . Such things always happen when two utterly alien cultures encounter each other for the first time. That's why I'm against sending earth people to other planets." His clear conclusion is that the mariner has become an all too easy target, a villain in a heroless universe.

IV

Two of the most fascinating scholarly books that preceded this controversy were written by an important Mexican historian and philosopher, Edmundo O'Gorman, and by the Colombian Germán Arciniegas. Originally published in 1958 and still a best-seller in Hispanic America—particularly in Mexico, where it has had enormous influence on intellectuals and artists, such as Octavio Paz—O'Gorman's *The Invention of America* went through many revisions and additions and appeared in somewhat different form in English in 1961. (The book is based on lectures delivered at Indiana University). Philosophical in nature and Aristotelian in method, it is divided into four parts. The first, "History and Critique of the Idea of the Discovery of the Americas," uses systemic logic and the related game of syllogisms to prove that in order for us to accept the idea that the lands across the Atlantic were indeed "discovered," Europe needed to have had some sort of intuition about its possible existence, a premonition, or an ideal picture. O'Gorman argues that there are no real accidents in history: all events can be seen as consequences preceded by immediate causes. Thus, for the New World to be discovered, it had to be waiting for a visitor, it had to be ready for an unmasking. Does that mean that for a gold mine to be discovered, it has to be waiting to be discovered? Yes, because the discoverer of a gold mine needs to have an appreciation for the value of gold as a metal that society deems precious. Otherwise, society would ignore the discoverer's finding.

The second part, "The Historical Horizon," explores the prevailing myths about the extra-European reality before 1492, from Christian theology to Marco Polo and Roger Bacon. The third part, "The Process of Inventing America," again using systemic logic, discusses the reaction to and aftershocks from Columbus's achievements. And the fourth part, "The Structure of Self in America and the Meaning of American History," investigates how the New World reshaped the ancient concepts of time, space, and humankind.

O'Gorman's nonfiction narrative, although at times convoluted and opaque, has one objective: to show that America is a creation of Europe.

Thus, his central thesis is that the New World is nothing but fantasy, a utopia like those imagined by Jonathan Swift, Charles Fourier, Edward Bellamy, and Ray Bradbury—an imaginary reality. (Saint Augstine, in "The City of God," is brave enough to give the Greek meaning of *utopia*: "There's no such place.")

The same argument is developed in Arciniegas's *America in Europe,* a book originally published in 1975 and translated into English in 1986. "When Columbus steers his three caravels westward," claims Arciniegas,

> he is not heading for the uttermost unknown. He is moving toward a magical reality. He sets out to locate a land already occupied: those populous regions, conquered already by fable. Medieval man, to whose society the admiral belongs, is more likely to believe in the fancifully elaborated than in the real and tangible. The giants and pygmies of fictional jungles exist for the learned and the ignorant alike with the same certainty as the folk they jostle in the marketplace or greet in the town square, see in church or pass on the highway to and from the countryside. The islands and the mainland of the other hemisphere have got to be the home of Cyclopses, of a whole race of big-eared people, of dog-faced tribes, of Amazons.

An essayist born in 1900 and the author of some thirty books, including *Latin America: A Cultural History* and a study of the chivalrous search for El Dorado, Arciniegas is bewildered by the fact that Western historians have emphasized the European perspective on what went on in and after 1492. He asks, What would our global reality be today without the New World? He goes one step further than O'Gorman: his goal is to rewrite the history of the world in reverse, to explain how during the sixteenth century and afterwards the New World reformed, transformed, and deformed the Old.

Divided into twelve chapters, *America in Europe* was not written for the specialist but for the lay reader interested in historiography. Unchronological in format, it uses rhetorical suppositions, anecdotes, and myths to set forth its convincing and solid ideas. Arciniegas discusses just about everything: the political agenda of Diderot's *Encyclo-*

pedia, the theological motifs behind the Inquisition, the so-called utopian science fiction of Plato and other Greek thinkers, the slave trade from Africa to Brazil, the Caribbean islands and North America, the foundations of the Industrial Revolution, the biological theses of Charles Darwin, even the military intervention of the United States in World War II. His conclusion is that France, Spain, England, Germany, and Italy have drastically changed their distinctive diet, art, philosophy, literature, morality, and politics since the admiral first set foot on Watlings Island. Instead of looking down on the Americas as virginal and inexperienced, we must reorganize our vision of history if we are to fully understand the profound transformation wrought by the event—a (re)discovery of the ancient by means of the new and invented.

V

Columbus died poor, forgotten, neglected. His life story is that of a journey from poverty to fame and back to invisibility. Yet for over a hundred years we have regularly celebrated his enterprise. In Hispanic America, 12 October, the date he set foot on non-European soil, is called Día de la Raza; in the United States, it is known as Columbus Day. There is a marked difference between the two names: the first commemorates the ethnic line formed as a consequence of his voyages, the birth of an entire civilization; the second glorifies not a collectivity but the mariner himself. The moment the mariner left this earth in 1506, rumors and speculations began to spread about his true identity, the secret of his success, his posterity. His metamorphosis into a mythical figure was instantaneous. People began imagining his origins, his loyalties, his true character. Was he a villain or a messiah?

Winifred Sackville Stoner, Jr., a North American, wrote in 1919: "In fourteen-hundred and ninety-two, Columbus sailed the ocean blue." In spite of the controversy over whether the admiral made an encounter or a discovery, one thing is certain: the Genoese is a key to modernity. Utopia—an earthly paradise, a fresh beginning—had been conquered. Only fifty years after the annus mirabilis, in 1543, Copernicus laid the foundations of modern astronomy by disproving the ancient conception of our planet as the center of the universe. More or less simultaneously, one of the supreme examples of Renaissance genius, Leonardo da Vinci, with his attraction to the infinite and passion for the architectural life of bodily things, made tremendous contributions to engineering, medicine, drawing, and music. And in 1516 Thomas More placed his own idea of utopia, presided over by an ideal government founded in reason, in the lands named after Amerigo Vespucci. After 1492 the vast globe was changed forever and with it, the limits of the Western imagination. Novelty became a craze: *new* fauna and flora, *new* patterns of culture, *new* idioms were incorporated into the catalog of the human adventure. Science and technology developed and religious dogmas gave way to liberalism and progress.

Bertrand Russell surely was right: if Columbus had not existed, somebody else would have done the job. While it is true that the Vikings landed in New England first, the admiral was the lucky one: applying a useful metaphor, he was there when the photographer was at hand. And for that alone he deserves credit.

VI

The continent Columbus found does not carry his name but that of another navigator, Amerigo Vespucci. Amending this injustice, monuments, cities, institutions, even nations, celebrate him by using his appelation. In fact, Simón Bolívar, during the internecine battles of revolution in nineteenth-century South America, tried to unify the countries in the region (Venezuela, Colombia, Bolivia, and so on) into one "Great Colombia," in honor of the man he considered the true founder of the Americas. But otherwise, history has approached Columbus tactlessly and ambiguously. Immediately after 1492 his achievements were ignored; in 1592, only a century later, his name was known to only a very timid few in Europe and the American colonies. But by 1892 he had been elevated to the stature of originator—a semipaternal figure in the United States and a role model for explorers in the Europe of Voltaire and Rousseau. And today his memory is troublesome to many: his legacy has been associated with slavery, conquest, disease, and humiliation.

Literature, on the other hand, has been gentler: its tribute to Columbus has been made without bloodshed, without any physical suffering (although not without pain). Washington Irving and Friedrich Nietzsche, Walt Whitman and Rubén Darío, Paul Claudel and Nikos Kazantzakis, James Fenimore Cooper and Alejo Carpentier—their various, magisterial artistic contributions are nothing but a proof of how life can be metamorphosed into fiction. Since fiction writers never presume to offer historical truth, the collective literary portrait of Columbus is a composite: we experience Columbus as both good and evil, intelligent and stupid, big and small in spirit. Ultimately, only the reader can judge Columbus.

My grandmother was right on target: the mariner's real-life adventure was in itself literary: his struggle to make it out of obscurity to glory, the suspense regarding the support of Queen Isabella and her court, his voyage of discovery as a rite of passage, his lonesome death. His existential plight seems at times to have been the creation of a talented Superior Author. He recalls three narrative characters who are equally sophisticated and rich in spirit and energy: Don Quixote of La Mancha, Robinson Crusoe, and Lemuel Gulliver.

Like Cervantes's protagonist in *Don Quixote,* Alonso Quijano—whose brains dried up because of his obsession with Amadís de Gaula, Tirant Lo Blanc, and other fictitious knights in his beloved chivalry books—Columbus was a victim of the act of reading. His fascination with Marco Polo's *The Book of Marvels* encouraged him to wander, to travel to unknown lands like Cathay and Cipangu, to find quasi-fantastic territories. And like Don Quixote, he dared the impossible: the geographers of his time were confident that the earth was a plane, horizontal and limited, but he navigated to the "end" of the world to prove that it was spherical and richer and more diverse than previously imagined. He encountered enormous obstacles yet remained loyal to his dream—or his lunacy, depending on who is telling the story. At the end he died misunderstood, lonely, and in misfortune; the entire world was laughing at him, and King Ferdinand had taken away the fruits of his achievement, thus jeopardizing his legacy. Like Don Quixote, Columbus opened up people's eyes to another dimension, another reality. He showed us a different way to read the book that is the universe. Indeed, somebody else could have done what he did—but in fact it was Christopher Columbus, born in 1451 and dead at the age of fifty-five, just ninety-nine years before the first installment of *Don Quixote of La Mancha* was published, who took upon himself the role of discoverer and has thus generated, since his departure from this earth, just as monumental an amount of fabulation as Jesus Christ, Buddha, and William Shakespeare.

Daniel Defoe's Robinson Crusoe has been compared with the Genoese by V. S. Naipaul, the Oxford-educated novelist from Trinidad. In a book review first published in the *Listener* in 1967, Naipaul equates Columbus's odyssey with *The Life and Strange and Surprising Adventures of Robinson Crusoe.* Both are stories of exploration and survival. Defoe's protagonist sails away, he is wrecked, and finds himself on an island in the Orinoco River; altogether, he spends twenty-four years there. His industrious spirit, his ingenuity, and his reading of the Bible help him overcome the difficult first period. Crusoe then meets a native, Man Friday, whom he saves from the cannibals. Their friendship is a proof of courage, patience, and dedication. In the end they both return to England. Defoe's two-part novel is a parable of man against nature, a metaphor for human capabilities in extreme circumstances, a dissertation on the pros and cons of civilization. In Naipaul's eyes, the journal of the first voyage is also a narrative of a pilgrimage into the unknown, an attempt to describe an exotic, foreign reality from a European perspective.

> *Robinson Crusoe,* in its essential myth-making middle part, is an aspect of the same fantasy [as the voyage of Columbus]. It is a monologue; it is all in the mind. It is the dream of being the first man in the world, of watching the first crop grow. Not only a dream of innocence: it is the dream of being suddenly, just as one is, in unquestionable control of the physical world, of possessing "the first gun that had been fired there since the creation of the world." It is the dream of total power.

Finally, Columbus can be compared with Jonathan Swift's protagonist in *Several Remote Nations of the World, by Lemuel Gulliver,* known by its shortened title, *Gulliver's Travels,* and written in 1720 but published six years later. A work of early science fiction and children's fantasy, its central character is a physician who makes four voyages: one to Lilliput, another to Brodbingnag, a third to Laputa, and the last to Houyhnhnmland. On the first voyage he meets inhabitants who are six inches tall; in the second, giants; in the third, "wise men"; and in the last, he encounters the Yahoos and the Houyhnhnms. Like Columbus reacting to the natives in the Caribbean, the voyager is always perplexed by the size and nature of these creatures; he is often forced to deduce meanings where his understanding of the language and customs falls short. Criticizing abuses of power and human reason, the satirist Swift went against the status quo of his time by antagonizing politicians and institutions. Similarly, the Genoese traveled to islands where European culture does not exist and another culture, quite different in customs and language, reigns. The pilgrimages of Columbus and Gulliver are almost identical in one respect: they are parables of man's search for himself beyond the limits of civilization.

What literature will the next century produce about Christopher Columbus?

During his illustrious literary career, Jorge Luis Borges wrote masterful short stories. But he also enjoyed writing scholarly reviews of nonexistent books. "Pierre Menard, Author of the *Quixote*" is on example: in it Borges discusses the art of a nineteenth-century French symbolist who decided to rewrite word by word, but not copy, the masterpiece by Cervantes. Menard is, of course, an invention, and so is his revisionist effort. Nevertheless, this literary device gives Borges the amazing ability, otherwise unattainable in a straightforward short story, to write nonfiction and fiction at the same time. Stanislaw Lem, a Polish essayist and science fiction novelist born in 1921, has also produced this type of semicritical invention. A couple of his books, *A Perfect Vacuum* and *One Human Minute,* include metafictional pseudo-reviews of nonexistent titles, and a third, *Imaginary Magnitude,* is a collection of introductions to fictitious volumes to be written sometime in the near future.

Why not speculate, as Borges and Lem do? Why not attempt a description of forthcoming volumes on the Genoese? Why not suggest entries to the Columbian library of the future? Most probably, by the time the twenty-first century is ending our ever-changing universe will no longer distinguish between Europe and the Americas as two separate realities. With the present fall of Marxism and the Balkanization of the former Soviet Union, mass media, foreign policy, and trade are likely to unify our overpopulated, ecologically sick planet into a homogeneous whole. Multiculturalism will no longer be only a sum of parts but a totality, a unity: everybody will be a mestizo—a mix of bloods and traditions. Yet the violent colonial past will not be buried. Rich international corporations hope to make outer space a fertile battlefield for technological power struggles, a stage for conquests and renewed domination of the haves over the have-nots. Will man repeat the mistakes of 1492 when expanding into the galaxy? No doubt.

What follows is a description of a handful of titles, some more intriguing than others, likely to appear in the next hundred years. The first, Haromir Slomianski Swedenborg's *The Labyrinth of History*, published in Boston in 2011, centers on the life of one Darian Columbus, a lawyer undergoing a midlife crisis. After a troublesome divorce and the death of his only daughter, Columbus has a miraculous vision during a picnic at Hanging Rock, a bucolic site in Australia; afterwards he receives, in a transmigrational reversal of a similar vision in James Joyce's *Ulysses,* not only the soul of his distant forefather Christopher but also that of the precursor of the civil rights movement, Fray Bartolomé de Las Casas. In dreams, the new, businesslike Columbus acknowledges the desire of the Genoese and the freedom-fighting priest to return to earth and proclaim the redemption of a kind of utopia they refer to as the Kingdom of Indies. Slomianski Swedenborg devotes little space to specifying what the utopia is really all about; instead, he concentrates on his protagonist's effort to convince the two most important leaders of the time, the president of the Confederation of Nations, Sir Jonathan Augenbraum, and the Jewish pope, Mosheus VIII, of the truthfulness of his celestial vision. But he is ignored, and the new Columbus, in a rampage of fury and religious passion, and emulating Henry David Thoreau, César Chávez, and Mahatma Gandhi, begins to perform acts of civil disobedience, such as obstructing traffic on busy highways and organizing marches and hunger strikes. To get attention, his mistress, the prostitute Judith Liweranth, videotapes him and mails the tape to TV stations and important trade magazines. People begin to notice. His activity escalates. Liberal groups, which have been active in debunking the prestige of Christopher Columbus, enjoy ridiculing him. In a final demonstration of heroic courage, Darian Columbus bombs crucial sites on the Iberian peninsula, kills thousands, and commits suicide. His last, ungranted demand is the restoration of his family legacy by the Confederation of Nations. He dies screaming, "The Americas are mine!" *The*

Labyrinth of History ends with Judith in an asylum, talking to a dead Darian Columbus through dreams. He now inhabits his solipsistic Kindom of Indies, where the wolf befriends the sheep, and the cat the bird.

A second invented title is *The Mind and the Pendulum,* a horror story by Joshua Hawthorne, about another direct descendant of Christopher Columbus, an anonymous biologist and archaeologist. One day he discovers, in a storage room of the Museo de Santo Domingo in the Dominican Republic, a sack of hair that belonged to his forefather, apparently saved by Don Diego, Columbus's son, immediately after his father's death. Attempting to revive the mariner in the bodies of other creatures, the scientist experiments with implanting cells in infants. Later, he arranges adoptions for the children, carefully selecting environments like that of Genoa in 1452, and parents similar in personality to Domenico Colombo and Susanna Fontanarossa. *The Mind and the Pendulum,* a tribute to Ira Levin's *The Boys from Brazil,* has the number three as a leitmotiv. Divided into three parts of thirty-three chapters each, the book includes two other characters as important as the scientist—two children who look and think like Christopher Columbus and grow up to be exactly like him. Published in New Delhi in 2079, Hawthorne's book will be celebrated as a masterpiece in the tradition of Mary Shelley's *Frankenstein* and will eventually become a classic. Hawthorne, a professor at Yale, will also write a guide to the science fiction elements of the Old and New Testaments, a bilingual Spanish-English edition of the previously unknown poetry of Gabriel García Márquez, and a comprehensive study of Sigmund Freud and his Jewish perception of monotheism.

Another title—published in Istanbul in 2003, in the not so distant future—by one Yerosaphim Venatar Shafbanijör, a Chilean poet of Hindu origin, is a rewriting of Barlow's *The Columbiad* from a Hispanic American perspective. Set in Ultima Thule (Iceland), the protagonist, an unknown pilot, is known simply as the Ancient Mariner, a name recalling the poem by Samuel Coleridge. Still another forthcoming work, *Colum-Bus,* published in Tel-Aviv in 2017 and written by Daniel Yehuda ben Nahson, a Palestinian Israeli, is an anachronistic piece in which ultramodern technology puts Columbus in the wrong historical contexts: at the battle of Waterloo; in Tlatelolco, a neighborhood in Mexico City, during the student massacre of 1968; by the side of Theodor Herzel during the First World Jewish Congress in Basel; as a stepbrother of Ludwig von Beethoven; and as the true self of Judas Iscariot. Nahson ultimately suggests that Columbus was nothing but an impostor.

Although these plots may seem ludicrous, the chance that these non-existent books might actually be published is not slim. The already immense library of works on the Genoese is likely to expand even more in both the near and distant future. They are narratives about the mariner, but also something more: texts to be thoroughly enjoyed in themselves. The literary voyage by Christopher Columbus continues. Humans can be understood only in effigy, said the Portuguese poet Fernando Pessoa, "when affection no longer compensates the dead person for the disaffection he experiences when alive." The miserable death of the Genoese in 1506, sad as it was, resulted in another birth—the rebirth of his true self. To paraphrase T. S. Eliot, in his end was his beginning.

[1991]

INDEX

"Triptych on Sea and Land" (Mutis), 148
TriQuarterly, 66
Tristán, Flora, 25
Tristes Tropiques (Lévi-Strauss), 68
"True History of the Encounters and
    Complicities of Maqroll the Gaviero and
    the Painter Alejandro Obregón, A"
    (Mutis), 148
Trujillo, Rafael Leónidas, 36, 38, 40;
    Alvarez on, 39
Tuchman, Barbara, 101
"Tuesday's Siesta" (García Márquez), 49
Tune in Tomorrow (film), 20
Tupac Amaru Revolutionary Movement
    (MRTA), 29–30
20,000 Leagues Under the Sea (Verne), 32
Twice-Told Tales (Hawthorne), quote from,
    68

Ubaldo Ribeiro, João, 201
Ulysses (Joyce), 162, 233
Unbearable Lightness of Being, The (film),
    106
Underdogs, The (Azuela), 200
"Un día después del Sabádo" (García
    Márquez), 56
United Fruit Company, massacre and, 46
Updike, John: on García Márquez, 41
Urbino de la Calle, Juvenal, 62
Uribe Uribe, Rafael, 45, 47
Urquidi Illanes, Julia: Vargas Llosa and,
    20–21
Uses of Literature, The (Calvino), quote
    from, 150
Utopia, 227, 229

Valenzuela, Luisa, 202
Valéry, Paul, 88, 205; Bianciotti and, 208–9
Vallejo, César, 97
Vallejo, Fernando, 179
Vargas, Germán, 54
Vargas, Morgana, 28
Vargas Llosa, Mario, 9, 44, 53, 61, 66, 100,
    111, 113, 129, 201, 202, 224; awards for,
    17; Bryce Echenique and, 127–28, 130;
    García Márquez and, 24–25, 42, 43, 56,
    64; Guzmán and, 11–12, 30; memoir of,
    26, 28; Paz and, 108; Peruvian persona

of, 19–20; phallus and, 186; rise of,
    16–17, 21; speeches by, 26–27
Varguitas, 20
Varguitas' Silence (Urquidi), 20
Varo, Remedios, 99
Vasconcelos, José, 102, 220–21
Vásquez Montalbán, Manuel, 122
Velasco, Luis Alejandro, 56
Verne, Jules, 32, 149
Versiones y diversiones (Paz), 107
Vespucci, Amerigo, 216, 229
Vicario, Angela, 63
*Vida e Obra de Fernando Pessoa: História
    duma Geração* (João Gaspar Simões), 86
Vikings, legacy of, 216, 229
Villa, Pancho, 95, 116, 137, 165, 200
Villaurrutia, Xavier, 179
Visión de los vencidos, 194, 202
Vitier, Cintio, 112
Vortex, The (Rivera), 54
Vuelta, 108, 109, 113, 114, 115, 118, 119,
    120; impact of, 116, 120
Vuelta Sudamericana, 120

Walcott, Derek, 113
Wang Wei, 106
War of a Thousand Days (1899–1902), 45,
    46
War of the End of the World, The (Vargas
    Llosa), 17, 18
Warsaw Ghetto, 5
Waugh, Evelyn, 128
Wells, H. G., 31, 34
West, Paul, 152
What Night Tells the Day (Bianciotti), 205,
    206
Where the Air Is Clear (Fuentes), 108, 165
Whitman, Walt, 43, 94, 199, 230; Colum-
    bus and, 214
Wiesenthal, Simon: Columbus and, 213,
    218
Wilford, John Noble: Columbus and, 213
Williams, Raymond L., 53; on *Chronicle of
    a Death Foretold,* 63
Williams, William Carlos, 158; Columbus
    and, 214; Paz and, 106
Wills, Garry: on multiculturalism, 224
Wilson, Edmund, 156